Sadulla Otamuratov

GLOBALIZATION AND NATIONAL SPIRITUAL SECURITY

Tashkent - 2021

© Sadulla Otamuratov
GLOBALIZATION AND NATIONAL SPIRITUAL SECURITY
By: Sadulla Otamuratov
Edition: February '2024
Publisher:
Taemeer Publications LLC (Michigan, USA / Hyderabad, India)

© Sadulla Otamuratov

Book   :
GLOBALIZATION AND NATIONAL SPIRITUAL SECURITY

Author   :   Sadulla Otamuratov

Publisher   :   Taemeer Publications

Year   :   '2024

Pages   :   330

Title Design   :   *Taemeer Web Design*

Discussed at the Academic Council of the Institute of Philosophy and Law. Ibragim Muminov of the Academy of Sciences of the Republic of Uzbekistan and recommended for publication (September 30, 2011 - Protocol No. 8).

Reviewers:

Doctor of Philosophy, Professor Karimov B.R.

Doctor of Philosophy V.A. Alimasov

Candidate of Philosophical Sciences, Associate Professor Khaitov Sh.I.

This book analyzes various threats to the nation and it is spirituality in the context of little-studied globalization in our country, including the relationship of globalization with modern civilization, the concept of national and spiritual security, it is causes, content, development of national identity. • tendencies, it iss manifestations in the understanding of national identity, the need to transform the provision of national and spiritual security into a national idea in the context of globalization.

> The book can be used by specialists in the field of social sciences and humanities interested in globalization and national spirituality.

Introduction

Revised Text with Professional Tone and Grammar Corrections:

Throughout history, humanity has navigated a complex landscape of challenges and contradictions, enduring world wars, the threat of nuclear annihilation, and a multitude of natural and man-made disasters. Today, globalization presents a new set of concerns, wielding its influence in distinct ways. The primary concern lies in the potential for highly developed nations to exert dominance over developing countries, not through brute force, but through the allure of scientific advancements, technological innovations, and economic integration. This influence extends beyond material wealth, aiming to capture the "hearts, minds, and psyches" of populations through various factors.

While the globalization process may appear mutually beneficial, the reality often reveals a skewed dynamic favoring nations with advanced intellectual capital, scientific prowess, and sophisticated communication technologies. Those lacking such resources may find themselves unwittingly drawn into the orbit of developed countries, unable to fully grasp the underlying implications. This occurs because globalization often operates under the principle of hegemony, manifesting across economic, social, political, and cultural spheres. Consequently, the national identities and spiritual values of developing nations, as well as their people, can become susceptible to the influence and material control of developed nations.

The intensification of globalization has significantly amplified threats to national spirituality, potentially eroding unique characteristics and homogenizing into a "mass spirituality" shaped by interconnected nations.

A nation embodies the collective spirit and sacrifices of its people, and its spiritual demise poses an existential threat to humanity. Therefore, safeguarding national identity, primarily its driving force – spirituality – becomes a crucial task in the globalized era. As globalization rapidly evolves, these threats escalate, and ignoring them risks irreversible damage to future generations.

Consequently, I propose incorporating the concept of "national and spiritual security" into political and philosophical discourse as a critical element of overall social and political security. Its scope extends beyond just preserving national spirituality; it encompasses the entirety of national security.

Guaranteeing national and spiritual security serves as the cornerstone of national security in general. This is because national spirituality reflects consciousness, worldview, psyche, soul, and morality. Shifts in these aspects directly impact national life, influencing political, social dynamics, and the country's stability.

Therefore, ensuring national and spiritual security translates to individual acts of patriotism: protecting the inviolable Motherland, nurturing devotion to the people and nation, upholding stability, prestige, and pride. Protecting our youth from harmful influences enables them to prioritize peace of mind – a critical value that spiritually impoverished individuals and nations may not possess, leaving them vulnerable to manipulation and negativity.

In conclusion, the erosion of spirituality leads to a domino effect impacting all spheres of life. As President Islam Karimov aptly stated, "Any threat to spirituality can become a grave threat to national security, interests, and the future of healthy generations, ultimately leading to societal crisis." Securing national security remains a fundamental issue of national importance.

Globalization is a product of the current stage of human development. Initially abstract, it has materialized into a powerful force shaping our world through advances in science, technology, and communication. This process, driven by human ingenuity and hard work, continues to evolve across various societal spheres. Therefore, advocating for its termination or isolation reflects a lack of scientific understanding and disregards its inherent strength and potential.

While nations, including our own, pursue development, are they aware of the threats to their national spirituality in the globalized world? Unfortunately, the answer seems to be negative for about two-thirds of the population, with young people being even less aware. This lack of awareness stems from the insidious nature of "mass spirituality," which consumes national spirituality under the influence of globalization and the technological advancements permeating mass media. Though these threats may not manifest directly as material forces, the achievements and influence of developed countries in science, technology, and capital penetrate the minds and hearts of citizens, especially youth. In the context of a market-driven economy, material interests often overshadow spiritual ones, creating a loss situation. This raises concerns about the future of national spirituality.

For nations to fully grasp these threats, their material well-being and intellectual potential must reach levels approaching those of highly developed nations. Additionally, they need to export their scientific and technological achievements. While our nation will undoubtedly achieve success in these areas, building upon the intellectual legacy of our ancestors, it will take time to participate on an equal footing with developed countries due to the increasing trend of using finished products instead of innovating at the level of modern requirements. This doesn't diminish our potential; on the contrary, our nation has a strong intellectual foundation. However, effectively utilizing it is crucial not only for success but also for preserving our national spiritual identity.

The rapid pace of globalization demands vigilance and the effective use of available opportunities to maintain our identity and keep pace with changes. Social mobilization plays a crucial role in fostering awareness, vigilance, and responsible social activism, as demonstrated by successful examples.

Beyond the material aspects of safeguarding our national spirituality, we must acknowledge the significant role of intrinsic spiritual factors. These factors are reflected in the consciousness, worldview, and attitudes of our compatriots towards the emerging phenomenon of "mass spirituality" in the global sphere. It is noteworthy that, since gaining independence, our citizens have experienced significant shifts in their awareness and perspectives. They demonstrate a growing desire to engage with their national and spiritual heritage, actively participating in the revival of traditions, customs, and values. This is particularly evident amongst our youth, where sentiments of national pride and patriotism are flourishing.

However, while this positive engagement with our national identity exists, some individuals remain indifferent to its future, gravitating towards "mass spirituality" and even contributing to its dissemination, consciously or unconsciously. Notably, this growing trend among many young people also presents an internal threat to the sustainability of our national spirituality. It is crucial to emphasize that this is not intended as a criticism of their involvement, but rather an acknowledgment of our collective failure to provide them with adequate resources to fulfill their burgeoning spiritual needs. This underscores the imperative to proactively address these potential risks to prevent a potential disconnect from our national identity.

As globalization unfolds, it becomes increasingly evident that both external and internal threats to our national spiritual identity are on the rise. While the means to counter these threats exist, their effective utilization is crucial to ensuring the continued security and sustainable development of our national spirit. This, in turn, requires fostering a deep understanding and commitment among all citizens. This book delves into the manifestations of these challenges, emerging issues, strategies for mitigating their root causes, and the increasing necessity for active and effective engagement from our community.

PART 1. THEORETICAL AND METHODOLOGICAL FOUNDATIONS OF THE GLOBALIZATION PROCESS

Globalization has become a ubiquitous concept, permeating nearly every aspect of our lives. While some view it as a catalyst for human progress and prosperity, others express concerns about widening the gap between developed and developing nations, potentially creating new dependencies. Some see it as a force fostering unity and embracing human and national diversity, while others recognize its foundation in power dynamics, whether explicit or implicit.

The concept of globalization remains in dynamic flux, reflecting it is multifaceted nature. While positive assessments of it is impact on the global economy have emerged, it is ramifications for individuals, communities, nations, and established ethical principles deserve further exploration. Key questions linger, including whether globalization will accelerate the pace of life and serve as the bedrock of modern civilization. Additionally, if globalization is indeed unfolding, what future processes await humanity upon its presumed culmination? Will we abandon its potential and seek alternative paths? Is it a permanent feature or a transitory phenomenon? Finding answers to these crucial questions necessitates further inquiry.

Therefore, we identify a critical gap in the prevailing narrative that equates globalization with human progress. We believe a comprehensive examination is imperative, both from scientific and practical perspectives. This section of our book delves into these complex issues, aiming to provide insightful and meaningful answers to some of the most pressing questions surrounding globalization.

1.1. THE REVOLUTIONARY ESSENCE OF GLOBALIZATION

Globalization encompasses social, economic, and political dimensions. Understanding it as a process or event raises questions about its inherent changes and the significance of these terms.

Process and event are intrinsically linked. While an event signifies a rapid, external change within an objective entity, the underlying process can be understood as a passive counterpart to that event. Conversely, the event itself serves as an expression of the unfolding process within a material entity.

The concept of process denotes the ongoing continuity of events and incidents within nature, society, and humanity. This continuity defines its very essence. As a phenomenon occurring within these spheres, it undergoes changes influenced by both objective and subjective factors. However, processes governed by objective laws are considered resistant to modification by subjective forces. Conversely, processes oriented towards specific goals become amenable to management, typically undertaken by individuals.

To accurately analyze the concept of "globalization," we must grasp the intertwined nature of these two facets within the process.

The accelerating pace of globalization, with its seemingly limitless reach, necessitates understanding it as a continuous process. However, this view is only one facet of this complex phenomenon. Globalization also represents an objective law governing societal and human development, unfolding regardless of individual preferences. This inherent characteristic aligns with the very essence of progress. Yet, despite its deterministic nature, globalization does not negate the human factor. In fact, science, technology, and modern communication technologies, the driving forces behind its materialization, are themselves products of human ingenuity and intellect. These advancements arise from the fundamental need to fulfill evolving human requirements. Therefore, even when viewed as an ongoing process, we must recognize the inherent link between globalization and the human element, regardless of its underlying objective forces. However, this recognition does not imply individual control over the process itself. Globalization stems from an inherent law of necessity, propelling humanity toward progress and a better future. In essence, it embodies the continuous evolution of human development. Consequently, while we cannot halt or impede globalization, we can influence its trajectory by accurately predicting its course through meticulously chosen, quantifiable indicators.

While globalization represents a product of humanity's intellectual potential and dedicated efforts, it currently faces the risk of contributing to spiritual impoverishment and potentially even the collapse of national spiritual identities. This unintended consequence highlights how humanity may, unwittingly, generate negative outcomes alongside its achievements.

The impact of globalization across all spheres can be compared to past revolutions that transformed nations and the world. However, the scale and potential of this process surpass any historical revolution in both its achievements and the uncharted territory it navigates. Given these aspects, globalization can be accurately characterized as a revolutionary force shaping a new era for humanity and society.

The term "revolution" carries significant weight in various contexts, encompassing political, military, social, and economic dimensions. Historically, revolutions have served as catalysts for societal change, ushering in new eras in science and technology and transforming social landscapes. Applying this concept to globalization, we argue that it possesses similar revolutionary potential, driving dramatic transformations across diverse domains, from individual lives to national and international structures. Politics, economics, spirituality, and international relations are all subject to its influence, as evidenced by the ongoing reshaping of the industrial landscape itself.

However, to adequately grasp the revolutionary nature of globalization, we must first delve into the core meaning and characteristics of "revolution." Only by understanding its essence and the factors that shape its course can we truly appreciate its intricate relationship with the ongoing phenomenon of globalization.

This revised text maintains the original points while improving clarity, structure, and conciseness, making it more professional and impactful. Remember to consider adding specific examples and evidence to strengthen your argument further.

Prior to the 1970s, the prevailing conception of "revolution" held that certain groups could radically transform society through any means, including socio-political, economic, and spiritual violence. Throughout history, numerous revolutions have unfolded in this manner, with the Bolshevik Revolution of October 1917 in Russia serving as a prominent example. This violent uprising led to dramatic societal shifts in Russia, including the abolition of private property, the establishment of state and collective farms, the restructuring of the political system, the formation of the Bolshevik Communist Party, the suppression of religious and national values, and the imposition of a singular communist ideology. However, such violent revolutions rarely achieve lasting change, often leading to societal crisis and ultimately collapsing. This underscores the criticality of basing societal change on objective development principles and the collective will and active participation of the populace. True revolutions, in this sense, are not imposed by force but rather emerge organically through a collective pursuit of progress and well-being.

The 1970s witnessed the emergence of a novel practice: applying the term "revolution" to describe the rapid advancements in science and technology experienced by certain nations. This unprecedented usage reflected the magnitude of scientific achievements during this period. Unsurprisingly, this "scientific and technological revolution" had a profound impact on the lives of people and nations, fostering rapid economic growth and enhancing the material well-being of populations.

The late 1980s and early 1990s witnessed the dramatic collapse and ultimate disintegration of the former Soviet Union (USSR), triggering revolutionary changes across the territories and populations of the former Soviet republics. This period was marked by a unique character, lacking military intervention despite its sweeping nature. While the USSR's fall may not have been intended by its leadership, it served as the culmination of a legitimate struggle for independence by the constituent republics. Each newly independent state embarked on a distinct development path, aiming for a radical transformation. However, the pursuit of "revolutionary" goals for societal and individual change has faced challenges in many of these nations, with some experiencing internal socio-political conflicts. Nevertheless, others have begun to see initial positive outcomes from their implemented changes.

Given the complexity of this transformation, it is crucial to revisit the concept of "revolution" itself. In light of the aforementioned events, does the term "revolution," denoting a drastic shift driven by specific forces, remain relevant in the context of globalization? This question will be explored further in the following sections.

Revolutions, as historical turning points, undoubtedly impact diverse fields, including science, technology, and society. In science, these revolutions represent significant leaps in progress, marking new eras with distinct characteristics and propelling further development. While revolutions in science and technology generally benefit humanity, social revolutions often lead to upheaval and significant societal suffering. Throughout history, such social upheavals have inflicted immense hardship on populations, and we must acknowledge the potential for unprecedented catastrophes in future societal revolutions, particularly as humanity embarks on a new chapter. Therefore, the evolutionary path of development, characterized by stability and gradual progress, appears to be a safer and more sustainable approach for fostering positive societal values like calmness, confidence, and optimism.

Historical evidence suggests that revolutions often prioritize the interests of specific groups rather than the common good. Their methods frequently involve violence, coercion, and the pursuit of narrow, often morally questionable objectives. Therefore, preventing such upheavals and pursuing an evolutionary path of development are crucial challenges for humanity today. The "Uzbek model," pioneered by President Islam Karimov, offers a compelling example of this evolutionary approach, guiding our nation's transition to a market economy and a democratic society. This model has garnered international recognition and is now being adopted by various countries. Notably, understanding societal dynamics and navigating towards sustainable development have become central themes in contemporary human progress.

The transformative nature of globalization presents a complex and multifaceted phenomenon. While humanity's inherent pursuit of progress remains constant, concerns surface among experts and theorists who evaluate development through the lens of universal values. This arises as groundbreaking discoveries permeate the global landscape at an unprecedented pace.

It's worth acknowledging the diverse perspectives regarding the precise inception and scholarly adoption of "globalization" – some even conflicting. However, rather than dwell on the continuation of these debates, a more productive approach lies in exploring the impact of this revolution on humanity, both present and future. By critically examining its trajectory within the context of globalization, we can illuminate its potential contributions to the betterment of our shared future.

Humanity today inhabits a novel civilization borne of its own intellect. The pace of life races forward at an unprecedented tempo, and we now live in an era where global populations instantly perceive even the most "minuscule" shifts transpiring in any corner of the world, thanks to radio, television, cellular communication, and the internet.

However, it is crucial to acknowledge that these very advancements can expose individuals to alarming displays of shamelessness, violence, tolerance, and moral decay. These concerning facets of society have unfortunately experienced rapid growth over the past two decades. Consider the mobile phone's ubiquitous rise in the modern world, now reaching nearly half the global population with over 28 million users in Uzbekistan alone, wielding approximately 20 million devices. Similarly, the internet has transcended urban boundaries, reaching even remote villages. These technologies empower individuals to instantaneously access and utilize information regardless of their geographic location.

Beyond mere convenience, these tools have demonstrably reshaped human perspectives and value systems. While their ability to disseminate scientific, technological, and engineering advancements remains impressive, their popularity pales in comparison to their potential for propagating negative societal trends.

This era of popularization has also ushered in profound transformations within the global economic landscape. National economies have become seamlessly integrated, forming a single, interconnected space. This intricate network fosters interdependence, rendering each national economy akin to a link in a chain. A disruption in any single link, as evidenced by the 2008 global financial crisis triggered by the US mortgage crisis, can cascade and render the entire system vulnerable. The crisis's repercussions, including surging unemployment, plummeting fuel prices, business failures, and widespread financial hardship, transcended national borders, impacting economies worldwide. This episode serves as a stark reminder of the interconnectedness of the global economic space, where purely nationalistic approaches are no longer tenable. This trend of economic integration further solidified over the subsequent two decades.

The political landscape of mankind has witnessed tremendous change in recent decades. The collapse of the USSR and the subsequent dissolution of the socialist bloc mark a watershed moment, representing a shift away from bipolarity and ushering in an era of cooperation in world politics. This coincides with the growing prominence of diverse political movements and forces, highlighting their influence on global issues and interstate relations.

A striking characteristic of this new era is the shift from violent territorial conquest to a subtler form of influence. Unlike the devastating world wars of the past, contemporary power struggles often play out in the realm of ideas and values, utilizing technology like the internet and mobile phones to shape narratives and influence hearts and minds. This information warfare, waged by leading powers, targets the material and spiritual wealth of nations, raising concerns about manipulation and exploitation.

The dramatic shift in foreign policy pursued by certain developed nations in the globalized era could be interpreted as a paradigm shift. This phenomenon is arguably driven by the ubiquitous dissemination of information through modern media. Even smaller countries, previously considered insignificant due to their size and population, are now privy to details about global weaponry, its deployment, and potential destructive capabilities. This awareness prompts them to prepare for potential threats within their capacity, while also seeking assistance from international organizations. Notably, leveraging these "soft power" tactics proves more cost-effective compared to military intervention. Ultimately, this approach allows these nations to exert influence over other countries with relative ease and affordability. This dynamic arguably represents a novel form of conflict, distinct from traditional warfare, and has been ongoing since the late 20th century, contributing to the ongoing transformation of global political landscapes.

The rapid evolution of foreign policy employed by certain developed nations in the era of globalization can be interpreted as a paradigm shift. This phenomenon is arguably fueled by the pervasive dissemination of information through modern media. Even smaller countries, previously deemed geographically or demographically insignificant, now have access to details about global weaponry, its deployment, and its potential for destruction. This newfound awareness motivates them to prepare for potential threats within their capabilities, often prompting them to seek assistance from international organizations. Notably, leveraging these soft power tactics proves to be a more cost-effective alternative to military intervention. Ultimately, this approach allows these nations to exert influence over other countries with relative ease and affordability. This dynamic arguably represents a novel form of geopolitical engagement, distinct from traditional warfare, and has been unfolding since the late 20th century, contributing to the continuous transformation of global political landscapes.

Furthermore, developed countries are investing unprecedented amounts of resources in transforming their ideas and ideologies into tools for shaping popular belief systems within less developed nations. On April 7, 2010, BBC Radio 7 reported on the existence of a state ideology within the British capital, London, with significant financial backing from the national budget allocated to its promotion.

Developed countries' efforts and investments in this area suggest a strategic focus on cultivating a "unified mass spirituality" that aligns their ideas and ideologies. We will delve deeper into this concept in a subsequent chapter. However, it is crucial to highlight that within the realm of globalization, the "formation of mass spirituality and its transformation into an instrument of global dominance" has emerged as a key strategic direction.

Our exploration into the "revolutionary nature of globalization" in this context stems from its significant impact on contemporary human development, particularly over the next two decades. We have previously elaborated on this impact, and in this chapter, we seek to draw upon the insights of leading globalisation experts and specialists to further substantiate our arguments.

Leading figures from diverse academic and professional backgrounds perceive globalization as a multifaceted phenomenon profoundly shaping the world we live in. Within the economic sphere, renowned figures like Nobel laureate Joseph Stiglitz (Columbia University), acclaimed philosopher Francis Fukuyama, and prominent economist Jagdish Bhagwati underscore its continuity and transformative impact[2]. Their perspectives highlight aspects such as increased trade, financial flows, and interconnectedness of production chains.

However, the conversation surrounding globalization extends beyond purely economic dimensions. Individuals like Mark Cyrwell, affiliated with the Yale Center for Globalization, and David King, Deputy Director at Harvard's Kennedy School of Politics, emphasize its political and state-level implications[3]. Their focus areas might include the influence of globalization on governance structures, international collaborations, and national identity dynamics.

It's crucial to acknowledge that while these examples represent prominent voices, the discourse on globalization encompasses a broad spectrum of perspectives, including critical viewpoints and alternative interpretations. Recognizing this diversity enriches our understanding of this complex and ever-evolving phenomenon.

Among leading scholars, diverse perspectives on globalization emerge.

Joseph Stiglitz, Nobel laureate and Columbia University professor, emphasizes its potential to enhance human well-being, particularly in developing nations, citing the globalization of science and its advancements in healthcare as a prime example [4].

Jagdish Bhagwati, a prominent economist, defines globalization as the continuous integration of the global economy, encompassing trade, direct investment, multinational corporation activities, international financial flows, and migration[5].

Vyacheslav Nikonov, President of the Political Foundation, highlights its impact on statehood, suggesting that globalization expands the scope of domestic and foreign policy and transforms the very nature of security policy[6].

Leading scholars concur that globalization is an ongoing transformation within the global economy. Its most evident effects are indeed economic, weaving the world into a more interconnected fabric. While developed nations experience this primarily through economic channels, a broader dialogue is crucial to address the potential impact of globalization on human, spiritual, national, and universal values. These deeply ingrained values, developed over centuries, often remain unreported in traditional media.

Should the ultimate goal of economic globalization be achieved, creating a singular economic space, questions arise about the influence of economic rules on spirituality, morality, and national identities. Can these elements resist the potential homogenization driven by economics? While some grasp the complexities of this process, others remain silent due to vested interests, while others find solace in the inherent instability of the economy and the distractions of daily life. However, ignoring the multifaceted forces shaping globalization's trajectory might carry unforeseen consequences.

Considering the transformative nature of globalization, it is crucial to explore its historical origins and diverse interpretations. While the aforementioned author touched upon this topic, further discussion and analysis are necessary to fully understand the "revolutionary" aspect of this phenomenon.

Scholars hold varying perspectives on when globalization commenced. Western figures like R. Cobden and J. Bright connect its emergence to the implementation of free trade in the early 19th and 20th centuries, citing the resulting economic growth. They view Great Britain, with its maritime, industrial, and financial prowess, as the driving force behind this initial wave.

Furthermore, they posit a "second phase" or resurgence of globalization, triggered by advancements in computer science and telecommunications during the late 1970s [7].

Professor Muhammadzhon Kholbekov, a renowned Uzbek philologist, argues that humanity's embrace of the term "globalization" signifies its growing relevance in the 21st century. He cites historical figures like Alexander the Great and Julius Caesar, who sought to unite vast territories and arguably initiated early forms of globalization[8]. Kholbekov further posits that the Middle Ages (4th-14th centuries) witnessed a literary globalization, marked by a tendency towards interconnectedness. He then highlights the 14th-17th centuries, when intellectuals drawing inspiration from Greco-Roman and Islamic traditions laid the foundation for the Renaissance in

Western Europe, contributing to the further globalization of cultural life. The 18th century, according to Kholbekov, saw the Enlightenment embrace and implement globalization principles, evidenced by the French Revolution in 1789. However, he notes that 19th-century literature did not fully uphold these principles. Today, scholars debate the future of literature and art in the 21st century, particularly how the anticipated economic and political globalization will impact the literary landscape [9].

To provide a comprehensive overview of various perspectives on globalization's initial stage, we present extensive excerpts from a relevant article. These excerpts capture the author's intriguing and, at times, contradictory ideas, allowing for a deeper understanding of their position on the topic before we engage in our own analysis.

Specifically, Professor A. Kadyrov links globalization to 20th-century technological advancements and automation. He emphasizes the rapid pace of progress during this period, stating that "the last twentieth century compressed several thousand years of socio-historical weight, momentous events, and significance for human civilization." He highlights humankind's achievements in various fields, including conquering the microcosm and unlocking the mysteries of human genetics.

Professor Kadyrov further underscores the 20th century's advancements in speed and control, not only in technology but also in human thought. He cites the creation of artificial materials, alongside breakthroughs in computer technology, robotics, automated control systems, and the global information network (the internet) as defining characteristics of this era. He concludes by noting the dramatic reduction in physical distances between countries and continents, emphasizing the swift exchange of information that became possible thanks to these innovations.

The diverse viewpoints expressed in this passage offer valuable insights into the complex phenomenon of globalization. Professor A. Kadyrov adopts a modernist perspective, emphasizing the acceleration of globalization in the 20th century due to converging economic, political, and cultural ties, fueled by technological advancements[10].This view connects globalization to the interconnectedness fostered by modern communication and transportation technologies, highlighting its rapid integration and transformative impact on the world stage.

In contrast, Professor A. Ochildiev takes a historical approach, tracing globalization's roots back to the 15th-17th centuries[11]. He identifies pivotal events like geographical discoveries and the Industrial Revolution as laying the groundwork for international trade and interconnectedness, demonstrating globalization as a longstanding historical process with evolving phases and influences. This long-term perspective allows for a nuanced understanding of the historical forces that shaped the interconnected world we experience today.

Finally, Bakhodir Umarov presents a more fluid and inclusive perspective, focusing on the accessibility of globalization's benefits[12].He argues that any country actively participating in international trade, attracting foreign investment, and embracing modern technologies can leverage these benefits. This emphasizes the ongoing nature of globalization, where active participation and adaptation are key to reaping its advantages, regardless of a nation's specific historical starting point.

The text you provided has no grammatical errors, but several stylistic choices could be made more professional. Here's a revised version:

Professor Ulugbek Saidov frames globalization as a continuous process of global integration:

He argues that interpreting globalization as a series of historical events fosters the understanding that it isn't a recent phenomenon. Saidov provides examples like the cultural exchange during the Crusades and the economic impact of the Industrial

Revolution on India, demonstrating globalization's enduring influence across eras and continents.

From profit to discourse:

Saidov further suggests that the pursuit of profit and income, intertwined with the evolution of capitalist relations, serves as a fundamental motivator for globalization. This emphasis on economic self-interest adds another layer to understanding the phenomenon, highlighting its potential interplay with broader societal and political shifts.

Beyond a single narrative:

It's crucial to acknowledge that Saidov's interpretation, while insightful, is not the only perspective. Other scholars offer contrasting or complementary viewpoints, highlighting different historical starting points, geographical scopes, and potential directions for this multifaceted phenomenon. Recognizing this diversity of perspectives is essential for a comprehensive understanding of globalization's impact on our world.

Engaging in a collaborative approach:
By engaging with Saidov's analysis alongside other scholarly perspectives, we can move beyond simplistic definitions and foster a more informed discussion. Examining globalization through various historical and theoretical lenses allows us to appreciate its complex evolution, diverse motivations, and far-reaching impact on our interconnected present and future.

Unveiling the Multifaceted Nature of Globalization

Several scholars offer diverse perspectives on the historical origins and characteristics of globalization, raising insightful questions. By limiting the discussion to free trade and economic growth (Professor M. Holbekov), globalization stretches back to Alexander the Great's ambitions in the 4th century BC (XX). Alternatively, Professor A. Kadyrov emphasizes the role of modern technology, while Professor A. Ochildiev focuses on the Industrial Revolution and geographical discoveries of the 14th-17th centuries as pivotal points. Bakhodir Umarov acknowledges the difficulty of pinpointing a specific timeframe, echoing Ulugbek Saidov's emphasis on interpreting globalization as a continuous process of global integration.

These contrasting interpretations naturally lead to several questions. Firstly, considering the term's relatively recent coinage in 1983 by Theodore Levitt, what historical precedents can we identify for this phenomenon? Why has the concept gained such prominence in recent times? Should terms like "integration," "internationalization," and "civilizational emergence" be disregarded, or are there significant connections to explore? Finally, can focusing solely on the economic aspects of globalization obscure centuries-old interactions in cultural and literary spheres, as well as efforts towards shared solutions to global challenges like preserving national identity? This paper explores the complex relationship between globalization and other significant concepts like internationalization, integration, and the scientific and technological revolution. It raises a critical question: are states positioned at the "forefront" of globalization perceived as sacrificing their own interests to achieve world domination through forced unification? Answering this necessitates examining potential "revolutions" within technology and other spheres impacted by globalization. Notably, established concepts like "internationalization", traditionally defined as a natural rapprochement of global populations, and "integration," often now confined to economic contexts, seem to have receded from academic discourse, becoming "victims" of globalization itself. However, it is crucial to differentiate between "globalization" and these other concepts. Globalization represents broader societal and cultural shifts, not solely industrial developments. Utilizing these terms within their distinct meanings reveals the "revolutionary" dimension of globalization. Furthermore, while the influence of "internationalization," "integration," and the "scientific and technological revolution" might appear to diminish across historical periods, their positive impact on personal development, worldviews, and shared values should not be underestimated. Building upon these ideas, this paper focuses on a comparative analysis of "internationalism," "integration," and the "scientific and technological revolution" vis-à-vis "globalization," investigating their specific manifestations within the contemporary world.

In Philosophy: An Encyclopedic Dictionary, internationalism, internationalism (Latin Inter - apo, nation - people) is a concept that expresses the international solidarity of people of different nationalities and races. The information provides "That this concept was not invented by Karl Marx, it was not included in science by him, it was absolute only during the times of the former Soviet Union..."[14]. «We are not talking about who introduced it into science, but about its essence and the fact that it serves, we must remember that it is based on two important factors. These are: firstly, the fact that in the process of forming nations and races and pursuing their own interests, these interests can be realized in cooperation with other nations and races; secondly, this concept does not mean the supreme power of anyone or any party, but the expression of mutual equality and interests of the parties, as well as the voluntariness and respect of the parties for cooperation or refusal to cooperate. Therefore, it is based on values such as kindness, tolerance and humanity. He does not intend to force the parties to cooperate violently. At the same time, «internationalism» is a natural process that laid the foundation for the conscious activity of mankind. But he always had the same name, "he said. In fact, its penetration into scientific consumption is associated with the emergence of the working class as an independent political force on the battlefield and its ideology of unification in the struggle against the bourgeoisie. Its main principle is equality of interests, prudence and naturalness.

The concept of «integration» is defined in the concise dictionary «Philosophy» as follows: «Integration (lat. Integer - complete, whole, indissoluble, whole) is a process or result of activities aimed at achieving community, unity»[15]. In «Philosophy: an encyclopedic dictionary» «integration» (lat. Integer - whole): 1) the union of separate parts and elements into one whole; 2) the unification of different countries, the merger of narrow economic and political groups. Forms of integration are studied in scientific, political, cultural, international and other types[16].

It can be seen that there are differences in the definition of these concepts even in dictionaries.

As noted above, the term "globalization" was introduced into science at the end of the twentieth century (1983, mentioned in T. Levitt's Harvard Business Review). However, as a process that arose in the IV century BC, XV-XVII centuries, late XIX and early XX centuries (this was discussed in detail above), various scientists expressed their ideas. If we compare the content of the concepts of "internationalization" and "integration" with the content of the concept of "globalization", the differences between them (when comparing the views expressed by scientists about them above) were almost invisible. In particular, we see that the concepts of "integration" and "globalization" have the same meaning. Now, in the 60-70s of the twentieth century, a high level of development of science, technology and engineering in the western countries of the world has entered.

Drawing on the Latin roots "inter" (between) and "natio" (nation), the concept of internationalism, as presented in "Philosophy: An Encyclopedic Dictionary," embodies the solidarity of individuals across national and racial boundaries. While the text clarifies that Karl Marx neither invented nor single-handedly introduced the concept to scientific discourse, it emphasizes the importance of understanding its core principles and values, regardless of individual attribution.

Key Foundations of Internationalism:

Internationalism rests on two fundamental pillars:

Collaborative Goal Attainment: While nations and races strive for their own unique aspirations, the realization of these goals can be significantly enhanced through mutually beneficial cooperation.

Equal Partnership and Respect: The concept explicitly repudiates notions of domination or hierarchical structures. It champions equality, shared interests, and voluntary participation in cooperative endeavors, emphasizing respect for individual choices to collaborate or decline. Kindness, tolerance, and humanity serve as the ethical bedrock of this framework.

The Natural Trajectory of Internationalism:

Furthermore, internationalism transcends mere imposition, existing as a natural phenomenon that laid the groundwork for conscious human collaboration. While the specific term may not be historically novel, its widespread adoption within academic circles roughly coincided with the emergence of the working class as a powerful political force. This class and its associated ideology of unification against the bourgeoisie championed the core principles of internationalism: equality, mutual understanding, and a natural inclination towards collaboration.

The phenomenon of integration resonates as a natural process deeply woven into the fabric of human history. Since the dawn of conscious action, individuals have inherently sought connection and collaboration. The very essence of self-awareness and personal growth is intrinsically linked to our ability to engage with others. This fundamental drive to connect, share experiences, offer mutual support, and cultivate positive relationships fuels the natural progression of integration, fostering a sense of "rapprochement" between individuals and communities.

This natural tendency towards integration manifests in three key ways:

1. Naturalistic Limitation: Integration remains inherently balanced, finding its boundaries organically. While fostering progress, it acknowledges its inherent limits and avoids excessive assimilation.

2. Vital Necessity: Integration serves as a fundamental prerequisite for individual and collective growth. Through collaboration and exchange, individuals and communities transcend limitations and achieve greater development.

3. Mutual Interest: Integration prioritizes the collective good, ensuring that the benefits and responsibilities are shared equitably among all participants. No single entity dictates the terms, but rather, a spirit of reciprocity prevails.

Therefore, integration emerges as an objective necessity, not simply an economic construct. Throughout history, it has served as a powerful catalyst for human progress, fostering collaboration and advancement across geographic and cultural boundaries. While the term itself may have gained formal recognition within academic circles, the underlying principles of integration have demonstrably guided humankind toward shared prosperity and mutual understanding since the dawn of our conscious journey.

Alongside the concept of "integration," "internationalization" has also found its place in scholarly discourse. It signifies the process of cultural and spiritual interaction between diverse nations, peoples, and ethnicities, fostering mutual enrichment. Notably, these terms – "integration" and "internationalization" – are not synonymous. While sharing positive intent, direction, and essence, they occupy distinct, although closely related, conceptual spaces. It is crucial to remember that, despite their proximity, they do not hold identical meanings.

Historically, the concepts of integration and internationalization served distinct purposes. Integration referred to the natural convergence of economies, while internationalization focused on the exchange of cultural and spiritual ideas across nations. While these terms have evolved beyond their original meanings, they remain relevant in understanding contemporary global dynamics.

Today, integration encompasses broader aspects of economic convergence, including trade, investment, and financial flows. This increased interconnectedness offers potential advantages like enhanced efficiency and access to new markets, but also raises concerns about uneven benefits and potential exploitation of resources.

Moving forward, a nuanced understanding of both the opportunities and challenges presented by globalization is crucial. This requires avoiding simplistic narratives and engaging in constructive dialogue to ensure that international cooperation benefits all participants. To bolster our perspective, we sought insights from renowned American sociologist and former presidential advisor Zbigniew Brzezinski. Responding to a query about mitigating globalization's downsides, Brzezinski emphasized relinquishing unearned advantages and fostering humanity in economic and ethical interactions, particularly with third-world workers. He underscored that globalization mustn't exploit individuals for profit, but instead serve as a cornerstone of global social policy, prioritizing the needs of a sizable portion of the world's population[17].

It is noteworthy that renowned sociologist Zbigniew Brzezinski recognizes the current trend of globalization benefiting primarily developed nations like the United States, while emphasizing the need for a broader approach that serves all populations. This perspective suggests that economic integration, once hailed as an enlightened concept, has potentially shifted under the influence of globalization, becoming a factor favoring specific interests rather than promoting universal progress. While its rapid development and widespread adoption might suggest a "revolutionary" impact on humanity and the modern world, it's crucial to engage in an objective and nuanced analysis to determine whether globalization truly lives up to its ideal of equitable development for all.

Echoing the sentiments of American scholar Thomas Friedman, globalization emerges as a "new system that replaced the Cold War system," reshaping the global landscape[18]. In the face of its current acceleration, concerns arise regarding the potential erosion of distinct national spiritual identities, potentially replaced by a homogenized "mass spirituality." This apprehension is not unfounded, as Friedman himself alludes to the shift from a bipolar Cold War to a more nuanced struggle for ideas, ideologies, and individual values. This paradigm shift marks a pivotal revolution in human development, propelling us towards a future significantly shaped by the battle for hearts and minds.

While the scientific and technological advancements of the mid-20th century, encompassing innovations in media, television, computers, and early internet and mobile communication, were undoubtedly significant, a profound chasm exists in their perceived impact compared to the contemporary landscape. The advancements of our era, spanning across numerous areas of science, technology, and engineering, exhibit a qualitative leap, yet our scientific literature curiously neglects to categorize them as revolutionary changes. When discussing globalization, the primary focus often resides on the concept of "integration." However, it is paramount to delve deeper and uncover the driving forces propelling this phenomenon. Globalization is not a spontaneous event; its true essence and scale can only be illuminated by analyzing the forces orchestrating its evolution.

In this light, the contemporary advancements in science, technology, and engineering can be viewed as akin to a 21st-century technological revolution. This revolution, intrinsically intertwined with globalization, represents a product of human ingenuity, marking a pivotal step in human development. Thus, the revolutionary character of globalization transcends the mere notion of uniting the world into a single political space. It manifests profoundly in the sophisticated nature and immense power of its driving forces, capable of accelerating the very rhythms of human existence.

1.2. DIALECTICS OF GLOBALIZATION AND CIVILIZATION

Rather than an inevitable force, globalization emerges as a carefully orchestrated phenomenon fueled by a multitude of influential factors and instruments. Notably, the entwined globalization of economics, politics, spirituality, and ideology signifies a unification process spanning individual, national, and regional levels. This complex orchestration hinges on the transformative power of modern telecommunications – including ubiquitous internet access, mobile connectivity, and diverse media platforms.

The remarkable technological advancements we witness today are undeniable testaments to human ingenuity and progress. They represent a pinnacle of achievement, surpassing any in our history. Many have rightly labeled this era of innovation and scientific breakthroughs as the "modern civilization." But a critical question arises: are these feats of creation truly reflective of the essence of this civilization, or merely instruments of material pursuit?

Examining the driving forces behind globalization, especially those facilitating its tangible impact, we discover their deep connection to human intellectual prowess and advanced development. However, we also observe a troubling paradox: while some experts hail globalization as a path to global well-being, its influence seems to threaten the distinct identities of nations, peoples, and ethnic groups.

Therefore, we must engage in a complex and essential discussion: can we consider globalization, or the tools transforming it into a material force, as a defining characteristic of modern civilization? If so, what evidence supports this claim? Conversely, if we believe globalization contradicts the true spirit of our era, what arguments justify this stance?

Sadly, this crucial inquiry has received insufficient attention, not only in Uzbekistan but across much of the academic landscape within the CIS region.

Currently, a sense of euphoria surrounding globalization's perceived benefits, particularly in the economic sphere, dominates the discourse. However, a more nuanced and balanced examination is imperative.

While the material well-being of all nations under globalization's influence captivates our attention, we rarely explore the potential implications on national identity. Imagine a future where disparate nations, peoples, and ethnicities coalesce into a single entity, a "flower of humanity." Would this unification, borne of prosperity, be a triumph or a tragedy for humankind's cultural tapestry? Alternatively, can we harness the positive aspects of globalization to preserve the essence of nations while fostering progress? If we consider these positive forces as markers of contemporary civilization, how do they coexist with, and perhaps even contradict, the preservation of distinct national identities? These are questions that continue to beckon for exploration.

Our current endeavor delves into the concept of "civilization," seeking answers through nuanced examinations of its varied definitions, established criteria, and diverse modes of manifestation. This exploration aligns naturally with the tenets of both political and cultural analysis, providing a comprehensive framework for understanding this multifaceted subject.

Within the scholarly landscape, both in Uzbekistan and abroad, including Russia, diverse conceptions of "civilization" abound. While there exist areas of convergence, significant divergences are also present. Notably, the "Popular Science Dictionary of Independence" offers a definition rooted in Latin etymology (Civilis – civil, social). The dictionary defines civilization as the "aggregate of material and spiritual wealth created by society throughout its development, along with the methods for their reinforcement and advancement"[1]. Drawing from various sources, this excerpt explores the multifaceted concept of civilization. One definition, offered by a dictionary, frames it as "the material and spiritual level achieved by society, an indicator of its success in improving the material and spiritual world"[2]. This definition highlights the unique human capacity to create an "artificial world" through intellect and labor, contrasting our built environment with the natural world devoid of such ready-made amenities. The level of societal development, according to this perspective, hinges on the "quantity and quality of these artificial objects."

However, "Philosophy: An Encyclopedic Dictionary" presents a more nuanced and historically grounded understanding. It defines civilization as a "socio-philosophical concept" with a "multifaceted and complex meaning." The concept itself, introduced by the Scottish historian and philosopher A. Ferguson (1773-1816), was initially employed by the French Enlightenment to describe a specific stage of human progress characterized by reason and justice.

Even after that, the concept of civilization continued to acquire a different meaning. In some cases, it was used as a synonym for culture, sometimes only as material culture, while the German philosopher O. Spengler, on the other hand, uses it in the sense of the antipode of culture, i.e., to characterize the stage of the disappearance of culture by the English sociologist and historian A. J. Toynbee, on the other hand, used it to describe unique and relatively closed societies. Even when defining the scope and content of the concept of civilization, diversity persists to this day. This concept includes: 1) the stage of social development following savagery and barbarism; 2) a certain stage in the development of human society as a whole (for example, neolithic, non-capitalist or modern civilization); 3) a certain socio-economic formation; 4) geographically separate units (for example, European and Asian civilizations); 5) cultural units that differ in their religious affiliation (for example, Christian or Islamic civilization); 6) units that differ in origin and planetary affiliation (for example, terrestrial civilization, extraterrestrial civilizations); 7) socio-cultural units that differ in ethnicity (for example, ancient Egyptian or Babylonian civilization) and a similar meaning"[3].

Within the esteemed Uzbek National Encyclopedia, the term "civilization" (derived from the Latin "civilis," signifying citizenship and the state) possesses multifaceted interpretations:

Broadest Scope: Encompassing any mode of existence for conscious beings.

Synonymous with Culture: Employed interchangeably with "culture," highlighting their close association.

Material Manifestation: Frequently used to represent the tangible elements of a specific culture.

Historical Timeline: Denoting a distinct phase in societal development, succeeding both savagery and barbarism.

Origins: The concept of "civilization" emerged in the 18th century, intricately linked to the notion of "culture"[4].

The concept of "civilization" remains elusive, with interpretations varying across philosophical texts. Notably, the ninth theme of the collaborative work "Philosophy of World Civilization and Independent Development," authored by scholars from Uzbekistan, dedicates a distinct subsection to "World Civilization." This section presents humanity as an integrated whole, conceptualizing the social system of civilizations as the very society of our planet.

In its broadest sense, this concept encompasses the totality of historical processes linked to the survival of states, societies, peoples, and nations. It reflects the shared space of life on Earth, uniting all individuals who inhabit our planet[5].

Within the pages of "Western Philosophy," we encounter the assertion that, during medieval Europe, "Christianity served as the cornerstone of civilization for all peoples, acting as a catalyst for the emergence of national states"[6]. Here, the text implicitly links civilizational development to the influence of Christianity, suggesting a causal relationship between the two.

Expanding on this theme, a philosophy textbook edited by the late Academician E. Yusupov delves into the concept of "civilization." Drawing upon the insights within the "Philosophy" encyclopedic dictionary, the textbook synthesizes existing perspectives, offers discerning observations, and presents independent arguments. Notably, it identifies three foundational pillars of civilization:

Technological advancement: Defined as "a certain technology of social production," this encompasses the tools and techniques that underpin societal progress.

Unique cultural tapestry: Each civilization boasts a singular "value of a unique culture, philosophical views, and moral norms." This rich tapestry shapes its identity and sets it apart.

Autonomous life principles: Every civilization adheres to its own "life principles," guiding its internal dynamics and fostering cohesion.

... only when the concept of civilization is applied to a lexical people, country (society), or to some of its qualitatively different stages, does it have a clear scientific content and, therefore, methodological significance. It is ethnic formations, countries that clearly show the specifics of civilization, the main characteristics ...

The relationship between culture and civilization is one of profound symbiosis. Civilization, with its tangible expressions, serves as a physical manifestation of a society's cultural DNA. Indeed, the very existence of civilization hinges upon the bedrock of cultural values, norms, and achievements. It is within the crucible of specific civilizations that individuals are shaped and refined, drawing upon the accumulated wisdom and riches bequeathed by generations past [7].

Further elucidating this intricate relationship, scholar F. Suleymanova delves into the nuances of civilizational expression in her monograph "East and West." Within this work, she presents cultural development as a defining pillar of civilizational character, highlighting the unique trajectories followed by Eastern and Western societies[8].

The late academician Zhondor Tulanov called a special chapter in his book «Philosophy of Values» «the first sign of the cultural and spiritual values of the Eastern civilization», in which he expressed his views on the history and culture of the peoples of the East. , the first political, legal, religious, artistic and philosophical views[9].

Russian scientists also made a number of interesting remarks about the concept of «civilization» and the peculiarities of its manifestation. In particular, V.P. Rozhins[10], B.G. Kuznetsev[11,ii], H.N. Momdzhyan[12], V.E. Davidovich[13,iii], A.Egorov[14], N.I.Konrad[15,iv] the formation of a formation (V.P. Rogin). Although 35-40 years have passed since the publication of their works and scientific articles, today they have a certain value for comparing the processes taking place in world, regional or human development, as well as for the formation of new views on "civilization".

It is noteworthy that contemporary academic literature has not comprehensively explored the evolving perspectives on the concept of 'civilization' and its potential entanglement with the increasingly intricate process of globalization, or vice versa. Furthermore, it appears that certain researchers remain tethered to traditional paradigms within the context of modern civilization. Conversely, numerous scholars have identified the advancement of culture, science, technology, and economics as hallmarks of civilizations, supporting their claims with substantial evidence.

In general, diverse perspectives on the concept of "civilization" can be broadly categorized into three main viewpoints:

Firstly, a regional perspective distinguishes between Eastern and Western civilizations. This distinction draws upon several characteristics, including the emergence of writing systems in the ancient East, the expression of folklore, the production of material goods (such as urban planning and architecture), the development of weapons, scientific advancements, philosophical schools, customs, traditions, and various other elements of spiritual culture.

Secondly, the term "Western civilization" was employed in the eighteenth century within the West to describe advancements in engineering and technology, particularly involving the development of mechanical energy production, utilization of underground resources, and other related areas.

Thirdly, "civilization" has also been used to convey the emergence of religions and their influence on human development, with particular emphasis on Islam, Christianity, and other major religions.

Fourthly, the development of society can be divided into historical stages, namely slavery, feudalism, capitalism, and communism. The lower stages were once used to define socialism, considering them as separate entities representing each new, higher stage of development. However, this approach has been criticized for its oversimplification.

Fifth, regional perspectives are also employed to analyze social development. These perspectives focus on advancements in specific regions across various fields like science, philosophy, religion, and industry. Notably, ancient China, India, Central Asia, Iran, and other regions are recognized for their periods of rapid development.

Sixth, civilizational approaches offer an alternative to the formation-based view of society. These approaches reject the emphasis on class struggle and instead focus on the overall levels of development achieved by a civilization. They propose stages like agrarian civilization, industrial civilization, post-industrial civilization, and super-industrial civilization, using indicators of socio-economic and cultural advancement driven by technological progress.

Thus, there are many views on the concept of «civilization», and the common denominator is that it is used in the context of expressing the level and indicators of socio-cultural development. At the same time, there are views on «civilization» as a synonym for culture, which we talked about above. It should also be noted that there are applications of «civilization» not only in the sense of a high indicator of development, but also in the sense of its opposite. Including the German philosopher O. Spengler used it in the sense of characterizing the stage of the disappearance of culture[17]. Similar views are found in the works of other scientists.

From this point of view, that is, from a one-sided point of view, this concept undermines the content of «civilization» as an independent philosophical category. Moreover, in some studies the point of view still prevails that "civilization" is the highest stage of cultural development.

Upon closer scrutiny, two pivotal questions emerge: Firstly, what criteria distinguish "civilization" and "culture"? Where do their boundaries lie, and can we truly rely on "civilization" as an indicator of cultural and socio-cultural advancement? Is categorization into distinct branches necessary, or what purpose does this concept serve? Secondly, within the context of contemporary globalization, a segment of the world's population fares well, having seemingly entered a novel stage of development marked by remarkable intellectual potential, talent, and material resources. This arguably reflects a new era characterized by stark differences in economic, socio-political, and spiritual-educational development compared to any preceding period. Notably, these discrepancies extend beyond mere advancement, encompassing the myriad contradictions inherent within it. While globalization fosters economic, technical, and technological progress, its impact on humanity's spiritual and moral values remains ambiguous. Does this current phase of globalization, with its undeniable benefits and drawbacks, represent a bona fide "civilization" or merely a novel stage in human development?

In our estimation, understanding the concept of "civilization" within the context of modern development necessitates a clear distinction between it and "culture," particularly regarding their philosophical underpinnings. While both terms represent positive indicators of societal advancement, and are not necessarily contradictory, conflating them would hinder meaningful analysis. Our proposed framework highlights several key differences:

Firstly, culture, irrespective of its stage of development, has been an inherent aspect of human conscious activity since its inception. As long as humanity exists, cultural evolution will continue. Conversely, civilization emerged not as a continuous process, but rather at a specific historical juncture. This distinction extends beyond the conceptual realm, encompassing differences in power, scale, quality, and the degree of advancement.

Secondly, cultural development is characterized by its continuous nature. It can flourish, stagnate, or even be reborn under the influence of various internal and external factors. Conversely, civilization, with its inherent essence, performance level, and impact on human progress, embodies transformative change at a "revolutionary" level. It signifies significant breakthroughs across diverse spheres, including society, culture, science, technology, and communication.

Thirdly, the impact of civilization on development exhibits a broader and more profound reach compared to culture. While advancements in specific fields like science, technology, or religion within a civilization can propel progress at a national, regional, and even global level, cultural development primarily manifests as a continuation of established traditions and practices.

Fourthly, while "civilization" is a distinct concept, its foundation can be identified as culture. However, this is not culture in its narrow and perpetually evolving form, but rather a "revolution" within it – a product of human intelligence at a specific historical stage and timeframe.

Fifthly, the notion of culture as the bedrock of civilization underscores that all achievements in science, ideas, techniques, and technologies are creations of human intellect and manual labor, brought to fruition through practical application. These materialized achievements are then refined and imbued with beauty through human "processing." At specific historical junctures, when intellectual potential reaches a critical threshold, cultural and spiritual life undergoes profound transformations, characterized by their transformative potential, scale, and lasting impact on human development.

While civilization may lie at the heart of societal advancement, it is not solely defined by material wealth or its mere existence. Rather, it is the transformative "revolution" that embodies the essence of change and progress. In this respect, civilization, much like the concept of culture, holds a distinct and multifaceted position within the philosophical realm. Its unique status is evident throughout history, where it acts as a catalyst for change across various spheres of life, public and private alike. Each instance of civilization marks a new chapter in humanity's journey, brimming with potential. It is not merely a seamless continuation of culture, but rather a decisive shift in its trajectory at specific historical junctures. This inherent ability to propel development forward through transformative leaps solidifies its position as an independent philosophical concept.

To fully grasp the interconnectedness of "civilization" and "culture" in the narrative of progress, we must acknowledge the inherent "tension" between them. Both are intricate products of human endeavor, meticulously crafted and refined through generations. They serve as testaments to the human spirit, embodying our collective identity and aspirations. Shaped by our hands and minds, they simultaneously elevate us to new heights, celebrating our capacity for material and intellectual achievement.

Cultural development, by its very nature, is an ongoing process. However, it is not immune to periods of stagnation or regression, often triggered by complex interplay of internal and external factors. Despite these setbacks, culture possesses the inherent resilience to re-emerge and continue its unique path of evolution. Unlike culture's ubiquitous presence, civilizations do not arise spontaneously in every corner of the globe. They emerge like radiant stars, illuminating specific moments in history with their transformative potential.

By meticulously examining the intricate relationship between civilization and culture, we unlock a deeper comprehension of the dynamic forces propelling human progress. Their distinct yet interconnected journeys serve as threads, illuminating the ever-evolving tapestry of human achievement.

Through the lens of two key conceptual pillars, we can refine our understanding of "culture" and "civilization," their significance, emergence, influence on human development, and current state. Firstly, it is posited that civilizations, regardless of geographical bounds, arise at a specific juncture where cultural development experiences a "pause." Secondly, we must consider the expression of "civilization" as a pinnacle, a "shining star" erupting from continuous cultural development and self-expression. Under this framework, assigning a negative connotation to "civilization" becomes untenable.

Samuel Huntington's concept of a "clash of civilizations" does not demonize these entities; rather, it serves as a warning to progressive thinkers about potential conflicts. Indeed, if humanity remains indifferent to the potential clash between its intellectual potential and its own creations, tragedy may ensue. However, civilizations themselves are not inherently to blame.

By harnessing our collective consciousness and approaching these entities with vigilance and foresight, we can foster harmony instead of confrontation between diverse civilizations. This would enable us to channel our achievements towards progress, longevity, and the continued flourishing of life on our planet. Failure to do so could pave the way for irreparable tragedies in future civilizations.

Given the scientific, theoretical, and political complexities of this issue, its comprehensive study as a unified problem, drawing upon insights from diverse experts, becomes paramount. While current research often compartmentalizes these aspects, a unified approach aimed at preserving civilization through collaboration is urgently needed. Recognizing the intricate nature of this problem and the necessity for interdisciplinary cooperation, we will delve deeper into the potential tragedies arising from clashes of civilizations in subsequent analyses.

Cultural development is an ongoing process. However, it is not always linear, and periods of crisis can interrupt its trajectory. Civilizations, representing a pinnacle of cultural achievement, emerge at specific historical stages characterized by a "pause" in continuous cultural development. They express their unique character through advancements in various fields, analogous to a luminous star. This concept necessitates a nuanced understanding of "civilization," avoiding negative connotations and instead acknowledging its potential for positive contributions.

Samuel Huntington's "clash of civilizations" thesis does not inherently paint civilizations as negative forces. However, it serves as a cautionary tale, highlighting the possibility of conflict arising from cultural differences. While such clashes can represent setbacks, they are not preordained outcomes. By critically examining and understanding these differences, humanity can forge harmony and utilize the achievements of various civilizations for collective progress. Failure to do so could lead to devastating consequences.

The driving forces of globalization are deeply intertwined with the advancements of contemporary civilization, manifested in scientific, technological, and communication breakthroughs. However, alongside these achievements, there exists a potential for negative impacts on cultural identity, ethical values, and traditional ways of life. Recognizing this duality is crucial in navigating the future of globalization. Therefore, the question arises: should we embrace the fruits of modern civilization or reject them altogether?

The assertion that we cannot reject globalization is undeniable. The contemporary era transcends mere "development" markers; it constitutes a distinct historical stage characterized by highly developed means and factors propelling globalization, fundamentally altering the lives of all humankind. Consequently, harnessing its potential becomes imperative. Neglecting to utilize it effectively risks marginalization in the global arena. Therefore, navigating this path necessitates a nuanced understanding of modern civilization, its potential, and its impact on nations and individuals, both presently and in the future.

Historically, civilizations emerged in diverse spheres. However, none were comparable to the ongoing phenomenon of globalization. Thus, defining its unique characteristics becomes crucial. We propose the following:

Firstly, previous civilizations were primarily localized, confined to specific regions or domains. Examples include regional civilizations, religious movements, and advancements in science and technology. While not entirely isolated, their influence wasn't immediate or global. For instance, scientific breakthroughs, though eventually spreading, initially impacted only specific disciplines. Over time, however, revolutionary scientific achievements in one field demonstrably influenced others, leading to a gradual integration of knowledge. The notion that scientific and technological progress should serve humanity's betterment manifested in practice,albeit slowly.

In stark contrast, modern civilization pulsates with globalization. No geographical or disciplinary boundaries constrain its reach. Scientific, technological, and innovative advancements in the United States, Europe, or Africa swiftly reverberate across the globe. Currently, advancements in physics, chemistry, biology, and medicine exhibit interconnected and harmonious development. Integration, rather than differentiation, defines the very essence of contemporary civilization.

Secondly, past civilizations were generally limited in size and scope. Notably, significant advancements in specific scientific, cultural, and other fields typically occurred within isolated networks, failing to achieve fully integrated development across all sectors. For example, progress in chemistry, physics, mathematics, or construction might flourish within certain industries, yet not spur simultaneous development in all directions. In this sense, their impact remained "narrow" and "quantitative," confined to specific areas and eras. In contrast, contemporary advancements at the civilizational level in science, technology, agriculture, and other domains trigger substantial changes not only within individual sectors but across the entire spectrum.

Thirdly, historical civilizations, even if considered groundbreaking for their time, often experienced lengthy implementation delays, hindering their real-world application. Their potential often remained unrealized until specific historical stages, when they were finally recognized and integrated as major achievements. For instance, in Central Asia during the 9th-12th centuries, groundbreaking scientific discoveries and concepts failed to gain immediate recognition and practical application. Today, however, any theoretically sound advancements in science, technology, and communication can be rapidly implemented and translated into material and spiritual productive forces. This expedited process stems from the significantly higher level of social and intellectual potential that exists today, along with increased opportunities for application.

Fourthly, past civilizations generally exerted a positive influence on human development. Notably, the early medieval civilization in the East significantly impacted the Western world, while subsequent Western advancements reciprocally influenced Eastern development. In essence, civilizations traditionally fostered closer ties and understanding between nations and peoples. Conversely, contemporary civilization presents a more nuanced picture, characterized by both positive and negative aspects. While some elements, such as powerful communication networks and economic potential, offer opportunities for collaboration, others, like certain Western countries' attempts at global dominance, generate significant discontent and conflict. A crucial difference between today's civilization and its predecessors lies in the impact of globalization. While facilitating interconnectedness, globalization also poses challenges to the distinct cultural identities and traditions of various nations and peoples, potentially impacting the overall prestige and standing of contemporary civilization.

Fifth, while past civilizations developed over extended periods, they often represented the interests of all humanity, not just specific countries or peoples. Their content and direction were not aimed at creating a "mass culture" serving the interests of a limited group. Instead, they emphasized the development of individual cultures within their own contexts, contributing to a universal culture through free interaction and enrichment. This formed a strategic direction for the positive development of past civilizations.

However, the main direction of modern civilization seems to be "mass culture," which serves to ensure the dominance of a select group of countries with access to material, spiritual, technical, and technological advancements.

This "popular culture," or perhaps more accurately, "mass spirituality," is not universal. It is not characterized by inclusivity or abundance. Instead, developed countries often attempt to establish global dominance and control resources, while simultaneously promoting a spirituality that is both ideologically shallow and embodies violence and moral depravity. This undermines not only developing nations but also the very people of these developed countries.

It is important to note that "mass culture" was not created by the ordinary citizens of developed nations. It was instead conceived and implemented by a specific political elite seeking to manipulate the masses for their own purposes. While ordinary people may have participated in activities promoting this "spirituality" in pursuit of material well-being, they have ultimately become victims of this process.

Despite their high material wealth, many individuals in developed countries now find themselves spiritually impoverished and alienated from universal values such as kindness, family, mutual aid, and kinship. These values, they realize, cannot be easily restored.

Therefore, it is crucial to recognize that ordinary people are not the creators of "mass spirituality" but rather its participants and victims. As globalization accelerates, this process threatens to spread further across the world.

The globalization process accelerates the growth of both material and spiritual needs, prompting a shift in traditional mentalities. This phenomenon fosters the emergence of a "mass man" archetype, characterized by a blend of conservatism and adaptability. While mentality generally lags behind period changes, in this instance, it aligns itself with material advancement, exhibiting a degree of conservatism compared to the surrounding context.

Within the contemporary globalization framework, "mass culture" significantly influences the transformation of traditional mentalities. However, this influence can have both positive and negative consequences. While fostering individualism, ambition, and a drive towards societal improvement, it can also harbor negative traits like greed, alienation, and disregard for others.

Therefore, a crucial strategic objective for modern civilization lies in navigating the globalization process, particularly the development of "mass culture," towards fostering a universal spirituality that counteracts the emergence of such negative traits in individuals.

In examining various facets of modern civilization, several key developments merit consideration:

a) The prioritization of democracy, equality, and human rights as core principles of human development.

b) The cessation of ideological divides and the active translation of diverse ideas into practice.

c) The growing emphasis on human interests over class-based interests.

d) The shift from a "formational" approach (viewing society through a class lens) to a "civilizational" approach (emphasizing productive forces and development).

e) The increasing priority of preventing global conflicts and fostering international cooperation.

These trends paint a positive political and spiritual portrait of contemporary civilization, marked by reduced global conflict and a rising awareness of the need for peaceful coexistence.

It is crucial to recognize that contemporary civilization transcends the narrow definition of culture. Its vast scope encompasses humanity's and Earth's most remarkable achievements, extending far beyond cultural boundaries. These advancements boast transformative power, having revolutionized the world and ushering in a new era where preserving national identities takes precedence over ideological conflicts.

Consequently, today's "civilization" stands unique compared to civilizations of the past. Notably, science, technology, modern communication tools, and other instruments now driving globalization serve as products of the human mind, testament to its potential, scale, and material power. Under their influence, humanity has attained remarkable progress, surpassing all previous achievements. Notably, human intellectual potential has grown significantly, leading to successes in diverse fields, with the exception of death's reversal. Our endeavors range from tackling complex issues like space exploration and artificial intelligence (with an estimated 4 million constructs already existing) to developing non-technologies in production, healthcare, and disease treatment. To characterize these accomplishments solely as "cultural development" fails to capture their true essence. They represent not just cultural progress but a 21st-century civilization propelling humanity to a new developmental stage. As mentioned earlier, "civilization" differs from mere culture; it signifies a revolutionary shift expressing materiality, periodically emerging as a product of human intelligence at specific historical junctures.

Here, the author joins other scholars in examining modern civilization, focusing on its potential and manifestations as an entity. Globalization, a prevalent phenomenon in today's world, increasingly amplifies the most significant outcomes of modern civilization.

While contemplating the unique characteristics of globalization-infused civilization, it is paramount to remember that humans are not merely passive participants but active creators and influencers. In essence, they actively engage in the globalization process, manifesting its positive and negative aspects. Most individuals participate based on their interests and needs, not driven by external dictates. This active involvement is inherently positive, for it fosters the awareness of leveraging globalization's opportunities to mitigate its potential downsides.

While humanity's contemporary civilization enjoys growing recognition under globalization's influence, it simultaneously grapples with a crisis. This struggle pits divergent interests against each other, witnessing advancements used for nefarious purposes—violence, indifference, and a spectrum of negative behaviors—eroding its prestige. Instead of fulfilling its potential and serving humanity, civilization finds itself under pressure from these negative aspects of globalization.

Essential markers of civilization extend beyond material well-being achieved through its advances. They encompass positive transformations in consciousness, worldview, and relationships. Unfortunately, the burgeoning deprivation and alienation of individuals, stemming from the aforementioned negative behaviors, manifests as a crisis of civilization itself. Globalization's negative impact intensifies this.

We posit that:

The pace of globalization outstrips the desire within individuals to realize their inner potential.

Material needs rise not from genuine civilizational advancement in consciousness, worldview, or psyche, but from negative external changes fueled by globalization.

Today, individuals, often unknowingly, cultivate dependence on external aspects of their psyche. Knowledge seamlessly integrates into the collective flow, fostering a growing tendency to prioritize external concerns over self-reflection and uncritical assimilation. This directly relates to the creation of behaviors aimed at expanding the "mass" and promoting imitation.

Globalization shapes contemporary value systems and lifestyles alongside the popularization of civilization. Notably, mentalities have undergone considerable shifts (as explored earlier). Changes in our way of life are demonstrably civilizational. Twenty years ago, rural weddings and celebrations revolved around felt and mats, with people seated on them. Today, restaurants host these events, and villages witness the construction of wedding venues. Remarkably, these restaurants thrive, reflecting the enhanced well-being and spiritual enlightenment within our society.

Three decades ago, a man with a donkey-drawn cart signified affluence. This evolved to motorcycles, then Zhiguli cars in the 80s, followed by basic Nexia models in the early 90s. Regardless of the quality of Uzbek-made cars, it seems a "tradition" has emerged where only those with two or three cars, not one, are considered "rich." Similarly, the design, appearance, furnishings, and amenities of contemporary houses, along with their cutlery, televisions, and recreational facilities, vastly surpass those of two decades ago. This progress within a mere twenty years underscores the advancements made. While these appear like natural progressions, it is noteworthy that humanity, throughout its historical journey, has never witnessed such rapid advancements concentrated in just the 21st century. These, in their scale, sophistication, and growing popularity, serve as potent indicators of modern civilization.

When considering the grand scale and potential of civilizations, it's crucial to remember their interconnected nature and deliberate creation. Unlike spontaneous phenomena, they arise from the concerted efforts of advanced intellectuals within a society, who act as a driving force. Through their activities, the general population becomes a material force, contributing to the collective advancement. This underscores the notion, championed by intellectuals, that a nation's wealth serves as a key indicator of its developmental level. Furthermore, intellectuals play a vital role in engaging the country and its people in the ongoing processes of civilization.

However, the issue of globalizing these aforementioned achievements demands careful consideration. A closer examination reveals an inherent disparity between civilization and globalization. While civilization represents a reflection and manifestation of positive, high-level development, globalization, in its ideal form, should serve as a process facilitating the widespread dissemination of these positive aspects. Unfortunately, current realities paint a more nuanced picture. Globalization carries the potential to not only empower and enrich populations but also to inadvertently contribute to the impoverishment of human spirituality and the spread of factors leading to crises. This highlights the contradictions between modern civilization and the globalization process.

These contradictions stem primarily from the influence of subjective factors. While civilizations are indeed established by intellectuals drawn from the populace, and some of their achievements undoubtedly benefit society, a concerning trend has emerged. Certain accomplishments are manipulated to serve the interests of a select group of highly developed countries. These nations prioritize objectives like wealth accumulation, global dominance, and exerting control over others, thereby undermining the essential universality that should define modern civilization.

Therefore, even if the driving forces behind contemporary globalization are rooted in the achievements of civilization, the fact that some nations exploit these advancements for their own agendas exposes a fundamental inconsistency. Addressing this multifaceted issue requires a comprehensive approach encompassing political, social, economic, and military considerations.

The repercussions of this dissonance extend to various aspects of human existence, encompassing national and spiritual development, interethnic relations, and interregional interactions. While these spheres are undoubtedly intertwined by shared interests and needs, completely directing all civilizational achievements toward the common good proves equally impossible as halting the tides of globalization itself. Consider the development of devastating weapons capable of annihilating humanity within minutes. While undeniably a testament to humanity's intellectual potential and a reflection of advanced science and technology, these weapons embody a tragic contradiction. They simultaneously represent a great achievement and a stark expression of modern civilization's potential for self-destruction.

This paradox raises profound questions about the true nature of our civilization. Can an entity capable of inflicting such devastation truly be termed "civilized"? Moreover, despite recognizing the tragic implications of these weapons, some nations continue to escalate the arms race, deploying them in various regions – a path destined to end in catastrophe. Given their capacity to erase humanity from existence, is such "civilization" even desirable? Does humanity possess the moral right to take pride in its creation?

These are pressing questions that demand our collective attention and concerted action. By acknowledging the complexities and contradictions inherent in both civilization and globalization, we can embark on a path towards a future where humanity's advancements truly serve the greater good, fostering peace, progress, and shared prosperity for all.

Indeed, if human thought and selfless labor are the driving forces behind civilization's emergence, can humanity itself hinder the development of detrimental aspects that lead to great tragedies? The answer is yes, but it requires addressing two crucial factors.

Firstly, global unity remains elusive. Although positive and negative changes resonate across the world, recognizing their universal impact has not translated into widespread, unified action. Courage and collective will are essential to harness the positive aspects of these changes for shared development while proactively mitigating the negative ones through strengthened cooperation and solidarity. However, achieving this universal task is challenging. Socioeconomic disparities abound, with significant segments of the global population struggling economically. This inequality hinders global unity and collective action against looming threats.

Secondly, developed nations hold a critical responsibility. They must extend financial and developmental assistance to less fortunate countries and their populations, preventing future tragedies arising from inequities. As Zbigniew Brzezinski cautioned, "globalization should not be misused to oppress people on the path to economic superiority." It is crucial to ensure aid is unbiased and prioritizes genuine human development over self-serving interests.

Developed nations, on the other hand, must also practice restraint in their resource consumption. While growth needs drive innovation, "containment" shouldn't stifle progress. The goal is not for developed nations to monopolize resources but to advocate for responsible and sustainable utilization by all. As resources are finite and interconnected, depletion in one region inevitably impacts others. This necessitates fostering a global culture of solidarity, cooperation, and mutual assistance. Failure to do so, particularly driven by the inaction of leaders and politicians from developed nations, could turn globalization into a "third world war," jeopardizing the very civilization humanity has built.

Hence, alerting the world community to this imminent danger is paramount. Recognizing the need for global cooperation to prevent this tragedy is a strategic imperative for ensuring the continued progress of humanity.

While the concept of "globalization" remains abstract, its driving forces – human intelligence and dedicated efforts – propel it to manifest as a concrete process. This process is yielding significant achievements in science, technology, engineering, and diverse communication domains. However, the transformation of these advancements into practical applications remains crucial for its transition from abstraction to materiality. Just as the advancement of science, technology, and communication fuels globalization, their widespread dissemination is equally reliant on the process itself. These elements develop in a mutually reinforcing symbiosis.

The current phase of globalization represents a distinct stage in human progress, significantly different from the "integration," "internationalization," and "cooperation" of the past. This acceleration is largely driven by the rapid conversion of scientific, technological, and communicative advancements into tangible societal forces. Consequently, globalization becomes an integral part of contemporary civilization, propelling development and transforming human achievements into shared resources.

However, a paradox emerges from this progress. While these advancements reflect the pinnacle of contemporary civilization, they also harbor the potential to become instruments of annihilation, jeopardizing humanity's very existence.

The primary danger lies in the potential for globalization to undermine the civilization it sustains. Unequal access and application of these advancements exacerbate existing inequalities, leading to further disparities in development between those who possess them and those who do not. This disparity, in turn, amplifies the risk of conflict. If allowed to escalate, it could result in the nullification of all human achievements to date, forcing humanity to rebuild civilization from the ashes.

In this context, preserving national identity and its associated spiritual values becomes crucial. These values embody the essence of human self-awareness and empathy, which can guide the resolution of conflicts through enlightened means.

Within academic discourse, interpretations of "civilization" vary. Some scholars include not only material wealth acquired through human ingenuity but also its potential disappearance. However, we propose a more nuanced view: "civilization" signifies the cumulative achievements of humanity at a specific stage of development, marking progress rather than destruction. It is not a fleeting cultural phenomenon, but rather the culmination of significant advancements within a continuous trajectory. Therefore, any advancements or crises that contradict the interests and progress of humanity cannot be considered a component of civilization; they are, in fact, its antithesis.

The "civilization" humanity has attained through its intellectual potential today differs significantly from its past in terms of the scale and speed of dissemination. This contemporary civilization, embodied by advancements in science, technology, and communication, is not just transforming individual networks; it is reshaping their interactions, impacting people's mentality, worldview, lifestyle, and moral values. Notably, the current process of globalization plays a pivotal role in transforming civilization into a "global" phenomenon. Just as globalization cannot exist without civilization, civilization cannot be imagined without globalization. This level of harmony is unprecedented in human history, and achieving it serves as a unique indicator of progress in the human experience.

However, only if humanity can harness this harmony for the collective good, transcending the interests of a select few developed nations, can it ensure a long and stable future on this earth.

Contemporary "civilization," shaped by humanity's intellectual prowess, exhibits a stark contrast to its past in terms of both the breadth and rapidity of its diffusion. Science, technology, and various communication systems fuel this phenomenon, transforming not only individual networks but also their intricate interactions. This, in turn, reshapes human mentality, worldview, lifestyle, and moral values. Globalization serves as a powerful catalyst in this metamorphosis, propelling civilization towards a truly "global" state. The interdependence between the two is undeniable: just as globalization hinges on existing civilization, civilization's trajectory is inextricably linked to the forces of globalization. This degree of integration is unprecedented in human history, marking a unique milestone in our collective journey.

However, realizing the full potential of this harmonious interplay hinges on humanity's capacity to prioritize the collective good over the aspirations of select developed nations. Only by channeling this force towards the betterment of all can we ensure a stable and prosperous future for humanity on this shared planet.

1.3. GLOBALIZATION, CIVILIZATION AND NATION

This analysis contends that the interconnected relationship between globalization, civilization, and the scientific, technological advancements driving them forms a unique perspective on modern civilization. These elements could potentially coalesce into a "universal spirituality." However, we have also acknowledged the potential negative effects of globalization, including the possible collapse of national identities, which could be construed as a "civilizational crisis" aiming to dismantle nations, ethnicities, and distinct peoples in favor of a single, homogenized identity.

Given these concerns, a crucial question arises: what is the fate of the "nation" in this evolving global landscape? To gain deeper insights, we must delve into the complexities of this issue.

Superficial vs. Deeper Perspectives:

Superficially, it might seem that developed nations like the United States prioritize "citizenship" over "nationality." The sentiment of "I am American" often takes precedence over "I am English" or "I am French." Conversely, in less developed countries, a stronger emphasis tends to be placed on national identity, often exceeding the importance of mere citizenship.

What explains this discrepancy? Is the dominance of citizenship in developed nations solely due to their higher economic well-being and perceived fulfillment of national and spiritual needs? Or is it perhaps a consequence of an underestimation of the potential threat to their cultural identity? Alternatively, does the very essence of "nation" hold an intrinsic connection to human existence and identity? These are indeed challenging questions.

Shifting Demographics and National Identity:

It's noteworthy that even in developed countries with declining birth rates among the native population, immigration plays a significant role in replenishing demographics. This raises concerns about potential cultural shifts and even a possible loss of national identity in the future. In response, leaders often resort to emphasizing a more inclusive "we" rather than focusing solely on the "nation," aiming to differentiate themselves from immigrants while still preserving a sense of national unity. While the specific terminology might vary, the underlying intention often points towards safeguarding the core identity of the nation.

Before delving into the specific questions, it's crucial to revisit the concept of "nation" and the factors contributing to its formation. We have extensively explored this concept in our previous works [1], drawing upon various perspectives to articulate our own understanding. While we refrain from reiterating those details here, it's necessary to provide the definition we established and the underlying rationale.

We define a nation as:

An independent entity possessing its own state, economic system, and territory. This entity is grounded in a shared language, a distinct sense of national identity and spirituality (in its broadest sense), cohesive customs, traditions, and values, and the ethnic unity of its people who generate and preserve their material and spiritual wealth.

This definition deviates from some existing academic interpretations in several key respects:

Emphasis on National Identity: We prioritize national identity as a fundamental characteristic, positing that its absence prevents a nation from distinguishing itself spiritually and forming a unified, independent entity. Only through self-awareness can a nation truly understand and affirm its unique "I."

People as Nation's Foundation: We highlight people as the embodiment of a nation. While "nation" may seem abstract, it manifests concretely through the natural, spiritual, and cultural organization of individuals residing within a shared territory, language, customs, and values. A nation devoid of its people is inconceivable, and belonging to a specific nation constitutes a core aspect of human identity (a topic we will explore further later).

State as Unifying Force: We acknowledge the state as a significant attribute of a nation, emphasizing its role in unifying, organizing, and solidifying the identity of people who share a common language, customs, traditions, and values within a specific territory.

It is acknowledged that some scholars hesitate or even reject the notion of the state as a symbol of the nation as a whole. This apprehension often stems from concerns about multi-ethnic societies and the potential aspirations of non-titular nations to establish their own states. However, dismissing the unifying role of the state based on such anxieties lacks compelling justification.

Historically, states have typically formed around dominant populations inhabiting specific territories for extended periods. These dominant populations often give their name to the state, establishing a "titular" status. Importantly, non-titular groups also have the potential to possess their own states in separate regions. Additionally, freedom of movement for individuals irrespective of their titular status is a widely recognized and valued human right. Furthermore, sustainable development can flourish in contexts where non-titular groups enjoy equal rights in all spheres alongside the titular nation.

Despite these points, the state remains a crucial symbol of the nation for several reasons:

1. Unity and Continuity: As mentioned earlier, the state fosters national unity and ensures the nation's continued existence. It takes responsibility for preserving and transmitting unique customs, traditions, and values, safeguarding the inherited heritage and nurturing future generations. Scattered and disunited, nations lose the capacity to effectively achieve these goals.

2. Global Context: In a globalized world, the preservation of national identity presents a complex challenge. Globalization presents the risk of smaller and less developed nations being absorbed by larger, more powerful ones. In such

circumstances, having a distinct state serves as a vital bulwark against cultural assimilation and political marginalization.

3. Inclusive Development: Contrary to anxieties about discrimination, a titular state does not imply indifference to the well-being of non-titular groups. In fact, a state's long-term prosperity hinges on its tolerance and commitment to the sustainable development of all its inhabitants, regardless of their titular status[2].

Today, the multiethnic existence of states has become a reality, and representatives of different nationalities and ethnic groups living in them achieve general progress in mutual understanding and support. As First President Islam Karimov noted: «The real wealth of the world is the diversity of values, the ability to exchange values and enrich each other»[2 v].

It is crucial to distinguish between globalization as a process and civilization as a stage of human progress. While globalization represents a new phase in human thought and integration into the global economic landscape, it should not be conflated with civilization itself.

1. Globalization: A Product of Intellectual Advancement

Globalization is facilitated by several key factors:

Enhanced intellectual potential: Human thought has achieved unprecedented levels, creating advancements in science, technology, and engineering.

Highly developed communications: Rapid communication networks accelerate the dissemination of these advancements.

Integration into world economic life: Participation in global economic systems fuels further development and exchange.

Without these elements, globalization would remain an abstract concept. However, it is important to note that these factors serve as enablers, not the essence of civilization.

2. Distinguishing Globalization from Civilization

Civilization represents the cumulative achievements of humanity at a specific stage of development, embodying progress and advancement beyond mere processes. While globalization facilitates the rapid exchange of knowledge and resources, it does not inherently embody the values and cultural characteristics that define civilization.

3. Hegemonic Tendencies and the Issue of Inequality

While globalization offers undeniable benefits, it also presents challenges. The concentration of wealth and intellectual capital in certain regions can lead to hegemonic tendencies and power imbalances, exacerbating existing inequalities. This raises concerns about exploitative practices and unequal access to resources, which contradict the fundamental ideals of a true civilization.

4. Recognizing the Challenges and Defining the Future

Acknowledging the potential drawbacks of globalization is crucial for guiding its future development. By establishing clear ethical and equitable frameworks, we can harness its potential for the benefit of all.

5. Conclusion: Towards a Future Civilization

While globalization represents a significant step forward in human progress, it is not synonymous with civilization itself. By addressing the challenges it presents and striving for inclusivity and equity, we can work towards a future civilization that leverages the power of interconnectedness for the shared betterment of humanity.

But, on the other hand, it cannot have the status of a full-fledged civilisation with its influence on the destruction of the future of the nation.Because it is known from historical data that until the end of the 19th century - beginning of the 20th century, when globalisation began as a process, the process of formation, development and improvement of nations took place in the world.Although it did not go smoothly, sometimes it developed and manifested itself in situations such as crisis at a certain stage and national revival and development at a certain stage, then we can see that the nation was not defeated by force.If we do not take into account the natural assimilation of small ethnic groups into large nations, the nation has always been progressive.And globalisation, despite the positive aspects mentioned above, is dangerous in that it can destroy the future of nations.

Globalization as a real process develops the spirit of «dependence» in the minds, hearts and worldview of underdeveloped or underdeveloped countries and their peoples, with a number of factors that ensure the priority of today's highly developed countries. In our opinion, they are caused by: a) the economic factor; b) popularization of the achievements of science, technology and technology; (c) Through efforts to disseminate and instill in the minds of the peoples of the world a «popular culture» that has emerged from the powerful economic, intellectual and creative potential of developed countries; (g) The economic and intellectual potential of the least developed countries, which are now on the path of development, and the peoples living in them, lag behind the levels of development of the processes of globalization.

Let us now try to back up our theses with concrete data. "According to international statistics, the share of poor countries with 20% of world income fell from 2.3% in 1960 to 1.4% in 1990 and 1.1% in 1994. The gap between the richest 20% of the world's population and the poorest 20% of the population was 30: 1 in 1960, 61: 1 in 1991, and 78: 1 in 1994. Between 1969 and 1989, the share of the richest 20% of world GDP increased from 70% to 83%, while the share of the poorest 20% fell from 2.3% to 1.4%"[3].

Statistics show that economically developed countries are developing more than developed countries, and poor countries are becoming poorer and poorer. Let's look at the facts again.

"How do Western analysts see the 21st century? Who rules the «ball» in this century? Naturally, a lot is in the hands of transnational corporations. So - the USA. Let's face it: In 1998, 74 of the 200 largest multinationals were under the US flag. Similar corporations accounted for 36.5 percent of the total turnover. The Americans «worked» most of all, when all TMSs taken together - 52.7%. Of the 50 largest companies in the world, 33 are located in the United States. They own 71.8% of all major shares on the exchange. Another living example. The United States, Britain, Germany and France account for 90 percent of the 201 largest industrial and financial companies in the world"[4].

This analysis draws upon data compiled by the World National Statistical Service and a specialized UN agency. It offers a glimpse into the rapid accumulation of material wealth by developed nations.

This raises a crucial question: what would transpire if developed countries held a larger share of available resources and manufactured goods? Given their substantial intellectual, technical, technological, and economic potential, might this process be considered natural? After all, within market systems, not everyone achieves entrepreneurial success, and equating them is inaccurate. Furthermore, market practices operate on the principle of "not for everyone, but for everyone;" those with substantial financial resources, intellectual potential, and entrepreneurial abilities will continue to flourish, while those lacking these attributes may be forced to rely on and follow them. This is the stark reality of globalization, where developed nations arguably leverage it to cultivate dependence in less developed counterparts.

Historically, powerful, developed states have employed force and weaponry to subjugate others and acquire their wealth. From Alexander the Great to the era of the World Wars, countless innocent lives were lost, nations plundered, and cultural heritage destroyed. Aggressive regimes imposed their own customs, traditions, and values upon conquered territories, eroding the national spirit of subjugated populations. While these nations ultimately achieved independence, the journey was fraught with immense hardship. Building unity and collective strength to resist common adversaries necessitated significant time and effort. The struggles for independence and the violence inflicted upon conquered peoples by occupying forces have been extensively documented and continue to be explored.

However, the contemporary landscape differs dramatically. Engaging in world wars through brute force is no longer a viable option for even the most developed nations. The global proliferation of weaponry renders containment virtually impossible. New weapons developed in one nation swiftly permeate others, highlighting the ease with which resources facilitating conflict can move freely.

Beyond this, the world has transitioned from a bipolar to a multipolar system. The dissolution of opposing power structures has diversified global interests, empowering nations to pursue independent policies driven by their own needs rather than external agendas. This significantly restricts the ability of major powers to unite and initiate a global conflict.

Moreover, the intellectual potential of humanity has reached unprecedented heights. We are increasingly aware of the consequences of global confrontation and the challenges of preserving civilization for future generations. The growing number of global challenges, such as environmental threats, necessitates collective action and collaborative solutions.

While the specter of global war may seem diminished, the arms race persists. Experts estimate that each individual on Earth currently carries the equivalent of a ton of explosives. This concerning reality is compounded by the constant development of even more destructive weapons. Despite these advancements, the risk of any nation triggering a global conflict remains minimal. Modern warfare guarantees no victors, and any initiator, regardless of their perceived advantage, would face certain defeat.

In this context, globalization has fundamentally reshaped the nature of war. The focus has shifted from direct physical conflict to the pursuit of economic and technological dominance. This "universalized" approach relies on sophisticated tools to establish dependence on developed nations. The primary weapon in this new war isn't brute force, but rather the intellectual prowess embodied in scientific and technological advancements. These tools are used to subjugate less developed or developing nations, making them reliant on the technology and expertise of their more powerful counterparts.

Developed countries leverage their resources to infiltrate developing economies, applying their scientific and technological achievements to extract material wealth. While competition exists among developed nations for these investments, it ultimately reinforces the existing power dynamic and perpetuates dependence. From the perspective of developing countries, this competition presents an opportunity to attract investment and accelerate their own development.

Further fueling this dynamic is the increasing liberalization of global migration. Exposure to the living standards of developed nations creates a natural desire for similar prosperity among populations in less developed regions. This, coupled with their own growing needs and aspirations, fuels a demand for advancements that their current technological capabilities cannot fulfill. The rapid pace of technological innovation ensures that even yesterday's equipment becomes quickly outdated, further emphasizing the need for modernization.

Therefore, developed nations cannot sustain their own progress in isolation from developing nations with untapped potential. The objectively higher development rates in developed countries create a natural draw for investment, technology, and expertise from these nations.

The main problem in this process is that highly developed countries do not allow less developed and now developing countries to realise their internal potential, to develop science, technology and engineering. Thus, on the one hand, these countries become accustomed to the development of the developed countries through the widespread use of industrial, scientific, technical and technological advances, ignoring their negative dependence on the developed countries and not realising its negative consequences. On the other hand, these countries are forced to use their training because they do not have the opportunity to develop science, technology and the organisation of production to the level of highly developed countries. From the outside, this may seem insignificant as a result of the strong pressure of globalisation, but in practice it leads to a high level of development of developed countries and their peoples, as well as to the dependence of peoples living in less developed and now developing countries.

In the process, the negative effects of globalisation will be intensified and the risk of ruining the prospects of nations will increase. In the process of globalisation, such a situation leads, on the one hand, to the interconnectedness of countries and the peoples living in them, and, on the other hand, to an increase in the potential of highly developed nations and to the attachment and dependence of less developed nations on them. .,

From the above, it is clear that science, technology and engineering, which are driving globalisation, are today leading to the formation of new interstate and interethnic relations. No matter how much they try to help the countries leading the globalisation process and the peoples (nations) living in them on earth with their investments, scientific, technical and technological achievements, as long as the aim is to make a profit, the priority of the nations in the developed countries will be and will continue to be strengthened. In this sense, no matter how glorious today's civilisation may appear to be, their interest in it is much less tragic than the interest of the advanced nations, and even more tragic for the nations that do not try to understand its negative consequences today. Because under the pressure of globalisation, any nation that is linked to other material and technological factors will lose its identity. This will lead to its ultimate failure due to the above factors and its integration into the developed countries.

From the above statistics and theoretical considerations, it can be seen that no matter how high the material factors in the life of nations are in the relations of globalisation and civilisation, they can ultimately lead to the loss of identity of any nation that is not aware of the consequences. and assimilation with developed countries. Thus, from the point of view of material development, a high level of development of science, technology and engineering is a great achievement of mankind, has a positive effect on its development and is a manifestation of the civilisation of the 21st century. Because in the past, mankind has not been able to reach the level of accelerating today's progress. This is an undeniable fact. But today's civilisation is radically different from the civilisations of the past, it has emerged simultaneously with the globalisation that is taking place in the modern world and is taking place under its strong pressure. Civilizations that arose in the past brought equal benefits to all mankind, they naturally moved from one region to another and had a positive impact on the mutual enrichment of peoples. Modern civilisation, influenced by the globalisation process, is rapidly gaining momentum on the basis of the inequality of the parties, serving to ensure the priority of the interests of the developed countries and the peoples (nations) living in them.

Let us try to reflect on the national and spiritual aspects of globalisation, civilisation and inter-ethnic relations.

Nowadays a lot is written and spoken about spirituality, because it is not only a national but also a universal problem. It is important to note that the issues of life and death are conceptualised at the level of spirituality. Moreover, some Heads of State, who until now have linked the development of countries only with the economy, have officially declared at various events in their countries that the expected results cannot be achieved without the development of spirituality. Today they realise that no matter how high the level of economic development in a country with poor spirituality, it may eventually collapse. Because on the basis of spiritual poverty, a negative process occurs, such as the emergence of instability in the country, the emergence of various conflicts, the formation of extremely dangerous attitudes, for example, to put one's own interests above the interests of any nationality or state and society. state and society. As a result, not only instability in the country can arise, but also economic and political crises, as the experience of today's most developed countries shows. Today, without relying on spirituality, it has become a fact that neither the economy nor the political systems are condemned to crisis.

Spirituality is one of the most important sources of sustainability in human relations, nations, states, societies and international relations. It embodies all the values of humanity, such as justice, peace, stability, honesty, impartiality, sincerity, piety, respect for one's rights, consideration of interests. In all countries and societies in which they operate, they ensure economic development, human well-being and political stability.

There is disintegration in countries and societies that do not pay attention to spirituality and do not try to use its educational potential effectively. The main reason for this is that all the universal values embodied in the aforementioned spirituality will disappear. Countries can reach a certain historical stage, high economic development, but the spiritual decline that occurs in the inner life of the country will inevitably eventually drag the economy into its trap. Because as a result of spiritual decline in the internal life of the country, "knowing oneself" in order to accumulate material wealth in any way, indifference to the life of the country, its processes, immorality and even a desire to replace material values. Such as man, family, nation, homeland. Of course, such negative situations are formed gradually, not overnight, and therefore are not visible in the life of the country in the early stages of economic and political life, which ensures the well-being of people. But as time passes, the processes of spiritual decline continue to influence economic and political life. The highly developed countries are going through the same process today. They are trying to use the economic factor to protect themselves from this spiritual decline. That is, they are spending large sums of money to rob them of their lands in order to capture the minds and hearts of the peoples of the world by using their high economic potential. They are pursuing the formation of a "mass spirituality" without national foundations in the localities as a strategic path for their spiritual rebirth. So why are highly developed economies trying to create a "mass spirituality" that can profit from spending unprecedented amounts of money on it? We believe the reasons are as follows:

First, there is a growing desire to understand the identity of all nations and peoples living in the world. This leads to a decrease in the possibility of influencing nations and peoples who want to understand the identity of the developed countries in the future. Today, titles in developed countries are increasingly dependent on the decline of nations and their replacement by migrants. This is becoming a major problem in developed countries. If this process continues in these countries in the future, the title will be associated with a sharp decline in the number of nations living in them and a growing need to prevent the risk of replacing migrants with spirituality.

Secondly, the aim of the countries that are interested in the formation of a "mass spirituality" and that spend a lot of money in this direction is to "persuade" the least developed countries, with the help of various forms of "discriminatory" aid, to give priority to the material (economic) factor: "persuade" them and make them dependent on themselves. The core of this policy is to achieve the spiritual superiority of the declining nations in the developed countries by using the still somewhat limited ability of migrants to occupy these countries. Despite the fact that he has become extremely poor, maintaining it with the help of existing economic opportunities and breaking it in the minds and hearts of countries that have not yet fully reached their Self and need financial assistance (for example, investment, science, technology, technologies The aim is to preserve their spirituality, first of all, to ensure its superiority and through this to gain dominance in the world, is to form "mass spirituality". The formation of "mass spirituality" is not a goal, but a means of preserving the developed countries (nations) and ensuring their domination over the less developed countries of the world and the nations living in them, using the fact that the nations have not yet achieved full equality.

Before going on to discuss the meaning of "mass spirituality", we will try to analyse its differences from "mass culture" and the question of compatibility.

The reason we draw attention to this issue is that the concept of "spirituality" is not found in the literature published in foreign countries where "spirituality" is embedded in "culture". Therefore, it is not used as "mass spirituality" but as "mass culture". However, in the scientific literature published in Uzbekistan during the years of independence, "spirituality" is used as a separate scientific concept. Thanks to the attention paid by the President to the development of spirituality as a separate direction, this concept became popular in the works and articles of Uzbek scientists. However, the concept of "mass spirituality" is not used scientifically, and the concept of "mass culture" is used with a mechanical translation into the Uzbek language, which is used in foreign literature. We believe that this raises a number of uncertainties today. In particular, it: a) undermines the status of spirituality as an independent philosophical category; b) leaves open the question of whether spirituality or culture is formed at all; c) which of the terms "mass spirituality" or "mass culture" can be used to describe the declining values of a person, nation, people, state and society, such as morality, values, national identity, national identity? g) what are the criteria for the relationship between them? d) the components of spirituality and the degree of their relationship remain difficult to answer. In our opinion, this may be due to the fact that the study of the problem does not take into account the fact that there is a point of difference between the levels of general methodology and the methodology of private science.

In fact, "spirituality" has a special status as an independent socio-philosophical category. Its status is also reflected in the fact that man is an inner potential and in his "I", which distinguishes him from other beings. Without the inner potential of man there is no difference to the animal world. He is radically different from other creatures in his consciousness, in his understanding of the world, in his desire to live as a human being in this bright world. It is in these aspects that he manifests his spirituality as a creator and consumer. Based on his spirituality, he creates material wealth, enters into various relationships and takes a worthy place in society.

If we interpret spirituality from the perspective of a nation, it is impossible to imagine a nation without it. For the originality, customs, traditions and values of a nation, as an integral part of its spirituality, reflect its "I". In this sense, spirituality has the same status and importance as material and political factors in the life of an individual, a nation, a state and a society. At the same time, it is only when these two factors are based on human spirituality that they can effectively develop an effective individual, nation, state and society.

It is clear from what has been said that spirituality has an independent status, not as a part of the structure of culture, but as a socio-philosophical category (concept). Of course, spirituality does not mean that it is completely independent of culture, economy and politics, they are interconnected. The independence between them is relative and at the same time they differ from each other in their specific tasks and functions.

Let us now try to reflect on the concepts of spirituality and culture and their relationship. First of all, since spirituality is an independent factor, we have to ask whether it or a culture was formed earlier. As mentioned above, spirituality and culture are intertwined. One cannot exist without the other. But in practice, spirituality takes precedence. It is impossible to form a culture without spirituality. Culture is formed only on the basis of high spirituality. At the same time, culture transforms spirituality into a material being. This means that the existing material heritage, historical monuments, technical, technological equipment are on the one hand an expression of culture, but on the other hand they are also an expression of spirituality. They reflect a person's world view, psyche, inner world, imagination, morality, intelligence, beauty and glory. Man creates culture on the basis of these possibilities.

Now, on the basis of this conceptual idea, we are trying to find an answer to the question whether we should think about "mass culture" emerging in the context of globalisation, or about "mass spirituality".

Today, from the scientific literature published abroad to the literature published in Uzbekistan, the concept of "mass culture" is used, not "mass spirituality"[5].

Recently, the concept of "mass culture"[6] has begun to be used. Authors who used it in their articles and monographs put forward a number of new ideas about the negative aspects of spiritual influences that today penetrate our national spirituality from abroad. We are not talking about their views on "mass culture", "culture of the masses", but to find out whether it is possible to use the concept of "mass spirituality" instead of these concepts.

In our opinion, when today we think about the weakening of national spirituality under the influence of globalisation, it is necessary to clarify the concepts of "mass culture" and "mass spirituality". This is due to the fact that the concept of "mass culture" is used in the scientific literature published abroad, including in Russia, and is still being published, and "spirituality" is embedded in it. "Spirituality" as an independent scientific concept does not appear in the above-mentioned literature. It is not even in the Russian dictionaries available today. But there are many opinions about the elements of which it consists, its role in society and human life. Thus, due to the fact that "spirituality" was not used as an independent concept in scientific literature, but was absorbed by "culture" and translated into the Uzbek language as culture, "mass spirituality" was not used as an independent concept and factor in scientific research. consumption has become common in the soaked state. This confusion in the use of concepts makes it difficult to fully understand the nature and status of "mass spirituality". In fact, "mass spirituality" has an independent concept and its own independent essence. Firstly, as mentioned above, spirituality is a comprehensive concept of culture, which includes a person's world view, morality, psyche, inner world, ability to imagine existence, intelligence, beauty, understanding and self-expression, attitude to various processes, nation, understanding of responsibility to society, self-awareness and devotion to oneself. This includes a person's worldview, morality, psyche, inner world, ability to imagine existence, intelligence, beauty, understanding and self-expression, attitude towards different processes, nation, understanding of responsibility to society, self-awareness and devotion to self. All this is not an expression of materiality per se, but manifests itself as a manifestation of spirituality. Secondly, 'culture' means the means of labour, housing, basic necessities, clothing, transport, communication, machinery, equipment and other material values created as a result of human activity. True, they are also a product of the development of human thought. But they are not as "abstract" as spirituality, they are material beings. They are created by human beings with their intellect, manual labour and activities. And they represent a real being in their own right. On the other hand, a real spiritual being manifests itself through the actions, contents, levels and effects of the created materiality. Thus culture transforms spirituality into materiality. The same dialectical relationship between 'spirituality' and 'culture' operates in the same process. Based on the foregoing, when we speak today of the collapse of national spirituality, we mean that the negative influence of the "mass culture" forming in the West is reflected primarily in spirituality. Because today "material culture" (tools, housing, basic necessities, transportation, communication, technical equipment), that is, material goods created by human labour, is not in crisis, but it improves and enhances people's lives, productive life is in the process of cultivation to help them to forgive. In this sense, when we talk about the influx of "mass culture" and its negative impact on national cultures, we must take into account the influx of "mass spirituality" and its impact on the collapse of national spirituality. In fact, all the negative aspects of national spirituality in our lives today occur under the influence of the "mass spirituality" formed by the developed countries.

What is "mass spirituality", how is it formed and how does it influence national spirituality? We will try to find answers to the following questions: Before addressing this issue, we believe it is necessary to clarify the process of revival of the concept of "mass culture". The fact is that the concept of "mass culture" has been used in literature since Soviet times[7].

It is not the essence of "mass culture" that aims to destroy national culture, but rather the ideological struggle between the two systems - socialism and capitalism, the "superiority" of the communist system over capitalism and the "crisis" of bourgeois society. ... This means that "mass culture" aims to protect the interests of the system and ideology in criticism. This concept is also used in literature published in Uzbekistan. But 'popular culture' refers to clubs, palaces of culture, parks, libraries and museums that are always visited and used by the public.

Thus, the concepts of "spirituality" and "mass spirituality" were not considered in the form in which we understand and express them today, before the collapse of the former Soviet Union and the subsequent collapse of world socialism. Today we believe that "mass spirituality" is aimed at undermining national spirituality, not in terms of class and system.

In addition to the above, Uzbek scholars today use not only "mass spirituality", but also, as mentioned above, the concepts of "mass culture", "mass culture". Regardless of how these concepts are used, all authors express their views on the negative impact of national spirituality on erosion. What is "mass spirituality"?

"Mass spirituality" is the spirituality of the "dying West" (Patrick Buchanan), which, in its efforts to maintain itself in this enlightened world, reveals its universal values and ultimately reaches material heights and content impoverishment. The spirituality of the advanced nations consists in stripping the peoples who have not yet reached the heights of progress of their identity, customs, traditions and values, and turning them into Manchus who will obey their will without hesitation. The "mass spirituality" is different from the universal spirituality in its structure, hierarchy and content, and is based on the spirituality of nations and peoples with economic, political and military power, which is capable of transmitting its influence to the world. Its influence is never natural, but is based on ideological and ideological strength and is the result of activities carried out with clear objectives and interests on the way to priority. From the point of view of the growing pressure and aggression of the nations and peoples living in the highly developed countries, the use of the opportunities available to them to serve their domination in the less developed or developing countries, as well as the nations and peoples living in them, is an expression of terror.

Universal spirituality, as opposed to 'mass spirituality', spreads naturally because it combines aspects of different nations that provide spiritual nourishment for other nations and has a positive impact on the spiritual development of different nations around the world. At the same time, the very process of forming universal human spirituality contributes to the development of national spirituality. For in this process, different nations and peoples have equal rights, freedom, will and opportunities and participate with the most progressive wealth inherent in them. In the universal spirituality formed in this process, each nation seeks to develop aspects that can bring joy, inspiration and spiritual wealth to others, and actively participates in its popularisation. It is not based on the goal of conquering the minds and hearts of other nations and peoples by force, but on universal values such as spiritual equality, sincerity, mutual friendship, brotherhood, mutual honour and mutual enrichment. Universal spirituality is formed by the whole of humanity, with its developed worldview and practical activities, regardless of nationality, ethnicity, region of residence, gender and religious beliefs, and serves human life. In this sense, it is also the property of all humanity. So, if today a "mass spirituality" is rapidly emerging, if the erosion of national spirituality is intensifying, does a universal culture have a future? At what cost does it survive and flourish?

Answering these questions is an extremely difficult task. Because today the rhythm (acceleration) of the levels of formation, development and popularisation of "mass spirituality" is stronger than the levels of formation of universal spirituality. This is a serious threat not only to the future of the less developed countries or the nations and peoples living in them, but also to the future of the countries living in them, nations and peoples trying to establish their dominance in the world. For the spiritually deprived world is doomed to destruction. So, metaphorically speaking, in this stream both the "king" and the "gado" suffer the same tragedy. Perhaps tomorrow it will be too late if both sides, i.e. those who form and promote "mass spirituality" and those who are under its influence, do not realise this today. The fate of the civilisation that humanity has created today, and therefore the fate of humanity tomorrow, will depend on the extent to which this truth is realised.

What we have said in the past does not mean that there is no 'spirituality' today, but that it is under great pressure. Today it is being formed by the most advanced people in the world, and it is inevitable that tomorrow such people will be able to live on Earth and use the opportunities they have for the future of humanity. However, we must not forget that they live together with people with evil intentions, who do not refuse to realise them, even at the expense of their own interests, even at the expense of great catastrophes that befall the whole of humanity. Will the formation of a universal spirituality be a priority in the development of the peoples of the world, or will actions aimed at the formation of a "mass spirituality" be a priority? The search for a solution to this question becomes a puzzle for all progressive people. The reason why we pay so much attention to this process is that, as the American professor Samuel Huntington warned9 , it is still difficult to imagine the future of a nation, a part of a civilisation, its spirituality, if the future struggle is not between systems but between civilisations. Since civilisations are the product of human thought, their preservation or destruction remains dependent on humanity. It should also be noted that, as a manifestation of the contradictions that arise today, we are witnessing the idea put forward by Western scientists to show the name through relations between peoples and migrants ("Death of the West" by Patrick Buchanan). It is not by chance that we are thinking about and paying special attention to the emerging "mass spirituality". For when national spirituality is defeated, the nation first dies spiritually and physically in its own land. This means that the nation becomes a "faceless" mass. In this sense, it is also necessary to preserve the nation in order to preserve spirituality.

It is no coincidence that today the leaders of Western states promote the idea of protecting their nation from the national spiritual influences brought by migrants in order to preserve it. On 2 February 2011, the Russian television news programme Voskresny Vremya quoted British Prime Minister David Cameron, German Chancellor Angela Merkel, French President Nicolas Sarkozy and Russian President Dmitry Medvedev as saying that "each country has its own country. The nation, its language, customs, traditions and values must be studied and practised by every migrant who enters these countries. Today, migrants who come to the West do not follow them but, on the contrary, develop their spirituality, customs and traditions and popularise them in our country. Others include the following. In particular, according to German Chancellor Angela Merkel, "promoting tolerance towards foreigners will lead to the creation of an enclave in Europe that does not speak the language of its new home, does not know its laws and does not obey them. This must be taken into account".[vi].

In January 2011, at a meeting with the leaders of the State Duma and the Federation Council, the Russian president raised the issue of "Russians" for the first time. "Russia must pay special attention to Russian culture," he said. This is the basis of our multinational culture"[vii]. Meanwhile, a survey by Russian sociologists (VTsIOM) found that 47% of respondents said that the state of inter-ethnic relations had worsened in 2010[viii]. This is also due to the fact that some politicians say things that offend the pride of other nations. In particular, Igor Lebedev, leader of the LDPR faction in the State Duma of the Russian Federation, said that "Russians should be the first in Russia"[ix]. "Clashes" between people of different nationalities in Moscow's Manezhnaya Square on 11 December 2010 caused serious concern among the country's leadership and the entire population, Russian media reported.

In fact, there should be no objection to the policy pursued by every head of state in his country, which gives priority to the language, customs, traditions and values of the titular nation. Indeed, unless the titular nation develops its customs, traditions and values at home and preserves its "image", there is no way of preserving them in other countries. Each nation can only sustain itself as an independent entity in its own country. If people of other nationalities want to live in a country, they must speak its language and respect its customs, traditions and values. Only in this way will inter-ethnic harmony continue to develop. But it is also fair to ask who is to blame for the formation of negative attitudes today. In our opinion, the reasons for the emergence of such relations are as follows: firstly, powerful states have always been hostile to states weaker than themselves, plundering their wealth and taking revenge for the acquisition of resources. At the same time, they have used various methods to exploit cheap labour. While this is not new to science, it should be borne in mind that it is developing rapidly on a practical level in the context of today's globalisation. The main problem here is that the disregard for the countries which the powerful states have occupied and enslaved, and the nations living in them, as a secondary "small", "unconscious" nation, ultimately paves the way for the formation of self-hatred. in the minds and hearts of others; secondly, to regard the development of a one-sided economy as a strategic task for the development of all related infrastructure, ignoring factors which ensure the survival of the nation, such as spirituality and education, leaving it to its own devices, preserving the nation. and its spirituality As a result of the practice of the idea that only wealth is necessary to live in the world, individualism in developed countries, the principle of "know yourself, let others live", everyone should live for himself, rose to the level of the values of the titular nation. As a result, universal values such as family, kinship, children, parents are being rejected and the number of titular nations is decreasing year by year. This, in turn, creates the conditions for migrants with cheap labour from less developed countries to meet this need in the face of the growing demand for labour resources, as well as for their solid foundation in these countries.

Today, the growing hatred of titular nations towards migrants has forced Western countries to pursue a policy of unilateral (economic) development, rather than migrants, neglecting the development of spirituality and education in line with economic development. We can say that this was caused by the formation of the spirit of the desire for wealth and the strengthening of the desire for domination. The basis for the negative attitude towards migrants that politicians are promoting today should not be sought in the migrants themselves, but in the highly developed countries themselves, which are trying to expel them from their countries. The danger of a negative attitude towards migrants today is that if it rises to the level of a priority policy of the developed countries: it will turn into a struggle; secondly, we can say that it also affects interstate relations and creates the risk that its effects will further complicate instability in such a complex world. But the development of tolerance towards them also increases the risk of dividing the world into two camps for their own interests, on the one hand the developed countries and the peoples living in them, and on the other hand the less developed countries or those on the way to development. ... At the same time, the migration of migrants to different countries should be seen as an objective law. Where there is a need for labour resources, the influx of labour resources from other countries of the world is an objective law of economic development. It is a law that always works. Consequently, restricting migrants is also a minefield for the countries that need them.

From the above, it is clear that the desire to preserve national spirituality is characteristic not only of nations under the influence of the "mass spirituality" shaped by the factors that drive globalisation, but also of any evil that shapes and enforces this "mass spirituality" in the minds and hearts of the world's youth. The fact today is that the risk of being late tomorrow will increase if both sides do not seek ways to work together.

The astonishing aspect of this situation that is arising today is that, on the one hand, the intellectual potential of mankind has developed to an unprecedented degree. He needed, or rather, today he has the privilege to rise to the level of performing all things except the resurrection of the dead. A number of nations in the world are being formed as independent entities and are following the path of development. At the same time, a number of ethnic units are formed as a nation. Thus, the achievements of mankind are many. On the other hand, man's appetite is becoming more and more susceptible to malnutrition. He even said that today, instead of strengthening cooperation in solving global problems that could ultimately lead to its total destruction - ecology, food, drugs, nuclear proliferation, increased pollution, the spread of dangerous diseases, reduced supplies of drinking water "," know yourself, let others know. "How does this negative state relate to civilisation? The question arises. If we consider civilisation as a high level of creation of all material and spiritual wealth created by human thinking, intellectual potential, we can see highly developed countries and peoples living in them (nations) together with less developed or developing countries and peoples; we can see the aggravation of contradictions between them as a product of globalisation, which occurred as a result of this high civilisation.

Thus, on the basis of the above considerations, we can say that there is a relationship between civilisation, globalisation and the system of nations, which, despite high rates of development, are experiencing a process of conflict. If we present civilisation today as a material being with a high level of development of science, technology and technology, we will see the results of globalisation in the crisis of national spirituality, when the nation becomes a leading factor in the formation of new policies for its use in the world. It is based on man's growing desire for self-realisation and, as an important part of this, the awareness of belonging to a particular nation. It manifests itself as an opportunity for man to live by striving for the future, to give himself new strength.

PART SECOND. INTERCONNECTION OF GLOBALIZATION AND NATIONAL SPIRITUAL SECURITY

The relationship between globalisation and modern civilisation is undergoing contradictory processes. It is still difficult to find a way to "soften" it. Today, humanity has made unprecedented progress in all areas with its intellectual potential, talent and selfless work. But inequality in the use of these resources also carries the risk of failure. This is particularly evident in the fact that the most developed countries, which are forming a "mass spirituality", are using it to destroy the spirituality of nations and peoples in less developed countries, in order to instil a "mass spirituality" in their consciousness and world view. This in turn leads to national and spiritual division. It is no exaggeration to say that this process is also accelerating the crisis we have reached today. Preventing it has become an urgent task for the whole of humanity today. Implementation is a very complex issue. The diversity of interests is one of the main obstacles. In particular, the development of a sense of belonging and self-awareness in people, which is an integral part of today's civilisation, makes it difficult to reconcile interests and to share equally the achievements of civilisation. For just as there is no nation without a person and no person without a nation, so there can be no nation without a person and a person who is its great value. This means that in order to preserve civilisation, it is first necessary to preserve a person and a nation.

In this part of the book we will try to focus on these aspects of the problem. At the same time, we reflect on the growing real and potential threats to national spirituality under the influence of globalisation and the nature of the factors and instruments that influence it.

2.1. THE NATION OF MAN AND THE NATURE OF ITS MANIFESTATION IN THE CONTEXT OF GLOBALIZATION

The relationship between factors such as globalisation, civilisation, man and nation is a complex socio-philosophical problem. In particular, one of the most important questions today is the search for answers to the questions of what is the position of man in today's globalisation, what values can he preserve or whether globalisation will lead to the loss of his values. Today, his responsibility is growing, especially in the area of preserving values. In particular, there is a growing need to think about the future of his status as a representative of the nation.

The conscious activity of man began, and to bring him to the level of a real "man" became one of the main tasks of philosophy. But this goal remains an invisible problem. It is a natural state. Since man is a living being, his self-knowledge is also difficult. His conscious activity has begun, and instead of preserving existing goods and passing them on to future generations, his spirit of self-sufficiency grows, his spiritual weakness grows more than true "perfection", and his alienation from himself, his nation and society grows. The increase in the number of these negative processes shows that there is no end to the study of the "human" problem. The more interest there is in studying it, the worse the problem becomes. In this sense, the great philosopher Miletus asked Thales: "What is the most difficult thing?" "Self-knowledge,"[1] he said. Due to the lack of self-knowledge, different views on the meaning and social nature of man have persisted from ancient philosophy to modern philosophy.

The purpose of studying a human problem in philosophy is to "help" him to understand himself, to reach his "I", or, more precisely, to find opportunities for his ascent to the level of personality and to use them effectively to reach the level of personality. For when a person is born and grows up, he enters into various social relationships in which his needs and interests are formed. In turn, social relationships create another fog of interests. Until they are balanced, contradictions will arise between them. They don't happen by themselves. It requires a wide range of educational activities. And there is no way to satisfy all the ever-increasing needs. The main reason for this is their infinity and immensity.

The level of man's becoming a "true man" is expressed in religious and secular science by the names "perfection", "perfect man", "complete man", "spiritually perfect man", "mature man", "man in all respects", "man in all respects", "man in all respects", "man in all respects", "man in all respects", "man in all respects", "man in all respects", "man in all respects". "and others. Whatever the name, it is based on the criteria of human self-knowledge. The beginning of perfection is also related to this.

One of the important criteria of perfection is connected with the high spirituality of each person or nation. There is a dialectical relationship between human perfection and spirituality. Having attained spiritual heights, a person, a nation can attain perfection. To raise both to a higher level will also be a great challenge. As First President Islam Karimov said, "The people, the nation, have been raising and enriching their national spirituality for years and centuries. Because spirituality is not a set of rigid beliefs, but a continuous process in constant motion, and as progress continues, the needs of spiritual life will constantly arise due to its rapid movement"[2].

In this sense, the task of forming a harmoniously developed personality, e.g. spirituality, is constantly changing and improving in accordance with nature and the requirements of time and space. The criteria for a harmoniously developed person are broad, as shown above, starting with the perception of oneself as a real subject in relation to parents, family, kinship, nation, society, human life, nature and other phenomena and processes. These relationships are very difficult to formulate on the basis of the needs and requirements of each era. This is because, on the one hand, there is an infinity of needs and interests and, on the other hand, there is the constant development and variability of the period itself. In this sense, the balancing of needs and interests and the "helping" of a person's self-awareness can be seen as the basis for the manifestation of the "human" level of all relationships[2].

So we can say that the highest manifestation of a versatile person is a person who is able to reach his 'I'. But does he have an end point in reaching this state? If we trace the process of a person's striving for this "I", we will see that his spiritual impoverishment increases. This process is reflected in the alienation of people, in the disappearance of the values of parents, family, children, nation, in the legalisation of homosexual marriages, in the most inhuman relationships such as transgenderism - in a word, in countries that are highly developed today and do not spare money to promote them. In other words, it is seen when humanity becomes a spiritual victim of its own intelligence. The search for ways to "protect" it from this tragedy, and the ability to implement them, will determine the future of the civilisation that humanity has reached today. If we take into account all the above negative indicators, we can say that the spiritual crisis of humanity has reached the "peak" and "end" of the level necessary for the collapse of spiritual civilisation, as exemplified by the highly developed countries. Now he must start from the beginning to express his spiritual self. Today, under the banner of democratic values, the process of forming the spirit of "freedom" of spirituality, far from universal human values, is gaining momentum. The fact that all the above negative conditions exist shows that it is time to find mechanisms that will ensure that the "I" of the person does not fall victim to "democratic values". Because in the process of spiritual impoverishment of humanity, the spiritual "I" of a person is destroyed, because he tries to develop "democratic values" which serve to destroy spirituality. If this process is neglected today, tomorrow man will have to start all over again to reach his "I".

The question arises. Why is mankind today moving towards spiritual poverty to such an extent? Is it inherent in his nature, or is it connected with the process of alienation from his psyche and consciousness, or is it a sign of reverse spiritual development after having reached a "peak" level in the context of his high intellectual potential? ? Of course, finding answers to these questions is much more difficult. This will require the general cooperation of existing disciplines in practice. So the world today is undergoing a process of general disintegration.

This, in turn, threatens the civilisation that humanity has reached today and increases the danger that it will be created and destroyed by humanity itself.

In our opinion, the best way to solve this problem is to start by preventing the process of "mutual alienation" of a person. Only when he understands his "I" through the values of his parents, relatives, family, nation, society and the whole of humanity, can his spiritual impoverishment be prevented. Today there are a number of theories along these lines. In particular, some argue that universal values can be restored by ensuring socio-economic and political stability in the world, while others argue that globalisation can be "limited", and still others argue that spiritual decline can be prevented through mutual integration. They are moving forward.

If we take a closer look at the ideas presented, these processes are more or less taking place. However, there is no possibility of their absolute (complete) realisation, nor can there be. It depends on the specific mentality, interests and needs of each country and its people. They can never be put into a "form". Therefore, taking into account this specificity, the diversity of interests and needs, it is necessary to find and effectively use the factors that have a positive effect on the prevention of general degeneration. One of them is "man" - the human factor. First of all, "helping" him to reach his "I", influencing him can have a positive effect.

But this is not an easy task, it cannot be done by lecturing or giving dry advice, by issuing appropriate regulations or by using force. It is necessary to find the main "ring" in the chain that has always existed in his psyche and spirituality, that "awakens" and moves him, and its effective use can prevent self-alienation and negative processes in this direction. Could this "ring" be economic, socio-political, spiritual and educational factors? Of course, none of them can be denied. Life would be impossible without them. But when the time comes, they will also have to find a "ring" that can exert its influence. Let this "people" show itself with its influence in the socio-political and spiritual-educational life of the economy.

In our view, this key figure in the whole chain of human development is the "nation" factor. So why should the nation factor be the main "ring"? The reasons are as follows: First, "nation" is an abstract concept that manifests itself as a material reality only through certain people. It is impossible to imagine a nation without real people. Human qualities such as honour, modesty, love, pride, arrogance, creativity, responsibility, patriotism, customs, traditions, values are reflected in the nation through communication with real people; secondly, a person comes into the world as a human being. He begins to understand his "status" as a representative of the nation only after his consciousness begins to form. He begins to assimilate it first under the influence of parents, family, society and other social institutions. At the same time, the deliberate "restriction" of ethnicity is not the last point. Otherwise, such a point of view would contradict the golden rule of philosophy, which always refers to events, incidents and processes with "suspicion", not taking any of them as the ultimate truth and not stopping them. In fact, the development of scientific and philosophical thought has enabled humanity to reach a high level of civilisation. So we can say that there is a reason to look at the formation of a person as a representative of the nation with "suspicion" and not to put the last "point". Thirdly, a nation is a "product" of a person, a person who gave birth to it, who gave it this "status", and the "status" assigned to it by various other institutions is a reflection of this reality.

This means that at the birth of a nation, all the positive and negative indicators inherent in it are also reflected in the "association" of the nation. In particular, the negative indicators mentioned above, such as honour, modesty, love, pride, creativity, patriotism, friendship, responsibility, tradition, values, or those that contradict these positive indicators, are "transmitted" from the person who is the creator of the nation to the nation. All the positive qualities inherent in a person surpass for him any material wealth, which is his life as a human being, the "sacred" spiritual potential that expresses his "I", the reaction to "life". As a result of these indicators, a person achieves material well-being and political perfection.

It follows that the prevention of the spiritual decay of mankind is one of the factors that can positively influence the existence of a person as a human being, that is, as a representative of the nation. Today, however, views on the "nation" factor are also diverse and even contradictory.

In particular, some of them deny the existence of the nation, while others believe that it should even be removed from scientific language. For example, one of the Russian scientists, P.A. Sorokin, said that "a nation does not exist as a social unit"[3x], and another, V.A. Tishkov, said that the nation was a political slogan and a means of mobilisation, but not a scientific concept. ... it has no right to exist and must be removed from scientific language"[4][xi].

According to some European scholars, "the problem of statehood in the West and elsewhere is gradually disappearing"[5][xii]. According to Ernest Gellner, a professor at the University of Cambridge, "in practice a nation is only an accident, not a state necessity"[6][xiii]. In their work Nations and Nationalism, translated into Russian, the group interprets the symbols of the nation as mutual recognition of the rights and duties of people[7]. In his opinion, the role and significance of spiritual factors in the broadest sense of the word or national values inherent in a person are "absent". Karen Momyan also agrees with T.A. Tishkov and believes that in the future the nation will have to be forgotten.

Another example is the introduction of the e-passport system in most European countries today, while 17 countries in the region have removed the "nationality" column from their passports. For them, nationality is the most important characteristic of a person. Our neighbour Kazakhstan has announced its intention to introduce such a system. But even those who do not support the idea are not yet in the majority. That is why there is a different negative attitude to the announcement of this regulation.

Will the transition to this system in general lead to people "abandoning" their "nation"? Time will tell. But should nations fighting for themselves give up their "nation"? Or will the deletion of the "nation" column in the passport lead to an "equal" life for people on earth, or to the full enjoyment of human rights? ...? - I have questions. In fact, none of them can be answered in the affirmative. For just as there can be no absolute equality, neither can they be absolute.

We believe that such ideas and actions are based on the following economic, socio-political, spiritual and educational interests:

Firstly, it is well known that the natural growth of "titular" nations in European countries is decreasing from year to year. This is due to the destruction of the values of family, child and generation. The population of the least developed or relatively developing (relatively "backward") countries of the world is growing rapidly. Part of the population of these countries is settling in European countries, and the diminishing "title" is replacing the nation and threatening to assimilate it. In order to prevent this negative process, the aim was at least to create a single "nation" of the peoples of Europe;

Secondly, the removal of the "nation" column from the passport is ultimately aimed at the formation of a single "European" nation. When a single European "nation" is formed, up to a certain stage of its development, Europe will strive to preserve its unique national "image" and, if necessary, gain time;

Thirdly, on the basis of integration and cooperation in production, the aim is to revive the declining world production and to ensure European dominance in this field once again;

Fourthly, the formation of a single "mass spirituality" based on the harmonisation of the spirituality of today's spiritually impoverished region and the peoples inhabiting it, preserving the culture of its close European peoples and achieving spiritual dominance in the world through its globalisation, such as goals and interests.

More precisely, the purpose of removing the "nation" column from the passport is to ensure the priority of contradictory private interests rather than universal ones. If Europe succeeds in popularising this on a global scale, it will have the chance to regain its dwindling position. Today it has some successes, albeit small. It is increasingly drawing the peoples of the world into its spiritual ocean. But this process is dangerous not only for the various nations, peoples and ethnic groups that are going out into the ocean, but also for Europe itself and the peoples who live there. Because this ocean will, in time, bring closer the period of the destruction of civilisation, which the whole of humanity has reached, and will lead to the material and spiritual destruction of the whole of humanity.

It is inevitable that these processes will be implemented in Europe today, when the future will be marked by the harmony of human and national factors, ensuring the priority of common human values and interests in the creation of a new civilisation.

But we cannot remain indifferent to the imitation of today's spiritually impoverished Europe, to the rejection of the "nation" factor and its transformation into a general principle of spiritual development on a global scale. For the imitation of European countries, the "tendency" to blindly accept their "values" threatens tomorrow to bring people to the level of "ignorance" of each other. The only thing that will distinguish these people will be the different levels of the material factor. This can gradually lead to the loss of inner riches such as human emotions, love, pride and dignity.

In fact, isn't it the fact that a person realises his "I" only through material goods that pushes him into the abyss? Doesn't the devotion to the same material benefits contribute to the mutual alienation of people, to the erosion of national and spiritual values that are so important for a person? Today, therefore, it is necessary to develop a scientific and theoretical concept for the revival of the "nation" of man, and not one of the main links in the chain that binds people together, which has manifested itself as a value from the very beginning of human consciousness.

Science studies the human psyche, his formation as a person, his relationship to various processes and events, the love he has, the causes of various diseases that appear in his life, and many issues related to his treatment. But to this day, his ethnicity is limited to considering only social and economic factors and the development of society. In fact, from the point of view of philosophical thinking, why should we put an end to such views? Isn't a nation, like a human being, a product of nature and divine power? This remains one of the questions worthy of investigation with the active participation of all disciplines. There are two reasons for this. On the one hand, it has to do with the rise of man to the level of perfection, with a sense of responsibility for the future, and, on the other hand, with the prevention of the process of mutual alienation of people.

The mutual estrangement of people means the erasure of the values that bind them together, such as parents, kinship, neighbourhood, home, homeland, nationality, citizenship, belonging to society, interests. Today people understand them better than we do. Today, the process of alienation is taking shape in a single "direction". That is to say, it can be observed as an all-encompassing process from the person himself to all social relations. It is necessary to find such a natural way to prevent this alienation, so that it can have a positive impact on the prevention of all the above-mentioned values, or at least on their further deterioration, and on their current state at the present level. In our opinion, one of these possibilities depends on the factor of ethnicity.

Because belonging to a "nation" is such a wonderful feeling, the understanding of which unites people with different views as one soul, one body. R. According to Samarov, "national identity manifests itself on the basis of a number of features:

- in the form of external signs
- socio-cultural characteristics (language, customs, traditions, etc.)
- in religious beliefs;
- on a socio-economic basis (way of life, production characteristics, resettlement or migration, agriculture or animal husbandry, etc.);
- The structure of political life;
- in ideas and ideological views8. In fact, it is thanks to these people that the nation is real. As mentioned above, human pride, honour, ego, emotions, love, anger, etc. are expressed in the nation through these people. If they act in an individual case peculiar to each person, then in a nation they manifest themselves in a peculiarly organised state. In this way they pass from individuality to community. The most important thing is that the process is natural, it does not need to be directed by anyone. Here the divine power that unites people "works" at the level of the nation itself.

The secret of this process in a region of the world that has made great progress and intellectual power, or that is still developing, or where some "backward" peoples have not yet renounced their nationality, is that the "nation" is naturally given to man by God? The question arises. In this sense, it is also necessary to look at "its absence" from a scientific point of view.

Is there really a nation, what will be its fate in the future and what is its relationship with man? If we acknowledge its "non-existence", on what factors should we base ourselves, and if we acknowledge its existence, on what factors should we base ourselves? ...?

Secondly, what should be the priority in assessing a person's social status as an indicator of his universal human value? Undoubtedly, he exists materially and spiritually. For when a person enters into social relations, he is not only a member of the family, a citizen of the state, a member of society, or a member of a particular property or social group, but he is also a "union" of the population. in the same broad material and spiritual communityWhat leads in this "association"? As we seek the answer to this question, it will be possible to pay more attention to the inner force that binds them together. So what is this basis? The reason is that people who are "organised" on the basis of their identity, when their dignity, honour, pride, "I" is violated from the outside, or when there are forces and actions contrary to their interests, they are not a profession, position or regardless of age and place of residence, gender, they unite and confront each other and unite as a single force to protect the honour, pride and dignity of their nation. Is it "politics" or someone else's action? No, of course not. It is the inner strength that holds this "union" together. The main thing is that the process was natural, there was no need to instruct anyone. Again, the divine power that unites people is manifested. Does this mean that today it is enough to link the process of nation-building with historical, social and societal development? We believe that we need to look at this process more deeply. That is to say, as soon as a person is born as a human being, he can begin to form with him some internal spiritual "elements" of nation, psyche, identity in the process of nourishment and growth in the womb. More precisely, we can say that it is a divine power that "penetrates" into a person through the blood and affects the soul. As a result of our many years of scientific interest and observation, we can give examples from real life: in real life we have witnessed a strong addiction to play. Or another example: children who have lost their parents and are brought up in an orphanage, even if they do not know their mother tongue, we often see in real life that when they grow up, their love for the customs, traditions and values of the nation to which their parents belong... We have seen this in the work of the great Uzbek artist Ruzi

Choriev and in our conversations with him. This man grew up in an orphanage, in his youth he hardly knew the Uzbek language, and even as an adult he spoke "without enthusiasm", but he was proud to be Uzbek and had a strong attachment to traditions, customs and rituals. Uzbeks were proud of their size and spoke with interest. Or another example: although the Uzbeks who fled to other countries in the 1930s have now died, their children not only speak Uzbek better than some of their compatriots in Uzbekistan, they speak it very fluently and are familiar with the customs, traditions and rituals. We saw this when some of them came to their homeland after our country became independent, laid the land of their homeland on their faces, shed tears, thanked Allah for the liberation of their homeland and wished it prosperity. There are many such examples. Here, too, there is no doubt that "blood" is "flowing".

The result is the conceptual idea that the laws of heredity apply to the formation of a person as a representative of a nation, and that genes belonging to a nation are naturally passed on from parents to children. Today it is scientifically proven that not only heritage, life experience, customs, traditions and values, but also a genetic affinity between generations and ancestors link them. In particular, it has been scientifically proven that when great intellectuals survive their ancestors, it is repeated in some generations, or when one of the ancestors suffers from a serious disease, it is repeated in subsequent generations or in any generation. So why do we now say that "nation" is a concept invented by someone, an invention or a "coincidence"; is it worth agreeing with ideas like "political slogan", "this concept has no right to exist, it must be removed from scientific language"? The question arises.

If the laws of heredity are applicable to humanity, nature and the animal world, then we can put forward the idea that the "birth" of a "nation" is linked not only to economic, social, political, linguistic, territorial and other factors, but also to heredity. but also with heredity. In other words, we can conclude that the laws of heredity apply to the formation of a person as a representative of a "nation" in the blood that flows in human veins, that genes belonging to a nation can be naturally passed on from ancestors, from parents to children. Unfortunately, this is a very difficult, but also very important question, which has not yet been studied in the scientific system. While its difficulty lies in finding and proving ethnicity in genes, its importance today lies in the strength of the aforementioned negative views on the factor of "ethnicity" and in some countries solving their demographic problems by removing the "ethnicity" column from passports.

If we accept them as "truth": firstly, from a political point of view, this is a process of uniting the hearts and minds of the people in the future, destroying their own thinking and, finally, "joining" them to the great world powers (although this is a secret today). Secondly, as mentioned above, in European countries today there is a process of reducing the weight of the "titular" nation and replacing it mainly with "foreigners" and "guest workers". Thus, in the future in these countries there is a danger that not only the "titular" nation, but also these "foreigners" and "migrant workers" will lead in all areas, will be given a priority position and will "assimilate" the "titular" nation to them. This is what worries politicians, statesmen and intellectuals in the developed countries today. The implication is that politics is more important than science, which underlies the idea that there is no such thing as a "nation". Thirdly, the process of human growth is measured not only by height, weight or other aspects, but also by the degree of socialisation. He is involved in social relationships from birth to self-realisation to the end of his life. First of all, a parent is a child, a family member, a representative of a certain social group or class, a citizen of a certain state, a being who professes a certain religion. He is also a representative of a particular nation. If we start from the above idea, then all the indicators of a person's socialisation arise in the process of his growth - the basis of the indicators as a representative of a nation can be associated with the period of his life in the womb and with himself. -realisation as a person. In his socialisation, of course, such indicators as mother, father, family, relatives are in the forefront. His nationality is formed on the basis of these.

Of course, the question cannot be closed with the conclusions of one small chapter. However, in our opinion, as long as a person understands that a child is a parent and a member of the family at birth and while growing up, the spirit of belonging to the nation is manifested through them. It is in this process that a person, under the influence of parents, develops a conscious attitude towards the status of a representative of a particular nation. In this sense, the understanding of a person's status as a representative of the nation in socialisation is "easier" and more pronounced than other factors. This does not contradict our view that feelings of belonging to a person are linked to heredity and genes, but rather that these feelings are manifested in practice and are linked to the process of human self-awareness. The political aspect of this process lies in the fact that in every independent state the "title" is the priority of education, the expression of national identity, the responsibility for the future of the motherland and the nation, the formation of national pride and honour. Because the stronger these feelings are, the greater is not only the eternity of the nation, but also the sustainable development of the country. From this point of view, the formation, development and improvement of the "nation" is a priority of state policy.

The disintegration of the "titular" nation, the emergence of contradictions within it, leads not only to its "feeding" to others, but also to the collapse of the state. The present and future of the state will depend primarily on the unity, cohesion and loyalty of the "titular" nation, on the organisation of other nations around it. Thus the existence of a nation is an important factor in the stability of the state, its functioning as an independent entity. The status of the "nation" as an object of politics will continue to exist in all periods of the existence of a state institution and will be improved to the level of modern requirements.

When thinking about a person's "nation", it is necessary to pay attention to the processes of "national awakening" that are taking place today in the world of national development. In particular, there are evil ideas and forces that are trying to seize power in exchange for the destruction of the nation, and ignoring them could lead to the disintegration of the "nation" in the future. In particular, we will consider the idea of building a single state based on the caliphate. In fact, this corresponds to the unscientific Marxist idea that "the proletariat has no homeland or nation, it has only one enemy and that is the bourgeoisie, the only dictatorship of the proletariat in the world". The factor that led to the destruction of the states they built was that the "nation" fell victim to the proletariat. The Bolshevik policy of uniting various other nations and peoples living in the former USSR around the Russian nation to create a single nation was also unscientific, tore the system apart and ultimately led to its collapse. The implementation of this policy of "unification" had a negative impact not only on all the nations and peoples of the former Soviet Union, but also on the Russians themselves. This policy led to the formation of the mentality of the Russian people, who had nothing to do with it, to be perceived as a common "enemy" in the eyes of other nations and peoples. In fact, the centre of this policy was not the Russian nation, but the politicians at the head of the government who carried it out. The nation will never be aggressive, aggressive or evil, but the politicians will cast a shadow over the great value of the "nation".

We must bear in mind that today in Europe it is not the ordinary people, the nation, but some theorists and politicians who are at the forefront of ideas and actions aimed at destroying the "nation".

The idea of building a unified state on the basis of the caliphate is the same as the evil ideas of people who want to seize power today, like the Marxists. The dangerous aspect of this idea is that, on the one hand, it creates confrontation between people of one religion, on the other hand, it negatively affects the reputation of our holy religion, and, on the third hand, it increases the risk of inter-ethnic conflicts and instability in the internal life of states.

The fact that different nations and peoples believe in a single religion does not mean that they give up their national identity, customs, traditions, values, rituals and ceremonies. A one-sided view of this is in itself unscientific. Putting it into practice can lead to the destruction of humanity on the planet on the basis of global national conflicts. In this sense, the presence of a person's "nation" is an important indicator of their identity. Understanding this has both theoretical and practical implications, so that people who are willing to sacrifice their lives to gain power on the basis of religion do not betray themselves and their nation. For one of the criteria for understanding one's identity as a human being is to feel like a representative of a particular nation, to live with pride and dignity, and to be selfless on the way to its future. This is a sacred feeling for everyone, even the most evil, if necessary. Because he has a consciousness that is inherent in the status of "person" anyway.

If we look at the processes of integration and globalisation in the world, there is a single "European Union" that unites the countries of Europe. - conditions are being created. So we can say that all the possibilities have been created for their unification into a "single nation". But if today a German, a Frenchman, an Englishman or an Italian - in the future you will unite as a single European nation, abandoning your language, customs, traditions and values - has been instructed or a law has been passed to create such a nation, inter-ethnic conflicts will spread throughout Europe. The "bottom line" of such an alliance is clear. In this sense, one of the reasons for the failure of efforts to adopt a unified constitution in today's region is the concern of the various peoples living there about the loss of their languages, customs, traditions and values. At the same time, the value of life can also influence this process, the feeling of being a representative of a nation that represents a great measure of humanity that is naturally passed on from ancestors to generations. From the above it follows that the nation was not created by any political forces, it is a flower of a person, an important criterion for expressing his identity, it is a gift of nature, while man enjoys its beauty, strives for it, it works under the influence of his psyche. As long as a man has a nation, it is natural for him to strive for his future, and a man without a nation is a man deprived of his identity. The death of a nation inevitably means the end of human life. In this regard, L. Ionin says: "Ethnicity is given to a person from birth and remains unchanged throughout his life. It is as strong as the ground... "also corresponds to the above ideas.

Just as it is impossible to be a man without a nation and a homeland, so it is this factor that determines his consciousness, his intellect, his understanding, his self-awareness and his spiritual aspirations. Man is not a herd of unconsciously organised people, but he is the greatest of all values, one of the great values, capable of expressing himself as a conscious being and as a representative of a nation that performs great miracles with its intelligence and potential. His "nation" gives him strength, strengthens his spirit of pleasure, beauty and aspiration for the future, and increases his confidence in a secure life.

In short, a nation is a man who belongs to a certain nation, who feels spiritually and naturally that he is its successor, who represents it and understands it in the same way as he understands the world of light, whose destiny, whose future is in harmony with his destiny.

This means that the nationality of a person is a product of the harmony of natural and social processes. It exists as a natural process and is one of the factors that is improved under the influence of social relations. While his sense of himself as a human being is strong, his sense of belonging to a nation as a natural state is equally strong.

The "death" of a nation inevitably leads to the "death" of humanity. For if man is the greatest of all values in the world, then a nation is the "flower" of these great men, a product of human self-awareness. Human values are also formed by the best and most beautiful qualities of the nation. The more of these qualities and characteristics there are, the more varied the beauty, the greater the possibilities of spiritual enrichment of mankind, the greater his desire for life and progress, the greater his confidence in the future, the greater his interest in life and goodness.

In this sense, in the process of self-realisation of a person, the strengthening of his potential as a representative of the nation remains one of the factors of the secure life of mankind.

But the process of globalisation can change the age of an individual and cast a shadow on the future of a nation. In particular, as mentioned above, there is a process of extinction of such values as fatherhood, kinship, brotherhood, sisterhood in human consciousness, worldview and behaviour. If in the past such negative situations were encountered from time to time, today they can be encountered every day. In our society today, we see people who, as children, put their parents in an old people's home, or sue their brother, sister or daughter-in-law for property, house and wealth, and finally become invisible.

When I think about these negative situations or encounter them in life, I am reminded of a recent conversation with a friend. He said that his grandfather, who lived and died at the age of 103, always said the same thing. There were four brothers, one with a single mother and one with a single father. The family consisted of 40 people who lived in one big house and ate from one pot. Any disputes or disagreements in the family were settled under the leadership of the eldest of the brothers and sisters. There will be very few such negative events in the family and they lived a very close life. Later, in Soviet times, the brothers scattered and each became a home for himself. But even then, the advice and words of the older brother had to be followed by everyone. More than 22 years have passed since their death. Therefore, I am witnessing the deepening of affection, mutual respect and a number of other values between the brothers and the relatives of the time in which they lived. Before, when I went to the village, they would be upset if I was not a guest at a relative's house. My friend said that now, let alone relatives, even brothers and sisters are not as 'sertakaluf' as they used to be.

We are now witnessing the unforgivable attitude of some children to the fact that it has become commonplace to take their parents to a nursing home. Sadly, it will be a tragedy for the current generation in the next 30 years if a child places a parent in an old age home. Such children will be forced to move from their home town to another place. Because public opinion was sacred, and those who did not follow it did not dare to look their neighbours in the face. This has now become commonplace. But if local residents want to comment or advise against the inhumane treatment of such disobedient children by their parents, it is now "valuable" for them to say that this is our family business and that you have no right to interfere.

Preventing such negative events is becoming more and more difficult, and the failure of parental, related values will inevitably lead to the collapse of the nation.

The main reason why we are thinking of the above-mentioned values here is that their superficiality is due to the fact that the process of globalisation has no "hand" or that the nation is losing its identity or, conversely, its "self-consciousness" as it is. has been growing for centuries and developing its spirit and intellectual potential"? Whichever of the three, these are the factors leading to the destruction of humanity. The most dangerous aspect of this process is that the process of globalisation leads to its popularisation and thus has a great influence on alienating man from himself and depriving him of the value of a nation that is sacred to him.

The alienation of a man from himself inevitably leads to the loss of his psyche as a representative of the nation, the need to understand it. Today, the search for factors that prevent such negative processes is an important condition for the preservation of all achievements.

2.2. THE SPIRITUALITY OF THE NATION

In the previous chapter we introduced the idea that a nation is formed by a person. Now let's try to consider the themes through which the nation can express itself.

The nation manifests itself as a real subject through its spirituality in the broadest sense. Its unique customs, traditions, values and mentality are expressed in its spirituality. In this sense, before thinking about the spirituality of the nation, we will try to dwell on the meaning of "spirituality" and its categories.

First of all, it should be noted that under the rule of the former Soviets, which was aimed at the destruction of peoples, "spirituality" was not studied as an independent subject or scientific research. It was added to culture and no clear ideas or concepts were formed about its meaning. It is based on political goals, because the creator and consumer of spirituality is a person and the nation itself, so talking about it "motivates" them to feel for themselves, "awakens" them to their aspirations for their land, and as a result, national movements for independence can lead into the future.

History has shown that the forces that seek to enslave a nation first and foremost seek to deprive it of its identity, history and culture. As the first president, Islam Karimov, said: "... the experience of many millennia shows that if the brutal and aggressive forces of the world want to enslave, enslave and seize the wealth of a nation or a country, we must first disarm it, i.e. the nation tries to lose its values, history and spirituality. The proof of this can be clearly seen in many examples from long and recent history. For the spirituality of any nation or people is undoubtedly of decisive importance in determining its present life and destiny, the future of its growing children."[1][xiv].

Suppressing the cultural and spiritual development of the peoples of the occupied countries is one of the age-old, historically proven ways of maintaining and strengthening colonial regimes by the occupying powers. The main aim of this policy is to gradually assimilate the conquered peoples, force them to accept their own ideology and ideas, damage their culture and prevent the development of a national language, national traditions and national values. The Chinese sage Confucius advised his emperor 2,700 years ago: "My lord, if you want to conquer a country and rule it for a long time, first deprive the people living there of their historical culture and deepen their spiritual crisis. A nation deprived of its own culture and in a state of spiritual poverty will not unite, will be caught in a whirlpool of internal discord, will not be able to resist you. It will not be difficult to govern the people and the country that have become like this"[2].

The intruders and invaders have always known that destroying culture and spirituality, preventing the improvement of the national language and traditions, is one of the most convenient and delicate ways to keep an obedient people under control. That is why the colonialists and invaders plan in advance what the Chinese sage said.

When Genghis Khan invaded Central Asia, he gave instructions to his commanders: "Appoint the ignorant, weak-willed, stupid people to rule the cities, support and praise them, and destroy the wise, educated and respected people from the local population". There were well thought out reasons for this policy. A nation that has lost its culture, its prestige and its wise representatives cannot be reunited and reconciled without spiritual guidance.

History testifies that at all times and everywhere, the rulers-invaders in the territories of the occupied countries carried out a policy in the spirit of the Chinese sage and Genghis Khan. The peoples of Central Asia were no exception. The tsarist government, which forcibly invaded Turkestan, one of the most advanced centres of science, culture and spirituality, considered keeping the local population in a state of dependence and slavery, political stagnation and spiritual poverty as one of the central issues of colonial policy. The tsarist government sent many scientists and other personalities from Russia to Turkestan with the task of making proposals and conclusions on where to start in order to develop the main directions for the implementation of this evil and insidious policy.

It is not easy to maintain a colonial order in an occupied country when science, spirituality and culture are many times superior to the occupying country. Our country is far superior to Tsarist Russia in spiritual, educational and cultural development. Following the advice of the scientists, the tsarist government, at least in our country, set itself the task of proving its superiority over the indigenous people and thus achieving a "decisive" victory.

Like the invaders of the past, the Tsarist invaders began their practical work in this region by depriving the people of Turkestan of their thousand-year-old history, culture, customs, mental and physical handicaps. It was a sinister policy, deeply thought out, far-sighted and planned. This policy was based on the complete protection of the interests of the Tsarist government and the transformation of the peoples of Turkestan, including the Uzbek people, into a group of people who had forgotten their past, lost their sense of patriotism and lost sight of the future.

As the First President said: "For a man, the loss of history is the loss of life"[3]; in other words: "There is no future for a nation that does not know its history and forgets its past. This fact must be taken into account"[4].

Spirituality and enlightenment help people to know their past and understand their future. It encourages us to love and be proud of our homeland, to fight uncompromisingly against enemies, invaders and colonialists, and to show courage for the sake of freedom and justice.

People deprived of spirituality and enlightenment cannot understand themselves nationally, they prefer to live and realise their destiny. Realising this, the tsarist dignitaries paid special attention to the issue of depriving the people of Turkestan of their spirituality, enlightenment and culture, completely forgetting honesty, religion and compassion.

The policy of tsarist Russia in Turkestan was aimed at the violation of national feelings, the strengthening of national values and their complete destruction.

M. D. Skobelev, one of the generals who introduced the colonial policy of tsarism in the East with blood and sword, said: "To destroy a nation, it is not necessary to destroy it; if you destroy its culture, language, art, it will soon decay"[5]. This "wise" instruction of his served as a guide to ignorance and vices of spirituality, enlightenment and culture in Turkestan. Tsarism was interested in keeping the peoples of Turkestan illiterate. Its aim was to rob and oppress the sleeping people who did not know modern science and technology, the achievements of the Enlightenment, undeveloped national identity and trampled on national pride. In Tashkent, Samarkand, Bukhara, Khiva, Kokand, representatives of the tsarist government in the colonies, such as the "half-king" Kaufman, the governor-general Kuropatkin, the executioner Golovanov, destroyed great monuments, mosques and madrasahs, arches and historical and cultural monuments. monuments. How can the culture, the spirituality, the enlightenment, the history of the oppressed peoples they control be higher than that of the invaders? Of course, they could not bear it. Their method was to destroy culture, language and history, everything that the peoples of Turkestan, including the Uzbek people, are proud of. As the first president, Islam Karimov, said: "History is the basis of people's spirituality"[6].

Educated, cultured, intelligent and wise children of our people have already understood the aim and purpose of the colonial policy of the tsarist government in Turkestan. Abdurauf Fitrat, a great man who exposed the colonial policy of the Tsarist government, called the people to freedom and liberty, knowledge and culture, supported our national values, suffered and died in this way, wrote in his pamphlet "Russians in Turkestan": "There is no country in the world more unhappy than ours... Did the old Russian government, which was the faithful guardian of Russian capitalists and Russian popes, do anything for the Turkish children in Turkestan for fifty years? We have no other answer to this question than "No! "Since our country has been under military rule for fifty-one years, we have not been able to meet with the cultural nations of Europe in order to benefit from their social and economic views," he wrote.

So, think about spirituality in the conditions of the former Soviet Union, study it as a scientific study, develop national consciousness, create a spiritual source for all the peoples of the former Soviet Union in the struggle for their independence. enlightened addiction. He pursued this policy so cunningly that he left no chance of getting rid of it. In particular, the production of conventional machinery or components of agricultural machinery in all the former republics of the USSR was impossible without the participation of any of them. This made Uzbekistan a cotton supplier republic. It entrusted the agricultural machinery and foodstuffs it needed to other republics, even if they could be produced in Uzbekistan itself, thus linking the republics with others and managing the entire economy from the centre, with some former Soviet republics in domestic and foreign policy. did not count, their wishes were not taken into account. Although the constitution of the former USSR provided for the right of each republic to secede independently, the republics in which these ideas or their elements arose were accused of "nationalism" and purged of "nationalists". In other words, those who fought for the freedom and independence of their nation were regularly subjected to physical destruction. As a result of this policy, the original children of our nation were destroyed by the violence of the former centre. Its policy of spirituality and enlightenment was above all. As a result of this policy, our nation has not only become economically and socio-politically dependent, but also condemned to lose its identity. The customs, traditions and values of our nation were destroyed, and there was a loss of identity and national spirituality. Realising that the reunification of a nation without identity was inevitable, the invaders intensified this threat to our nation. As a result, a spirit of dependency gradually emerged in the minds of our people.

So what is dependence, what is it? Spiritual dependence is the subordination of subjects to spiritual and mental power, which, for objective and subjective reasons, leads to the use or weakening of their land, limited opportunities for independent development and growing dependence on other subjects. the resulting process.

Spiritual dependence is a process that is forced upon itself by the power of other subjects, not the result of the desires and aspirations of the subjects. Spiritual dependency extends to a person, person, citizen, family, nation, people and country. Its main aim is to gain advantage, to use others for its own benefit.

Spiritual dependence is such a dangerous process that it can lead to the loss of identity, the inability of a citizen to think independently, to defend his destiny and rights, and ultimately to the collapse of the family, nation, people and country as an independent state. organisation. The most "subtle" aspect of spiritual dependence is that it is linked to the inner potential to which the mind, worldview and psyche are connected. If a nation seems to fall into a state of spiritual dependence on other nations, it will be difficult to get rid of its complications for a long time, even after it gains political independence. For there is no way to get rid of spiritual dependence in a year or two. When spiritual addiction completely takes over the mind, the thinking and the world view, it will be necessary to change them, first of all by using their lands to free themselves from it. This is a very difficult task that takes time and much dedication. After all, dependence means obeying the will of others, living according to their instructions. Spiritual dependence is spiritual obedience to others, obedience, mental and spiritual dumbness.

The spiritual dependence of a person is manifested in the weakness of the inner potential and faith, the paralysis of the will. The spiritual dependence of a nation leads to the loss of self-expression and ultimately to the feeding of other nations. Spiritual dependence is a terrible factor that condemns a nation to death. Islam Karimov, the first President of the Republic of Uzbekistan, wrote about the struggle of our people to protect themselves from spiritual dependence: "We are well aware of the hardships of our country, which amazed the world with its culture, prosperous cities and villages. ... But even in such a terrible period, despite all the oppression and arbitrariness, our people did not lose themselves. It kept its language, its religion, its faith"[7].

Indeed, our people have become politically, economically and socially dependent on others, but no matter how cruel they may be, they cannot make our people spiritually dependent. The same factor played a key role in achieving the political independence of our country. The experience of the development of our nation is reflected in the fact that a nation with its deep spiritual foundations is spiritually vigilant and naturally able to protect itself from spiritual dependence.

In fact, without unfolding the inner potential of the individual and the nation, without achieving their self-awareness, it is impossible to achieve the development of society as a whole, as mentioned above. From the same point of view, after independence, the study of spirituality, the realisation of our national potential, the development of a sense of national identity, the development of a harmoniously developed personality became a priority of state policy.

During the years of independence, a number of interesting articles on the concept of "spirituality", its role in the development of society, nation and personality have been published in the country, scientific conferences have been held and are being held at various levels. In these published articles and conferences an attempt is made to define the concept of "spirituality", to reveal its role in the development of society, man and nation.

The basic definition of spirituality was developed by the First President Islam Karimov. He writes: "Spirituality is an incomparable force that purifies a person spiritually, encourages him to grow in his heart, strengthens his inner peace, expresses his faith, awakens his conscience, is the criterion of all his views"8 . This definition reflects all aspects of spirituality.

The most important aspect of spirituality is that it is an important factor in a person's self-awareness, in determining his place in society, in ensuring that the nation is an independent ethnic unit, and in the development of society. Spirituality is not only the inner psyche of a person, the "blessing" or positive indicators given to him, but also the processes of its consistent development, formation and use in the development of a person, nation and society. He develops not only the human nation and society, but also himself.

Spirituality is formed and developed in human relationships, throughout one's life experience. From the moment a person realises himself as a person, he continues to form and develop his spirituality until the end of his life. Man's need to develop his spirituality is a never-ending process. It forms, develops and evolves throughout a person's conscious activity. In this sense, spirituality is not only an existing factor, but also includes the ability and desire of a person to consciously act in the development and improvement of existing factors.

Spirituality is a concept that expresses the inner world of a person. The inner world of a person can be compared to a deep sea full of diamonds. No matter how much you take from this sea, the inner world of a person manifests itself deeply, boundlessly, colourfully. The deeper a person goes into his heart, into his inner world, the more diverse he becomes, revealing his new facets. In the same sense, these aspects are included in the perfect definition of spirituality. Moreover, this inner world can be imagined and understood by everyone. From this point of view, the definition of spirituality given by our President has a general methodological significance.

Spirituality is formed at birth under the influence of mother's milk, her goddess, love, paternal education and inherited values. Factors such as family environment, social cohesion and government policies will play an important role in shaping it.

The transformation of spirituality into a material force is reflected in the behaviour of each person, in the extent to which he understands himself, understands and follows his place in the family, nation and society, in his attitude towards the motherland and nation. Man is not born spiritual, he inherits something from his ancestors. But he assimilates spirituality through his relationships with parents, family, nation and society. In the same sense, the improvement and development of spirituality, the formation of family relations based on humanity, the growth of the feeling of love for the nation, selflessness in its interests, stability in society and its service to the interests of man are important factors in human development.

Enlightenment is a factor in the development of spirituality. Enlightenment is the next branch of spirituality. Enlightenment means knowing, knowing, knowing and knowing. That is, a high level of knowledge, self-knowledge of a person, a high level of knowledge naturally leads to his spirituality. Of course, this does not mean that people without higher education (higher education, Ph.D. or doctor, professor) are "immoral". Even if people do not have enough knowledge, they are devoted to their family, parents, nation and homeland, loving, humane, hardworking, shy, pure of heart, sincere in relationships, strong in hating consent, loyal, faithful, honest, pious, can embody such qualities as compassion, fairness, honesty. People with these qualities are spiritual people.

If he possesses all levels of knowledge, if he does not benefit his family, nation, homeland, if he does not have the ability to do good to others, if his actions and relationships are ignorant, disgusting, unclean, etc., then such people are considered spiritually poor and helpless. Therefore, it is wrong to understand enlightenment in a narrow sense, that is, only in the sense of mastering a certain field of science or obtaining higher education, but it is better to bet on the fact that it has all the positive qualities inherent in humanity.

Indeed, perfect mastery of a particular field of science is one of the aspects of spirituality. But as a double wing of enlightenment, he can only rise to the level of a spiritual person if he combines all the traits of humanity. Professor A. Jalolov expresses the necessity of spirituality as follows Moreover, the formation of a harmoniously developed personality is not only a spiritual need, but also a spiritually conscious economic, social and political necessity[9].

At the same time, it should be emphasised that education is the most important factor in the development of a person, a nation and a society. The deeper a person gains enlightenment (knowledge in the broadest sense), the more his spirituality develops. A person who possesses true knowledge (i.e. perfect knowledge of secular knowledge, religious knowledge, profession, etc.) will be free from negative vices such as ignorance, unbelief and evil. Therefore, the role of education in the development of spirituality is invaluable.

The transition of humanity from one society to another, from one stage of history to another, begins with enlightenment. The most mature, conscious people of the nation and of their time, who knew black and white, who lived selflessly as my people, my nation, my country, visionary spiritual people, who knew enlightenment as the most important factor in providing perspective, showed dedication in the way of its improvement. This, of course, is not in vain, for enlightenment removes spiritual dependence, fear and hesitation, and gives man incomparable divine power, unprecedented potential and inspiration. Freedom and liberty of the individual, the nation and the country are ensured through education. Enlightenment is the support of spirituality and their unity is an example of a bridle. Together they protect people from all negative, evil actions, i.e. lack of spirituality. Therefore, our ancestors and forefathers always lived with the desire for enlightenment and lit the torch of spirituality and enlightenment. Thanks to high enlightenment and spirituality, the Turanian land became famous on earth.

The transformation of spirituality into material power is reflected in the behaviour of each person, in his family, nation, home and in his relations with other people. These relations recognise sincerity, mutual respect, respect for the integrity of the family, responsibility for the destiny and future of the nation, sincere love for the motherland, its stable needs, respect for the peoples living next to it and for their own interests. These are clearly visible. But it's also important to remember that these relationships don't happen spontaneously. The influence of qualities such as the education of children, the education system, national values, humanity and the environment in society will play an important role in their formation.

Values such as peace in the family, sincerity in relationships, respect, attention, the power of national unity in the development of the nation - stability in the life of the state, are one of the criteria for determining the majority of spiritual people in certain families, nations and states. This means that spirituality in the family, the values of the nation are formed and developed through the activities of parents and the state, and in turn serve their strength and perfection.

The role of spirituality in the life of an individual, family, nation and society is enormous. It also forms the basis of economic and socio-political factors in society in terms of its importance and potential. We know from the bitter experience of historical development that it is possible to satisfy hunger, to clothe the naked. But overcoming the spiritual poverty of a generation is a difficult task. It is the inner strength of a person that determines his actions, his goals, that gives him strength and power. From this point of view, it is possible to solve today's human problem, to "humanise" the whole of humanity, to transform the nation into a great value of humanity, to solve the existing problems in the economic, socio-political spheres of society.

From what has been said, it is clear that spirituality is an all-encompassing factor and its role is increasing. At the same time, there is a growing need to study aspects of its role that have not yet been studied and to use them effectively in human development. One such aspect is its categories (concepts). The main point here is that certain categories of spirituality are also used in the ethical and aesthetic sciences. Therefore, there are different views on whether "spirituality" is a relatively independent field or science. In our opinion, such "repetition" does not mean that spirituality is an independent direction or "does not have" its own concepts, but the scope of its application is wide, combining many aspects of ethics and aesthetics, expressing the inner potential of a person, nation or people. At the same time, "spirituality" also has its own independent concepts, which are not repeated in other sciences. Therefore, we try to think about the concepts (categories) of spirituality.

A concept (category) is a form of knowledge that expresses general, important, necessary, special properties of objects and events. When we talk about the categories of spirituality, we mean the aspects that express its most important, necessary and special features. As mentioned above, some concepts of spirituality appear in a state of harmony with the sciences of ethics and theology. However, if his concepts are considered in terms of the relationship between the factors of society and spirituality, they can be understood independently of the two disciplines mentioned above.

Accordingly, the categories of the Foundations of Spirituality can be conditionally included in the following concepts related to the life of a person, nation and society;

Self-awareness, knowledge, purity of heart, generosity, sincerity, kindness, faith, honesty, loyalty, piety, purity, honour, modesty, compassion, conscientiousness, honesty, justice, respect for parents, loyalty to family, faithfulness, decency, etc. In a person's status as a representative of a nation: National identity, national pride, nationalism, patriotism, responsibility for the fate of the nation, sense of priority of national interests, national language, national education, literature, art, customs, traditions, values, respect for the state system, respect and obedience to the law, serenity, enterprise, mastery of one's profession, awareness of the internal and external activities of the country, its support, indifference to negative processes in the nation and society, social, political, economic and spiritual activity of the country in life, etc.

In the status of a person as a representative of society: the responsibility to increase the prestige of the country in the world, to achieve the achievements of world civilisation, not to be indifferent to the universal problems of the peoples of the world, to understand the harmony of the nation and universal interests; perhaps.

It is clear that all the above concepts of spirituality are associated with the inner psyche of a person, which elevates him, the growth of his soul and the expression of his "I", which covers the spiritual level of a person, his status as a representative of the nation and society.

These concepts are associated with the status of a person as an independent entity. In this system of concepts, a person's self-awareness also determines the levels of other concepts. For if a person does not understand himself, if he does not seek to raise the level of his personality, he will remain a spiritually poor person. The pursuit of knowledge cannot purify the heart, purity, generosity, sincerity, benevolence, loyalty, honesty and other qualities of spirituality.

Self-knowledge is the achievement of oneself in public life and in various relationships. That is, if he can rise to the level of his 'I', he will rise in all spheres and reach the level of personality. Of course, the attainment of the "I" does not mean that he has such negative qualities as arrogance, self-esteem and indifference to others, but it is the criterion that he has a high spirituality, free from them. The late Professor Begali Kasimov wrote about human qualities: "Of course, everything has a certain standard. Abuse of human dignity leads to arrogance. Too much gentleness - humility - will humiliate a person. On the other hand, humility leads to objectivity. And here the iron law of the relationship between form and content manifests itself in a peculiar way. True human dignity manifests itself only in the combination of knowledge, virtue and good manners. On the other hand, it is a sign of high morality and virtue to feel the norm in every behaviour, to conform one's character to the laws of humanity"[10].

With the help of this idea we can see that the scientist points out that the harmonious development of such qualities in a person is an important sign of spirituality.

Returning to the subject, it should be noted that all the above concepts (categories) of spirituality are qualities inherent in a mature person. One of the categories that unites them is faith.

The true humanity of a person is measured by his faith, religion, kindness, purity and honesty, humility, and so on. We can generally express this with the concept of humanity. Humanity exists only in believers. Here we are thinking of a precious power in matters that are common to all human beings.

If each of us correctly understands the essence of the concept of faith, we will also learn the essence of piety, honesty, decency, kindness, justice, purity and honesty, and humility, which are the interpreters of faith. Only believers follow the path of purity and honesty, piety, goodness, kindness, generosity and mercy. That is why we thought it appropriate to explain in detail the concept of faith, its essence.

Believers understand deeply what it means to fear Allah and to be ashamed of a slave. Knowing Allah as One and our Prophet as His Messenger is the most important sign of faith. Believers always try to behave correctly and honestly in all their lives, at work, in their activities, at home, on the street, in their relations with others, with their families, with their homeland. They have no prejudices in their relations and dealings, they abstain from taste and filth. In everything they do, they think not only of this world but also of the future life. They try to subordinate all their actions and behaviour to Him.

As a spiritual and moral quality, faith is a spiritual phenomenon unique to mankind. There is no place for faith in any creation except man. Therefore, man differs from all other living beings in that he believes in something and holds it sacred, that is, he believes. Faith is the root, the foundation, the basis of man's spirituality and morality. No matter how sharp the mind of an unbeliever, no matter how strong his will, and no matter how proud he is of himself, he has never entered the ranks of true human beings. Indeed, the unbeliever is not afraid of Allah, nor is he ashamed of his slaves. He is an obedient slave to his own desires and does not turn away from debauchery and contempt. May Allah protect us all from this. To do so, we must follow the path of faith.

The essence of faith has always been the source of the universe and mankind, the place of man in the universe, the meaning of human life, what mankind is called to and what it is capable of.

Therefore, the basic conditions of humanity - piety, compassion, purity and honesty - include the concept of faith. For only a person who has faith will have piety, compassion, purity and honesty. These cannot be expected of the unbelievers. It is because of these and other qualities that we use the word "unbeliever" to refer to some people.

Let us now turn to a brief explanation of some of the categories of faith. A deep understanding of their content, essence and practical meaning and application in our daily actions will always lead us to a higher humanity, to perfection, which means that our faith will be strengthened. The beginning of faith is piety. Piety is the fear of Allah and the avoidance of evil deeds. A God-fearing slave lives honestly in the family and society, does not touch haraam, does not betray anyone's rights, does not give bribes, does not swear, does not deceive, does not lie, does not betray people, motherland, etc. God bless us all to be godly. Everything depends on us.

Morality is very much the same recognition. Morality is a word that makes everyone feel ashamed to refrain from inappropriate, bad behaviour. In Xadisax it is shameful to say that a person first of all has a long life. A person who is ashamed of his own misdeeds, wrongdoings and misbehaviour does not condone other misdeeds. He who is not ashamed of himself will not be ashamed. So shame is a sense of responsibility for one's wrongdoings before one's conscience, one's religion.

Hayo means shame in Uzbek. When I say "shameless, seductive", we mean a person who is not ashamed or immoral when he acts shamelessly. Shyness is more common in women than in men. Some words that a man can say easily, women cannot say because of various experiences and embarrassments, shame does not allow them. Imagination is not just about not saying an embarrassing word. It has a much broader meaning and content than that. Shame does not allow a person to be degraded like an animal. Feelings of shame for bad behaviour are unique to humans. "Morality, chastity is not an invention," wrote Professor B. Kasimova, "it has been formed for centuries together with the idea of a person. It is difficult to imagine human decency without modesty and chastity"11. Raising children so that shame begins in the family. This is an important aspect of national education and an integral part of spirituality.

One of the signs of a believer is a breast. Morality is a feeling of shame, embarrassment and disgrace about something unworthy or unworthy of oneself. Or it means being afraid of something.

On the other hand, feeling is not only a feeling of honour, but also a feeling of honour and dignity. Usually aristocrats do not remain indifferent to humiliation, degradation and disrespect for themselves and their families, their relatives and respect others.

Honour is chastity in the sense of virginity, which means maintaining one's status, honour and respect, a sense of shame, and not insulting the honour of one's family and ancestors. When a person, his family members or his ancestors are unjustly insulted, and this person is indifferent to it, they are often asked if they have honour or dignity. Our ancestors, our people, have been noble and aristocratic for a long time, so they considered it a disgrace that their country, their land, their mothers and children should be trampled on in other places. Obviously, in the essence of honour and patriotism, there are feelings of patriotism and nationalism.

Another sign of a believer is that he is religious and conscientious. Religion and conscience are closely related concepts. Religion and conscience are in harmony with people's sense of justice. Religion and conscience is a sense of moral responsibility for one's daily activities, actions and behaviour, first to oneself and then to one's family, society, community and homeland. A person of conscience and religion is angry at unjust and unfair acts, resists them, is satisfied with the good aspects of his activities, dissatisfied with the bad aspects, is psychologically oppressed and suffers from a bad conscience. There is no punishment more severe than remorse for a man who knows himself. That is why our people have a saying that the pain of conscience is a great pain. This proverb has a deep meaning.

Compassion is also one of the characteristics of faith. As above, compassion is a characteristic of our people. "Mutual love between people, wrote the ancient Chinese philosopher Mo-Tzu (Mo-Di) in 480 B.C. - (about 400 years ago) - treats other people's property and household as one's own, and teaches us to understand everyone as they understand themselves"[12]. These ideas of the thinker have been confirmed for centuries. Today, compassion is usually a feeling of material and spiritual support for orphans, the elderly, the homeless, the disabled. Continuing the traditions of our ancestors, the leadership of our independent republic sets an example of high compassion for orphans, street children and the elderly, as well as for the disabled in the transition to market relations.

In these days of Uzbekistan's independence, the task is to create in people, especially in the younger generation, a sense of purity and honesty in the spirit of independence. The humanity of a person is measured by his purity and honesty. That is why our ancestors have always encouraged us to be clean and honest and called on us to distinguish between halal and haram. For Muslims, especially Uzbeks, this is the basis of moral law, that is, the basis of faith. Cleanliness and decency are one of the main characteristics. It is impossible to be a believer without purity and honesty.

On the other hand, being a believer is rooted in a person's purity and honesty. Goodness does not come from a person who is not pure and honest, he has no compassion, humility, honour, shame and modesty. Clearly, purity and honesty are at the core of all faiths. That is why our ancestors paid special attention to cleanliness and decency.

Honesty is a collection of good, positive actions, things that people can do, things that can be earned through hard work, and a range of clean and pure foods. The broader aspects of honesty are honesty in marriage, honesty in society, honesty in business, honesty in dealing with friends, and so on. People with pure hearts and pure minds who follow the path of honesty will always be calm, reasonable and healthy. Mahmud al-Zamakhshari, an encyclopaedist from Khorezm, advises:

Honesty begins with the family. The Uzbeks have a saying: "What you see in the bird's nest, you do". This means that if the parents are clean and honest, the child will grow up in the same spirit. Good deeds and actions in a child are an honest bite.

The conclusion is that cleanliness and honesty are the basic conditions of the believer. What is good or bad in a person depends on his faith, that is, on his purity and honesty. Therefore, constant vigilance on the path of faith, purity and honesty is an important factor in the sustainable life of a person, nation and people. This is especially necessary in the transition to market relations.

Above we discussed the basic characteristics of the believer, which are one of the concepts that are an integral part of spirituality. You must know that each of them is an ornament for a man. Here it is impossible not to dwell on another ornament that is extremely necessary for a person. Without it a person cannot be perfect. It is also a sign of humility. Humility adorns a person, increases his reputation and enlarges his circle of friends.

Humility is a manifestation of the inner spiritual world. If there is no softness, generosity, decency, shame, honour, dignity in a person's blood and heart, no matter how hard he tries, he will not be able to look humble in people's eyes.

In the traditions of the Uzbek people, in our national values, arrogant, deceitful, boastful, arrogant people are strongly condemned. It would not be foolish to say that humility is perfection and pride is perfection.

From these ideas about spirituality it is clear that its formation has always been a difficult problem. Spirituality is manifested in the subjects of man, nation, people, society and state. Its potential in relation to a person and a nation is different. They are the first "developers" of spirituality, so we have already thought about the human aspects of spirituality, and now we will try to think about specific aspects of national spirituality.

It should be noted that the revelation of the role and significance of spirituality in defining a nation as an independent entity is one of the most pressing issues today. This is because the experience of historical development has shown that no matter how much humanity is globalised, the number of problems, dangers and threats that it needs to solve together is growing. This means that people's desire to express themselves through their national countries is becoming more important than the desire to fight common threats together.

From the above, it can be seen that the spirituality of the nation is all-embracing, and depending on which side the authors focus on, it is possible to reveal the essence of its various aspects. We have focused here on the fact that national spirituality operates at the level of material power, based on the idea that all the characteristics arising from a person's status as a representative of a nation, and of course all the characteristics inherent in him, belong to the nation. Since a nation (as we discussed above) is an abstract concept without people, it manifests itself as a material being only as a result of the union of people who embody common traits. It is the uniqueness of the people, linked by common characteristics, that unites the nation and contributes to the achievement of a common goal. Therefore, all the positive and negative aspects of the people who represent the nation are reflected in the nation. If we consider all the aspects inherent in people, we can say that their status as representatives of the nation means a new direction in the view of national spirituality. For all the scientific literature published so far discusses the peculiarities of the nation, the processes of its formation and development. But the question of who is its subject, who made it a material being, remains unanswered. Consequently, there was also ambiguity about the power to protect national spirituality from the negative effects of the globalisation process. Having clearly addressed a number of such questions, we tried to think about the spirituality of the nation, the spirituality of its representatives in the image of the people, its spirituality that embodies its inner and outer potential.

This is actually normal. Because a person who does not have a nation cannot rise to the level of a full person, and his prospects will be limited if development is not based on national foundations. National soil is a bridge between the past and the future. It is a source of beauty, inspiration, strength and power for development. In this sense, it is of theoretical and practical importance to keep in mind that national spirituality, based on its own foundations, allows us to solve many problems that exist in society and national development. So what is national spirituality? What is its place in the life of the nation?

National spirituality is an intellectual and spiritual force that reflects the unique characteristics, traditions, customs, values and mentality of a nation, reflects its "I", defines its identity and guides its development. There is no nation without its own spirituality. And in this sense, spirituality is the brightest, most conspicuous factor that distinguishes nations from one another. A nation acquires the status of a true nation only when it can have its own spirituality, which is not repeated in other nations. For example, virtues such as shame, honour, religion, faith, conscience, modesty, pride, faith, justice, purity, honesty, and fidelity may exist in some form in all peoples, but the degree of their observance or their perfect manifestation will not be the same in all nations. Even if some of them develop or do not develop, they may find expression in other concepts.

However, they are the most important factors that ensure the 'self' of the nation and express its identity, regardless of the level of development or manifestation.

National spirituality manifests itself in the following ways

a) The transformation of national identity, pride, customs, traditions and values into a real material force in the life of the nation;

b) Awareness of the identity of the nation, its responsibility for its history, heritage and future, as well as the acquisition of "I";

c) cultural (material and spiritual) manifestations and possibilities of human influence;

g) The ability of the national idea and ideology to influence the glorification of the nation and its striving for good and progress;

d) the desire of the nation to occupy a worthy place in world civilisation with its intellectual potential;

j) the equality of the nation in the world and the strengthening of its prestige. Just as a nation is not dead, so is its spirituality. It is a factor that unites generations, ensures their spiritual closeness, gives the nation joy, passion, inspiration, beauty, inspiration, and motivates it for the future.

National spirituality is a "shield" that embodies the unity of the nation, ensures its longevity, and preserves and protects all its characteristics. In this sense, the following views of the First President Islam Karimov, which define the theoretical foundations of our national revival in the conditions of independence, are noteworthy. He writes: "We do not know people by name, but by their culture, their spirituality, we look at the roots of their history"[13] [xv].

The unity of a nation with high spirituality and solid foundations will also be strong. Such a nation may be temporarily dependent on itself because of countries or nations that have powerful and modern weapons through violence and the use of weapons, but this cannot be overcome spiritually. For the psyche is the inner strength and power of the nation. Its main characteristic and ability is that it cannot be seen with the eyes and heard with the ears. These same invisible and inaudible factors constantly "wake up" the nation and encourage vigilance. Of course, a spiritually strong nation will not lose its identity under any circumstances; it will fight for freedom and independent development. In this sense, a spiritually strong nation can be temporarily enslaved by weapons, but it cannot be completely defeated.

To confirm our opinion, let us present the following thoughts of the Russian scientist V.V. Bartold (1869-1930). He made several scientific journeys to Russian-occupied Central Asia to study the country and its people. Reporting the results of these trips to the Cultural Council of the St Petersburg Academy of Sciences, he said: "Until now we have occupied the lands of peoples whose cultural level is much lower than ours. Now, in the case of Turkestan, we are faced with a completely opposite situation... The Turkestanis have recognised our military superiority, but not our moral superiority. The challenge is to admit it... Until we admit it, we cannot say that we have won a decisive victory. "From this point of view, it is clear that the will of a nation with a strong spirituality, with strong roots, will be strong, it may fall into a state of temporary dependence, it may face various difficulties, but it will never disappear. For this reason, peoples who live with their future have always considered the preservation and development of spirituality as the main source of ensuring their eternity and have followed this principle.

Thinking about the role and importance of spirituality in the life of an individual, a nation and a society, it is necessary to think about the factors of its formation. Because it is often said and written that the perfection of the individual is an important source that ensures the eternity of the nation and the leading factor in the economic, socio-political development of society. However, the question remains unanswered as to the factors and sources on which it is based. In fact, spirituality is not a spontaneous factor. Its foundations are associated with the emergence of humanity and the formation of a nation. It is associated with the perfection, the creative activity of people who have represented the nation for centuries.

Only from this point of view can we fully understand the nature and content of spirituality. It follows from this idea that the appearance, existence and creative activity of people on a particular land also shaped their spirituality.

Avesto embodies the dreams of the creation of the world, the improvement of man as a people, the fight against evil for good, freedom, creativity and ingenuity.

The teachings of Zarathustra, "good thoughts, good words and good deeds", propagated in the Avesta, still call humanity to do good, purify people spiritually and lead them on the path of spirituality[15][xvi].

Since spirituality is a product of the historical development of mankind, it is clear that the spirituality of the Uzbek people is not in some "empty", "naked" place, but in the wealth created by its ancestors. It is also because its lands are strong that no matter how much effort is made to destroy them by foreign invaders, they are again a source of restoration of its power and demonstration of the identity of our nation.

World recognition of the Uzbek people, creation of a whole civilisation, great thinkers and scientific discoveries created by them are not spontaneous, but are connected with achievements in material and spiritual spheres created in this motherland. Muhammad Khorezmi, Ahmad Fergani, Ibn Sino, Abu Nasr Farobi, Abu Raykhan Beruni, Imam Bukhari, Najmiddin Kubro, Az-Zamakhshari, Jaloliddin Manguberdi, Amir Temur, Ulugbek, Alisher Navoi, other inhabitants of Babur and a number of other material states and spiritual riches from which they received spiritual nourishment and divine power. The vast inheritance they left secured the future of the Uzbeks. These material and spiritual resources were and are the source of freedom, independence and development of the Uzbeks.

The spirituality of the nation is such a pearl that it shows its "I" in every situation. As the nation rises to the level of spiritual maturity, the beauty of this pearl will increase. No other nation has such a beauty. As our teacher, academician Erkin Yusupov, noted, "There are specific national criteria for determining spiritual maturity. According to Uzbek beliefs, waiting for a guest with your hands on your chest and greeting others is not an example of obedience, but a sign of moral maturity. Some people may not understand this tradition. To understand it, it is necessary to be an Uzbek at heart, to know the historical conditions of this people, national ethics and psychology"16. They have been formed by our ancestors over the centuries and have become an integral part of the spirituality of our nation. In this sense, the effective use of the heritage left by our ancestors in our national and spiritual revival will once again help to raise the level of our nation.

We have said several times above that national spirituality is an important factor in ensuring the freedom and independence of the nation. So how does it accomplish this task?

In our definition of the concept of national spirituality, we focused on the fact that it is the inner psyche, which reflects the "I", that reveals the identity of the nation and defines its "identity". Not worth it, of course. Because the inner psyche is such a powerful force that it urges the nation to preserve its identity, to fight for its chest, its pride, its prestige in every situation. It enriches national feelings and ideas. Although these processes are invisible and unseen, they manifest themselves in the "differentiation" of nations from other nations in the struggle for their freedom and independence, in the striving for success and progress. Although the main driving force behind these processes is the understanding of the identity of the nation, the main source that provides its continuing energy is national spirituality.

Consequently, through the simple development of the intellect and strength of a person and changes in ideas about the system of values, some of the ix "obsolete" will be replaced by new ones, and the status of the national buddha of the spirit of news as great Because the nation understands itself in the enormity of the possibilities of spirituality and through it strengthens its status nation. The survival of the nation in values is an important factor that gives beauty, freshness and life to this vibrant world, capable of "reproducing" itself and motivating humanity to creativity. An important aspect of the ego as a unique value is that one of the main criteria for determining the true humanity of people today and in the future is their ability to maintain their "image" and the characteristic qualities of a representative of the nation.

This means that while a nation 'reproduces' itself, its identity, interests, goals and aspirations will continue as an ongoing process. Therefore, no nation capable of self-realisation can live in dependence on anyone. It sees the acquisition of freedom and independence as its main goal and will do everything possible to achieve it, even if dependence on others, living in a colonial state, brings it prosperity and economic perfection.

What does independence mean for a nation? It is not limited to getting rid of political and economic dependence. This is only one side of independence and the part that leads to true independence. The nation becomes spiritually poor and incapable of self-realisation, which makes it incapable of fighting for political and economic independence. Therefore, independence for a nation is to get rid of the scourge of spiritual dependence, the ability to breathe freely, to reach "I" before others.

It can only be completely liberated from political and economic dependence when it is aware of itself and feels its "I". If a nation gains political independence and has the opportunity to form its own national statehood, but does not use it in time, it inevitably falls into a state of dependence on others. As Professor Isa Yabborov rightly notes, "the development of the national psyche, social consciousness, family and spiritual life in accordance with modern requirements, the freedom of the people, of course, is directly related to its state structure"[17xvii].

For the same reason, in the struggle for independence, direct political liberation is carried out in harmony with the initial spiritual and intellectual preparation of the nation, the growth of its self-knowledge, self-awareness is the most important task. Only when this task has reached a certain stage can the nation fully and decisively achieve its independence.

Thus, the attainment of political and economic independence in turn leads to spiritual dependence, freedom from muteness and spiritual liberation. For this reason, pragmatic statesmen, who have the potential to foresee their own future, see their development in line with the task of restoring spirituality and not with economics and politics as the main directions of their policies.

If a nation gains independence while economic and political reforms are accompanied by spiritual renewal, it will have a great opportunity to strengthen its independence and to embark on the path of development it has chosen. While this question may seem very simple and straightforward in theory, in practice it is an extremely difficult problem. We are talking about a radical change in the minds and hearts of the majority of the population, who are the representatives of the nation.

However, this complex task requires a certain amount of time and consistency. Moreover, it is not enough to increase education. Although it is absolutely necessary, it must be organised in a complex and harmonious way. That is to say, the goal of developing national self-awareness will only be achieved with the unity of theory and practice. The important role of spirituality (culture, which in Soviet times was considered a part of spiritual culture) in the life of an individual, a nation and a society has always been emphasised, and attempts have been made to use its potential for one's own purposes.

However, the tasks of the spiritual sphere during the transition of society from one system to another include: changing people's consciousness, enriching it with national ideas, developing the self-consciousness of the individual and the nation, giving priority to spiritual renewal in the economic and social spheres. -Political reforms, etc. have not always been considered as important factors. If we look at the results of this approach, it is clear that the enormous gains have been one-sided. In particular, many countries in the world today have made great strides in the economic and socio-political spheres. This is not news to anyone. However, as a result of the fact that these achievements have not been carried out in accordance with the processes of spiritual renewal, the narrow self-awareness of the individual (living only for his own interests) and the importance of some very important relationships in national values have decreased. In particular, in a number of developed European countries, the sanctity of the family (marriage, childbirth), the disappearance of parental responsibility, kinship, etc., are the result of insufficient attention to spiritual renewal. If the shortcomings in this area are not remedied, the achievements in the economic, socio-political sphere, no matter how great, will lead to the spiritual impoverishment of the people and the nation, as well as to the collapse of society from within.

The historical experience of the development of man, nation and society shows that economic development is not the last measure of height. If this height does not serve the formation of a perfect human being, the glorification and development of national values, their enrichment in keeping with the times, the stability of society, the elimination of greed for other countries and peoples, spiritual poverty will persist in this bright world... This leads to the loss of human sincerity, prejudice, unbelief, irreligion, kindness, national, racial, religious conflicts, various conflicts and contradictions between countries.

Today we are witnessing these negative events. The saddest thing is that the same situations are causing great tragedies for humanity. At the same time, the most dangerous danger is that the process of spiritual impoverishment will become one of the most pressing global problems (various diseases, drug addiction, food shortage, nuclear threat, etc.). The emergence of these negative processes is influenced by universal poverty. In order to prevent them, it will be of practical importance for nations to seek development by relying on their own countries. Unfortunately, this process is slowing down. There is a growing tendency to adopt the "mass spirituality" of the developed countries of the world rather than the self-reliant development of nations. This in turn threatens the development of the spirituality of nations on the basis of their uniqueness, beauty and potential.

The collapse of national spirituality will inevitably lead to its assimilation by the developed nations. This, in turn, affects the inconsistency of the spirituality of the whole of humanity. In this sense, in order to achieve the harmonious development of a person, nation, people, society, it is necessary to find and effectively use the factors that ensure the spiritual security of a person and a nation.

We have considered above the connection between the spirituality of the nation and the human factor that is its representatives. According to this point of view, the protection of the spirituality of the nation from the negative consequences of the globalisation process should consist, first of all, in the preservation of human spirituality. The more people realise that their nation is passionate, selfless and responsible for its own interests, the more the spirituality of the nation develops, the more chances it has to protect itself from any external influences.

2.3. THE CONCEPT OF NATIONAL AND SPIRITUAL SECURITY AND THE REASONS FOR ITS EMERGENCE

The escalation of globalisation is also accelerating the disintegration of the spirituality of the nation. The threats to it are increasing. Today, the preservation of the nation and its spirituality has become one of the common problems of mankind. For when it comes to preserving the spirituality of a nation, it is necessary to keep in mind the preservation of the people who are its representatives, their spirituality. The spirituality of a nation cannot be preserved without the preservation of the human being. They should be considered together. Today people are forced to live under strong ideological, ideological and informational pressure. Threats against them naturally affect spirituality. Today, the growing number of these threats puts on the agenda the task of ensuring national and spiritual security. This is a very difficult task, the implementation of which again depends on the people who are the representatives of the nation. That is why we have analysed the problems of the "creator" of man and the spirituality of the nation, expressed our views on their interrelated features of development. Now, given the importance of the spirituality of a nation in human development, we will try to clarify the meaning of ensuring its security in the face of growing threats.

Although the concept of "security" originated in the era of the emergence of states, in the twentieth and early twenty-first centuries it rapidly moved into the social and humanitarian sphere. The main reason for this is that from that time on, actions aimed at perpetuating their dominance over the entire earth by capturing the minds, hearts and spirituality of an individual and a nation began to intensify. But because this is an overarching concept, it still lags behind today's demands.

The concept of "security" is not defined as a philosophical category in various dictionaries and scientific works. However, the National Encyclopaedia of Uzbekistan defines the concept of "threat" as "threat (by law) - one of the crimes against an individual: the inability to help a person whose life or health is threatened and who is deprived of the opportunity to defend himself"[1]. "Philosophy:

Encyclopaedic Dictionary and Idea of National Independence: Basic Concepts, Principles and Terms (Brief Explanatory Dictionary)[2] define the concept of "ideological security" as follows "Ideological aggression, which manifests itself in various forms, is a concept that characterises the degree of protection of various ideological centres from destructive effects"[3].

The concept of "security" has also been defined by Russian and a number of other scholars. While some have tried to define it comprehensively, it can be seen that others have applied the concept to some of its forms. In particular, one of the Russian scientists V.N. Kuznetsov believes that "the essence of security is life without danger... the phenomenon of security arises only when there is a possibility of danger to the object"[4]. Another Russian scientist V.I. Mitrokhin argues that "the concept of security requires an understanding of the level of protection of values, honour and dignity of the individual, social groups, the state, society and civilisation as a whole"[5]. ON. Severev and V.K. Dednov characterised the concept of security as "the state of protection of vital interests of the individual, society and the state against internal and external threats"[6].

Moreover, the concept of "security" is defined "narrowly". In particular, according to R. Yanovsky, "economic security is the material and financial characteristics of production, the role and stability of the economy in the geopolitical sphere"[7][25]. A.I. Kravchenko, on the other hand, focuses on the concept of social protection and defines it as follows -measures"[8][26]. Information security has a direct impact on social security, with a special place for the information transmitted, the message received and the attitude towards it. Information security is defined as the state of a country in which no significant damage can be inflicted on citizens, society and the state by affecting the country's information sector[9][xviii].

The military tried to define military security on the basis of its territory. Among them, A.S. Skvortsov, D.A. Kruglov characterised: "... this is an important component of national security, from its content it is necessary to understand the state of protection of the individual, society and the state from external and internal military threats. The main goal of military security is the assessment, localisation and elimination of military threats, the creation of favourable conditions for the existence and development of the country"[10][xix]. "Military security is an important component of national security, which determines the state of the country's defence capability and the ability to defend national interests with the help of the armed forces", - said Voloshko[11][xx]. He describes military security as the ability of the state to prevent the outbreak of war and, if such a situation arises, to minimise its destructive consequences for the national security of the country. The author believes that military security, along with political, economic, environmental, informational, etc., is one of the most important and key structural components of national security, with which it has an inseparable dialectical relationship[12][xxi].

There is also a growing interest in Uzbekistan in defining the concept of "security" and studying its meaning. While some Uzbek scholars tried to give a general definition of "security", others tried to define its branches. In particular, Doctor of Philosophy Professor R.S. Samarov considers security as a certain system and defines national security as one of the security spheres as follows: "it is a set of conditions created institutionally to protect the material and spiritual wealth of society, social norms and constitutional order, sovereignty, territorial integrity of the state from various external and internal threats"[13][xxii]. At the same time, the author interprets national security as an integral system related to the national: social, economic, political, military, environmental, etc. Researcher F.M. Yesayev analyses the concept of military security and defines it as follows "... military security is an important component of the national security system, which means the degree of protection of vital interests of the individual, society and the state on both sides. external and internal military threats". It sees military security in the national security system"[14][xxiii].

Another Uzbek scholar, A.E. Ishmukhammedov, said that "the concept of security is very broad and covers almost all issues related to public life - border security, regional peace, extremism, absence of ethnic groups, corruption, crime, etc."[15][xxiv]. Professor Abdulkasimov, an economist, said: "The concept of security is multifaceted and has different meanings. However, they also have a common idea, according to which security is protection, a guarantee against the dangers that arise in various spheres of human life. Risk is a potential or real force that threatens the development and normal functioning of the state and society. "Acute forms of threat include natural and social disasters and shocks, crises and emergencies, revolutions and uprisings, wars and armed conflicts"[16][xxv].

In addition, a number of foreign and Uzbek scholars have given scientific definitions to a number of concepts such as "national security", "military security", "border security", "personal security". However, there is still no consensus on the definition of this concept. This is not surprising, as it is a complex concept that is linked to the need to secure all spheres of human life, society and the state. For this reason, there is a growing interest in defining the meaning of this concept, its place and importance in all areas.

However, from the above definitions it is clear that first of all it is necessary to develop a definition of this concept that expresses the philosophical essence embodying all directions. The above authors have given definitions of this concept in connection with specific objects. Of course, their definitions have both theoretical and practical significance for the correct understanding of the meaning of this concept and for determining the possibility of interaction. Without denying any of them, let's try to analyse this concept in a general philosophical key.

It is well known that an event, an occurrence, a process and various relationships do not arise spontaneously, but as a reflection of a need, a necessity, an interest, an inequality or an imbalance between the parties. It is a process that manifests itself in all areas of human life, nature and society. The most important thing is that they are always there, and as a result progress will continue. But the main problem here is that needs, necessities, interests, inequalities, inequalities arise in an event, a process, and in various relationships that are not always in balance, but in a state of aspiration of a particular party for priority. This in turn forces the "weak" side to become completely weak and to "obey" the strong side. The continuation of this process creates a state of anxiety and fear in the "weak". The use of balancing factors to avoid this is a process applicable to the activities of the "weak" party. That is, the desire to preserve one's "I" is a characteristic of all events, incidents, processes and relationships in which there is danger as a result of "inequality" and "unequality". Therefore, in order to defend itself against them, to get rid of them, to strive for balanced development, the weak side must ensure its own security. Achieving "security" will therefore continue to be a perennial challenge.

On the basis of these considerations, the concept can be defined as a philosophical category: Of course, this definition reveals the meaning of the concept of "safety". As we continue to improve it, we are aware of the need to fully disclose aspects that we do not understand. In particular, some scientists, experts and researchers call it a "factor", others a "state", still others a "life without danger" and still others a "level of protection". Some of our scientists say that "security is a state of protection of a certain object (internal and external), in which all dangers should not exceed the norms".

Of course, as they noted above, they approached the question on the basis of which side of the issue they were studying. In this sense, none of them is objectionable. Our definition embodies the general philosophical aspects of "security". One of its key messages is expressed when we consider "security" as defence potential.

The "defence potential" we are talking about does not contradict the definitions given by the authors above, but implies that ensuring "security" is not only related to "power", but also to intelligence. Here, "potential" is a broad concept that includes not only "power" but also "intelligence". Especially in today's world, where more and more attention is paid to the use of "intellectual" capabilities rather than violent methods to ensure security, if we see security as "protected potential", then the times are synchronous.

"Security" is divided into national, regional and international and has its own system, which includes social security, economic security, political security, spiritual security, ideological security, environmental security, personal security, military security, resource security and others. They have their own characteristics and are caused by different factors.

In this system, "national security" occupies a special place, which in the broadest sense includes the forms of "security" that make up the system. Its complexity means that "national security" means that all people living in the country and on its territory, regardless of nationality, race, gender, religious beliefs, social origin, are protected from various negative influences, threats from evil forces and ideas. At the same time, "national security" is protected from the negative impact of various hostile forces that may arise outside and within the borders of the state. That is, "national security" is not a concept of a particular nation, but the whole country, all its material and spiritual wealth, the whole population living in it, is protected from various negative influences.

In this sense, the term "national security" is now used in scientific and theoretical concepts and practices. At the same time, depending on the specificity of the problem, the concepts of "border security", "environmental security", "ideological security" and a number of other concepts are used.

Today, however, the concept of "national and spiritual security" is not used in the "security" system. It is mostly seen and presented "within" national security as an integral part of it. That is why it has been excluded from scientific consumption. Today, however, it is necessary to study it as an independent concept and problem. There are two reasons for this: first, the role of national spirituality in the development of mankind and the world is growing as never before, it is becoming an important factor in capturing people's minds and hearts; second, despite the fact that the intellectual potential of mankind has risen to a high level, its spirituality is weakening and impoverishing. As a result, the most heinous manifestations of spiritual poverty, such as evil, violence, selfishness, immorality, premeditated murder, human trafficking and drugs, which completely destroy human genetics, are intensifying; and third, the growing threat of "mass spirituality" to national spirituality. In response, there is a wave of aspirations of nations, peoples and even a small number of ethnic groups living on the planet to preserve their identity, to assimilate their heritage, to rely on their own lands; fourth, in developed countries for many years a new person, family, parents, relatives, homeland, nation and other "values" formed under the influence of alienation between ancestors and generations, high economic development, have reached their "peak" level. ... still can't answer for the next perspective. Today they are looking for a way out of this negative situation, and as one of these possibilities they realise the need to "return" and turn to the spiritual factor.

In this process, which is an important direction in the development of their spirituality, they achieve their superiority, assimilate the "mass spirituality" into the national spirituality and weaken it. The weakening of national spirituality, which develops on its own soil, ensures the dominance of "mass spirituality" throughout the world, and leads to the dependence of the countries that have formed and popularised it on other countries, as well as on the nations and peoples living in them. In other words, spirituality becomes a means of ensuring the dominance of the developed countries on the planet.

All this increases the role of spirituality and the desire to use it effectively.

At the same time, the intellectual potential of humanity in the world today has reached a high level of development. Now it can solve the most difficult problems that serve its own interests and general development. As a result, in one part of the world economic, socio-political and spiritual-educational life has developed, while in another part people still live in difficult conditions, education, health care, social and economic life are in the most vulnerable position. Solving these problems is still a universal task. In such conditions, the highly developed countries try to establish their hegemony on the planet not only in the economic, political, but also in all spheres of the spiritual life of the peoples. If in the bipolar world there was a struggle for land between them, today the political landscape of the world has changed dramatically and in the conditions of its multipolarity the number of forms of struggle for dependence of the least developed countries, peoples and peoples living on them has increased by one due to spirituality. In particular, today there is a threat to the state, the nation, the individual and society, as well as to national spirituality. The main reason why it becomes a big problem is that the threats against it are "harmless", "novelty", "pleasure", "passion", "spiritual food", "spiritual" for people full of uniformity and completeness. exaltation" and "inspiration" seem to be initiated. It is therefore difficult to determine their negative impact on national spirituality. It should be noted that these threats are primarily directed against national spirituality. There are two reasons for this: first, the countries of the world today are multiethnic and differ in a variety of spiritualities. In such a situation, their tendency to "innovate" from outside will be strong. Secondly, it shows that the possibilities of the method of "conquering" countries from within, rather than openly fighting them with open arms, are greater.

Threats to national spirituality have always existed, but it is known from the processes of historical development that cruel countries first enslaved other countries and peoples by force of arms and then began to take possession of their spiritual life. That is why they could not maintain their rule forever. Examples of this are the conquests of Central Asia, India and other regions, and the subsequent acts of violence against the spirituality of the peoples living there. The spirituality of the peoples of these regions is strong and the strength of their roots gave them the spirit of strength, power, inspiration and unity to overcome the rule of violent invaders. That is why these peoples gained independence and agreed to restore their unique national and spiritual characteristics.

At the end of the twentieth century and the beginning of the twenty-first century, the highly developed countries, which are prone to violence, changed the style and direction of their dependence on other countries and peoples, no longer using force but spiritual influence. ... The danger of this method is, firstly, that it is convenient for the developed countries, which will be able to try to achieve their main goals under the pretext of 'helping' the underdeveloped countries in various directions. In such conditions, they will be able to achieve their main strategic goals of penetrating and capturing the spirituality, consciousness, heart and psyche of the peoples; secondly, the costs in this style are also cheaper than in arms; thirdly, in the eyes of the world community, these countries are not "invaders" but "helpers", "saviours", "humanists", "developers" of universal "spirituality and enlightenment".

By applying this method, these aggressive countries will be able to seize not only all the wealth and resources available in other countries, but also all independent states, and will be able to perpetuate their rule over them.

Thus, a new style of struggle for a united world power is emerging today and its application is in full swing.

Certainly, some peoples today are concerned about the growing threat of such threats to their national spirituality. This is reflected in the rise of national processes to a new level in the modern world. In particular, the desire to preserve the identity of nations, to restore their national and spiritual foundations, to make them the main sources of their development, is growing as never before.

At the same time, as mentioned above, in highly developed countries the alienation of people, the legalisation of same-sex marriage, individualism as opposed to parental, family, children, relatives and a number of other universal human values, the practice of self-knowledge and the desire to popularise it are growing. This popularisation is dangerous, first of all, because it is aimed at people with poor spirituality and, through them, at the whole nation. Thus, providing a new, national and spiritual security for the existing system of security forms has become a global problem in the development of peoples and nations of the world. After all, the collapse of national spirituality will inevitably lead to the collapse of the civilisation that humanity has reached today. Therefore, the preservation of national spirituality becomes a task for the whole of humanity, its charm and potential.

National spirituality occupies a special place in the national security system and has its own components. It thus answers the question of what is meant by national and spiritual security.

In our opinion, national and spiritual security means the existence of conditions, prerequisites, opportunities for sustainable development of national spirituality, protection from various spiritual, intellectual, moral and aesthetic threats that contradict its specificity and the ability of national spirituality to become natural. necessity and practice of national development.

As mentioned above, the growing need for national spirituality is explained by the inability of the "new values" formed under the influence of globalisation to correspond to the future. When it comes to the manifestation of spirituality through specific themes, the main threats come from a focus on individual and national spirituality. The two are inextricably linked and it is impossible to imagine a nation without a person, a person without a nation. In this sense, when it comes to ensuring national and spiritual security, we must understand them consistently.

Above, we have listed a number of reasons why ensuring national and spiritual security has become one of the most urgent tasks of our time. As a logical continuation of this, we can mention the following: First, national spirituality, as its name implies, belongs to a particular nation and expresses its specific customs, traditions and values. The stronger the spirituality of nations, the less likely the formation of a "mass spirituality". Its characteristic feature is that it arises naturally on the basis of the equality of the parties, and not through the oppression of some highly developed countries. Today, the threat to national spirituality is reflected in the growing pressure; secondly, although the pressure on national spirituality is not felt from the outside because it is exerted through the possibility of economic heights, in practice it remains one of the main factors in the erosion of national spirituality. Since it is natural for different nations and peoples of the world to envy, "love" and aspire to highly developed countries and the nations and peoples living in them, underdeveloped countries easily fall under their influence not only economically but also spiritually. Under their influence, new values are introduced into the national spirituality which are completely contrary to its nature and originality. The danger is that they capture the minds and hearts of the people. As a result of this process, national spirituality is in danger of gradually losing its external and internal charm and beauty.

From the above, it is clear that the spiritual, intellectual, moral and aesthetic threats to our national spirituality today are various factors, methods and patterns of behaviour (we will try to show them in the third part of this work), which are acute in terms of space and time. Another dangerous aspect is that, due to the pressure of modern media, national spirituality cannot develop on its own soil. In this real life, not only young people, but also our compatriots with a certain experience of life, the desire to study or imitate films, music, lifestyles broadcast on the Internet or television, develop over the national heritage, traditional art and folklore of our people... It is not news that this single threat is rapidly penetrating our national spirituality today. At the same time, the fact that this process is seen by some of our compatriots as a sign of simple 'progress' is a serious threat. As this process changes attitudes towards national spirituality, psyche, morality and beauty, the main criterion in it remains foreign, not national values. As First President Islam Karimov noted, "... the greatest danger of our time is the incessant ideological struggle for the hearts and minds of people. "Now the struggle is not in the nuclear sphere, but in the ideological sphere"[xxvi].

Indeed, the attitudes, norms, thoughts and thinking skills that have penetrated the mind, the worldview and the heart and become an integral part of them are extremely dangerous. Because it will take years and a lot of money to get rid of them, to direct the spiritual development to the foundations of the national lands. In this respect, the prevention of threats to national identity in terms of spirituality, psyche, morality and beauty remains an urgent task.

Just as a nation is not dead, spirituality is eternal. It is a factor that unites generations, ensures their spiritual and moral closeness, gives people joy, inspiration, beauty, flavour and motivates them for the future.

National spirituality is a "shield" that embodies the unity of the nation, ensures its longevity, reflects, preserves and protects all its characteristics. In this sense, preserving national spirituality and ensuring its security is an important task for the present and future of the nation.

Ensuring national and spiritual security is the sacred duty of every nation, the way to preserve and express its identity. Another aspect is that this is not a narrow concept, but also covers the specifics of the country and other nations and peoples living in it, protected from various threats. As President Islam Karimov noted, "... any threat to spirituality in itself can become one of the most serious threats to the country's security, its national interests, the future of a healthy generation, and ultimately lead to a crisis in society"[xxvii].

In fact, the factor of spirituality can be used to create various dangers. Because it has the following aspects: A) It is linked to the human mind, worldview and heart, which are the main blood vessels of spirituality. The conquest of the mind, worldview and soul by an idea that contradicts progress leads to self-denial, and when a person is in such a state, he becomes "soft" and "soft" obedient. For the mind, the outlook and the heart are the most subtle feelings of a person. It is easy for a person who is deprived of them to become dependent on others. When a nation consists of uniting people, the sense of obedience to others in people's minds, world views and hearts is also reflected in the national consciousness, world view and heart. B) Changes in the national consciousness, outlook and heart are reflected in spirituality. This means that national identity, which constitutes national spirituality, is also manifested in customs, traditions and values. Considering that a change in the national consciousness, worldview, heart and soul, or their complete conquest, is a key factor in gaining national spirituality, it is enough to deprive a nation of this potential without using a terrible weapon for subjugation or destruction. It. It follows from the above that ensuring national and spiritual security is a key factor in ensuring the security of the nation.

"National security" includes national and spiritual security, economic security, political security, military security, environmental security, resource security and others. That is, ensuring national security also means eliminating all threats to national development. But where is the main mechanism of national security? If we compare security to an inextricably linked chain, threats to national development cannot be eliminated without finding their main link. The main link in this chain is national and spiritual security. So why this key ring? Because, as we have said, national consciousness, worldview, psyche and soul are reflected in national spirituality. Consequently, economic, social, political, military, border, environmental and other security can only be ensured as a result of its stability and sustainable development. If we combine them into a system (chain), it can be expressed as follows.

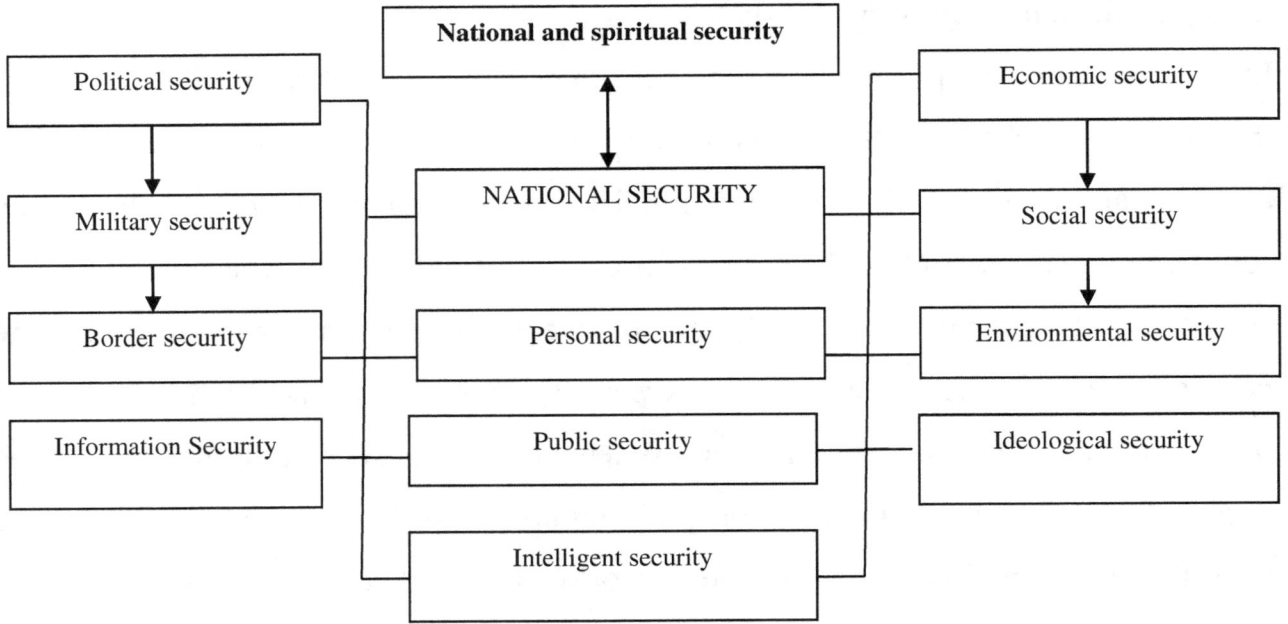

If the key figures in this chain are national security, then the key factor in ensuring it is to ensure national and spiritual security. Why is this a key factor? Because a) national security in the national consciousness, worldview, mind and heart cannot be achieved if the representatives of the nation do not understand that this is the main condition for the preservation and development of the nation; b) political instability arises in a society with national and spiritual poverty; c) a nation with poor spirituality will not be able to defend its homeland. The people of such a nation will not refrain from betraying their homeland. g) National spirituality will be strong in people who strive to protect the motherland from all evil forces, to help strengthen its borders. The strength of the borders of their homeland is a sign of the high spirituality of those who see the security of their homeland as the strength and security of their family. In the case of economic security, the economic use of the country's resources, the prevention of their plundering and export, is also linked to the morality of the people. The preservation of the country's wealth by spiritual people, like the apple of the eye, the emergence of a feeling of hatred towards those who try to exploit it illegally, is also associated with spirituality; d) The maintenance of inter-ethnic harmony, religious tolerance, friendship, cooperation and stability in relations between different social classes in society is also associated with spirituality. If spirituality is developed, there will be a balance of interests in the relationship between them, and society will continue to develop steadily; e) keeping the environment clean and tidy, protecting the country's nature, wildlife, forests and water resources, and preventing air pollution are also associated with spirituality. Spiritual people are well aware that these riches are necessary not only today but also for their descendants in the future, and they try to preserve them within their means. On the other hand, spiritually poor people cannot have such feelings; j) Ideological security means the strength of the national idea and national ideology against all external evil ideas and ideologies aimed at weakening the nation, protecting the national consciousness and world view from their influence, and ensuring that national interests are glorified and reflected in practice. Achieving this also depends on a highly developed spirituality; z) Today, people and nations live under strong information pressure. Developed countries, through the high level media at their disposal, spread various destructive ideas, moral misery and slanderous messages, information and data among world public opinion in order to ensure their dominance in the world. Under such circumstances, their choice is connected with spirituality to be aware of the aspects that are contrary to the interests of a person and a nation. Only people and nations with high spirituality can be vigilant and protect themselves from their influence; i) Today it has become a tradition for the developed countries of the world to "steal" scientists and specialists with high intellectual potential from different countries of the world. They manage to attract such scientists and specialists to their countries by promising to create all material possibilities, technical and technological conditions. Thanks to these activities, on the one hand, they save money and time spent on training such personnel and acquire ready-made scientists and specialists; on the other hand, they try to weaken countries intellectually and ultimately make them dependent. Under such conditions, people with high spirituality, the spirit of love for their people and homeland, refrain from travelling to other countries in exchange for material benefits. Only people with high spirituality can follow this. On the other hand, people who are spiritually impoverished are susceptible to the suggestions of others. It should also be remembered that there are intellectuals who go to other countries and benefit themselves and their country, which is important for national development. In this sense, ensuring the spiritual growth of the intelligentsia remains a necessary condition for national development.

From the above, it is clear that national security cannot be achieved without ensuring national and spiritual security. All the forms that make up the national security system remain dependent on how national and spiritual security is ensured. We also see this in practice. For example, those who claim to own the globe today are more and more interested in pursuing human consciousness, worldview and heart rather than using destructive material weapons. That is why the concepts of "ideological pressure", "information attacks", "ideological threat", "ideological immunity" and a number of others, which did not exist 20-25 years ago, have a firm place in scientific consumption. Today they are becoming stronger and stronger. At the same time, it is impossible to ensure sustainable national security without eliminating them. To do this, we need to achieve national and spiritual security. If we can achieve this, we can achieve national security, which is the basis, the core of all security.

First of all, it is necessary to find out the reasons for the threats to national spirituality. What are the reasons, factors and means that can lead to the emergence of threats to national spirituality? Before answering this question, let us try to dwell briefly on the concepts of "danger" and "threat".

A "threat" is a threat in a state of stagnation. The danger is that the 'threat' becomes a practice, 'works' and begins to influence something. When the threat of "threat" is applied to national spirituality, it becomes clear that it is in the process of internal and external collapse. For although 'threat' is a dangerous force, if it does not reach the level of practice, it will be difficult to understand the status of its impact. Risk is a process that is always in motion. It happens as a result of a 'threat'. At the forefront of risk is the "threat". If there is stagnation in a "threat", then risk is always a fluid process. Which of these has the greatest influence on national spirituality today? If we ask a question and look for an answer, we can say that both are becoming stronger and stronger. This means that as the threat grows, so does the threat to national spirituality, and the process of its disintegration "from within" and "from without" is intensifying. However, they are closely intertwined and act as a single force.

Threats to national spirituality arise in the following cases: a) as a result of the nation's dependence on others; b) as a result of the weakening of national unity; c) as a result of the alienation of the representatives of the nation from their national spirituality; d) as a result of the separation from education; e) lack of respect for the rule of law in the country as a result of increased corruption; f) as a result of the development of democratic values lagging behind the needs of national development.

Let's try to focus on each of them. It is known from the experience of the development of nations that the enslavement of a nation is naturally aimed at depriving it of its spirituality, assimilating its language, customs, traditions and values by the countries that made it dependent. As a result of this policy of the colonial powers, the representatives of the nation leave their homeland and national consciousness, world view and identity are weakened. This process is not sudden, but gradual. Its characteristic feature is that the stronger the foundations of the nation, the more it seeks to preserve and gain its independence, the earlier its desire to preserve its identity and gain independence begins, and the less the influence of the colonialists' actions on its destruction. national spirituality. But there is a danger of collapse. Of course, the direction in which this process will develop will depend on the nation's ability to achieve freedom, its ability to unite as a single force against the enemy, its reaction to external influences, and the ability of the colonial countries to maintain their dependence. However, the experience of similar processes in the world has shown that, first of all, no nation can easily become dependent on other nations; it regards gaining independence as its highest goal in every situation and eventually achieves it. But countries that have become dependent on their spirituality, consciousness, worldview and mentality manage to keep nations under their influence for a long time. It will take years to free them from the consciousness, worldview and spirituality of the nation. The main problem in this process is that there is also a risk that the dependent nation, once it has achieved this, will be somewhat weakened compared to the level of struggle before it gained independence. As a result, the possibility of returning national spirituality to its "pure" image, in which elements of the spirituality of the peoples of the colonial countries are preserved, is limited. This jeopardises the development of nations that have gained independence and are experiencing a national and spiritual revival. For in such a situation, the tendency to accept external influences in their consciousness and world-view may appear. Therefore, the dependent peoples must continue their national and spiritual revival even after gaining freedom and form a "pure" national spirituality on the basis of their national land in accordance with the requirements of the new order and development. Otherwise, the threat to national spirituality will not be completely eliminated; it will be able to survive and survive in a new form.

The weakening of national unity is also a threat to the development of national spirituality. This process can take place in the following cases: a) with the material stratification of the nation and its division into rich and poor; b) localism, the emergence of tribalism; c) increasing distance between theory and practice in the life of the country.

The material stratification of a nation is an objective situation that arises in the context of a country's transition to market relations. The market creates the conditions for everyone to realise their full potential and ensure their own well-being, but it does not allow anyone to live without working, without working for themselves. Those who are successful and enterprising will live prosperous lives; those who do not have these qualities will not be able to achieve the prosperity they dream of. They may have a kind of protest attitude, to put it mildly. This creates certain contradictions between those who can make effective use of the opportunities offered by market conditions and those who cannot. As a result, the unity of the nation is in danger of being undermined. In this situation, the state implements a policy of social protection for the "poor", the helpless and the disabled. However, this is not implemented in all countries. In this respect, the implementation of the social protection policy in Uzbekistan has prevented a sharp material stratification of the population in the country. In our country, we can see that the definition of social protection as an integral part of the task of transition to a market economy is bearing fruit. However, in addition to providing social protection to those in need, the state is also obliged to adapt it to the requirements of the market. The effectiveness of this process will lead to a steady reduction in material stratification between nations. This, in turn, leads to the preservation of national unity. It should be noted that material stratification within a nation is also reflected in national spirituality. That is, two views are formed in the national spirituality: material and energetic, the spirituality of those who have great potential, a way of life and an attitude to life, and the spirituality, a way of life and an attitude to life of those who do not have such an opportunity. This creates contradictions within the national spirituality. This process also reflects the danger of the material stratification of the nation for national spirituality. Its dangerous aspect is that if this stratification takes a firm place in national spirituality, it will take a long time to eliminate it. At the same time, if the split in national spirituality is not resolved carefully and calmly, conflicts will arise within the nation, and if this is not understood in time, there will be a danger of external evil forces being used.

The weakening of national unity is also influenced by localism, the preservation of tribalism or its revival. In fact, localism is a condition characteristic of the period before the formation of ethnic unity at the national level. Its survival is one of the signs that the nation has not yet been formed. However, the experience of today's developed countries shows that in order to manage the state effectively, every leader has the practice of gathering trustworthy people around him. Of course, this approach has been accepted as one of the main conditions that it does not contradict the common interests of the state and the people. But no matter how it is established, there is a danger that it will create a spirit of distrust among the representatives of the nation and undermine national unity. The survival of or adherence to tribalism is the greatest threat to national unity. For it leads to the disintegration and eventual division of the nation from within. In this practice, talented, promising and intellectually gifted cadres of people in responsible positions are left on the sidelines and are primarily reflected in their efforts to promote representatives of their clan to appropriate positions. As a result of such activities, on the one hand the development of the country suffers from the arrival of uneducated, incompetent people in responsible positions, and on the other hand it leads to the formation of a spirit of distrust in the state, the division of the nation. A key factor in ensuring that people who are promoted to leadership positions are people who are surrounded by mutual trust, closeness and experience, so that others do not have a spirit of mistrust towards them. If this style of leadership serves the development and effective implementation of management, it will benefit people in general. But for this method to work effectively: a) It is necessary to develop a strong sense of national identity. This will help to maintain national unity. That is, a nation with a developed national identity "realises that it serves the common interests of localism". (b) At the same time, employers must have a sufficiently developed tendency to pursue personal interests in harmony with the common good. Only when "localism" becomes a factor of common interest, and not of the interest of individuals, groups or individuals, will it be possible to prevent the collapse of national unity. If it is not, the development of "parochialism" will lead to the collapse of the nation and the disintegration of the state. Therefore, in order to take advantage of this factor, both parties, i.e. the representatives of the people and the leaders who serve in the system of government, must be prepared in terms of talent, responsibility and interest. Of course, this will not be easy. It will take a long time for both parties to understand the laws of market relations. The aim of the market is to ensure strong national unity and prevent national and spiritual disintegration, because both sides understand the legitimacy of increasing efficiency with less effort and resources, and not who works with whom. The main condition for this process is a high level of development of the nation, the absence of racism in its consciousness, the awareness of the priority of national interests over all other interests. But it should always be borne in mind that achieving this is a difficult process.

The lack of coordination between theory and practice in the life of the country is also a threat to national spirituality. This is reflected in the fact that in the life of the country the development of concepts is aimed at its development, laws and various regulatory documents are adopted, but they are not implemented in practice or are not effective in implementation. If the developed concepts, adopted laws and regulations do not have a practical effect in the life of the country's population, on the one hand they will remain on paper, which in turn will lead to a loss of public confidence in the future, the state and the condition, leading to distance; on the other hand, this process will lead to the division of the nation and the spiritual impoverishment of society. An example of this is the various "theories" of a "great" future developed in the former Soviet Union, and the fact that as a result of their implementation, people lost confidence in the state and the country collapsed. Under communism, developed under the former Soviet regime, the unscientific theory of "from each according to his abilities and needs" led the country into economic crisis, escalation of inter-ethnic tensions and ultimately to the complete collapse of the state. The unscientific nature of this theory was such that it was rejected as an objective law according to which human needs are unlimited and can never be satisfied, and at the same time it is an important factor in development. It follows from this that it is practically important that any theories developed do not go beyond existing possibilities, are applied in real practice, are supported by people and are reflected in their real lives.

Indeed, theories are born before practice. This does not mean, however, that the possibilities of application in practice should be ignored. On the contrary, every theory is based on: a) the resources available and the possibilities associated with their use; b) should be developed taking into account the level of development of the country's population, its way of life and traditions. Only in this way can the theories that are implemented be inseparable from life and have the expected effect.

The role of the unity of theory and practice in ensuring national and spiritual security lies in the fact that the existence of this unity has a positive effect on the sustainable development of the country, strengthens solidarity and cooperation among various social groups, balances the interests of nations, and strengthens mutual trust. The backwardness of the theory in real life leads to the failure of these very important factors and to the spiritual impoverishment of society. This is due to the fact that the separation of theories from real life is a very dangerous source of chaos that will eventually occur in the life of a country. Any disintegration of society is the most dangerous factor leading to its spiritual impoverishment. The only way to prevent these negative processes is, first of all, to develop and apply theories based on existing possibilities and not on abstract "possibilities", and their results will be reflected in people's lives. Only in this way will there be spiritual unity in the life of society and the possibility of ensuring security will increase.

Another factor in ensuring national and spiritual security is the promotion of national spirituality, its development at a higher level than the development of "mass spirituality" in the world. In the context of globalisation, it is important to intensify the promotion and dissemination of customs, traditions and values, material and spiritual heritage, which are components of national spirituality, in order to raise them to the level of modern requirements. The main problem in this process: Firstly, the developed countries of the West, which form the "mass spirituality", have all the means for its dissemination and diffusion, and they have the opportunity to make spiritually and substantially poor spirituality attractive and thus to disseminate and diffuse it among the population. young people. They also have the opportunity to spare no expense in promoting their "mass spirituality", and this is reflected in practice; secondly, "mass spirituality" is spreading so rapidly in the world today that it is impossible to limit it. In the context of national and spiritual revival in the life of developing countries, highly developed countries that are experiencing spiritual "decline" are taking the initiative to capture the minds and hearts of young people by any means and by any means. ... National spiritual revival - the activity, skill and intellectual potential to make the national spiritual heritage an integral part of the minds and world views of young people - is lagging behind the popularisation of "mass spirituality" in developed countries; Third, the fact that young people are more interested in others than in themselves, and the inability to get the "charm" and modernity they expect and live in, also leads them to seek it from abroad. Of course, "charm" and "modernity" do not mean the promotion of spiritually impoverished spirituality, but the promotion of unique world masterpieces in our national spirituality at today's level of development. This affects their alienation from national spirituality. To prevent this danger: a) Develop national spirituality at a higher level than "mass spirituality", which with its content, essence and charm can replace young people's need to master "mass spirituality". Advocacy should be carried out to the extent that young people have a comparative potential and realise that their national spirituality is rich and beautiful; b) the promotion of national spirituality may have the expected effect of increasing opportunities for advocacy and protection, rather than limiting others, but focusing on the priorities of national spirituality. For any attempt to limit this or that spirituality leads to an increase in interest in it. Thus, in the context of the contradictions between "mass spirituality" and national spirituality in content, essence, charm, propaganda and propaganda, the achievement of the supremacy of national spirituality in the modern world "who" is an important factor in national spirituality. spiritual security. Delay, negligence and, if necessary, irresponsibility in this regard remain a great danger to the future of national spirituality.

Another factor in ensuring national and spiritual security is the integration of education with upbringing. The fact that the prosperous economic life of the peoples of the world today and the well-being of the peoples living in them are not yet a sign of real progress confirms the processes of spiritual impoverishment that are taking place in the developed countries of the world today. Over the next ten to fifteen years, they realised that this process posed a dangerous threat to the establishment of the titular nation. Many scholars, experts and even politicians in these countries are now beginning to realise that education has been cut off from education, partly because of the emergence of such threats. Although the narrow ownership of a particular part of the educational system played a positive role in the development of these countries, its removal from education ultimately led to spiritual impoverishment. Now they are trying to use their economic achievements (material opportunities) for the spiritual, social and moral collapse of the country, the restoration of the spirituality of the titular nation and its priority in the country (we will try to discuss this in more detail later).

The experience of the developed countries shows that, although prosperity is not a sign of high development, it is only in the mind, outlook and heart that "knowing oneself and leaving others", where there is a prosperous life and no concern for the future of the motherland, country and nation, leads to the formation of feelings such as "living for peaceful pleasure". If we look closely at the emergence of such a mentality, it is not only a very dangerous factor for national spirituality, but also proves in the modern life of developed countries that the future of the whole country can be threatened. Thus, this experience will become a unique lesson for any country that considers national spirituality and self-preservation to be the highest values. In our country, the combination of education and upbringing is a priority of state policy. Therefore, our country is developing steadily, social cooperation and inter-ethnic harmony are functioning in our society, the process of our national and spiritual revival is underway. However, these achievements do not mean that all the problems have not been solved and that there are no problems in providing comprehensive education. There are still problems in this area that need to be addressed. In particular, it is necessary to raise education to a qualitatively new level, to increase its prestige, to form intellectual potential that will give us strength and opportunities to ensure equal participation in the context of globalisation. The stronger the education and enlightenment of a nation, the stronger its spiritual security. For both form the basis of national spirituality. Therefore, the consistent improvement of the harmonious conduct of education and training to strengthen our national and spiritual security is still of practical importance.

Another factor of national and spiritual security is the rule of law and the application of democratic values in the country. Although in theory they seem to be "far" from spirituality, in practice it is impossible to imagine high spirituality without them. In particular, the violation of laws is a sign of spiritual poverty; the fact that everyone lives according to the law, that it applies to everyone equally, is a manifestation of the development of spirituality. The effective application of the law is an important guarantee of equality, freedom and the fulfilment of all human rights. In a law-abiding society, corruption, betrayal, violence, immorality and spiritual poverty are prevented, and sincerity in human and inter-ethnic relations is strengthened. The role of the rule of law in ensuring national and spiritual security is that: a) Legal consciousness and culture are an integral part of spirituality. As spirituality develops, so does legal consciousness and culture. In a spiritually poor society, people's legal consciousness and legal culture lag behind in their development. They, in turn, lead to the development in the minds of the people of the society of the mentality of using various illegal means to achieve their goals by circumventing or ignoring the laws. In such a society there is economic, socio-political, spiritual and educational chaos. It is important to develop spirituality to prevent such a negative process. As spirituality grows, people's legal consciousness and legal culture grows, a culture of solving all problems that arise in society within the framework of the law is formed. If we look at this process in harmony with national spirituality, we can see that a high level of development of the nation's spirituality is an important factor in the development of its legal consciousness and culture. With the development of legal consciousness and culture, the values of harmony, tolerance, mutual cooperation and reconciliation of interests, which are important indicators of national spirituality, become natural and strengthen national and spiritual security; b) Observance of laws is important for the development of the spirituality of all peoples. Since the laws guarantee the equality of all nations, their implementation creates equal opportunities for the preservation and development of the national spirituality of all nations and peoples in multi-ethnic countries. The peoples who use them effectively will be able to develop their national spirituality, and this will create conditions for strengthening the national and spiritual security of all the peoples of the country. The provision of national and spiritual security in multi-ethnic countries also strengthens the feelings of interethnic harmony, trust, mutual support and mutual sincerity. Thus, observance of the law is, on the one hand, one of the important indicators of the spiritual development of nations and, on the other hand, an important condition for creating the necessary opportunities for national and spiritual development. Their harmonious manifestation will ensure the strengthening of national and spiritual security.

Another factor in ensuring national and spiritual security is the rule of law and the development of democratic values. An important factor in the formation, development and improvement of democratic values is the rule of law. Democracy will also fail in any society where the law is broken. Democratic values are inconceivable without the rule of law. Democracy is not only an indicator of political rights, freedom, liberty, direct or indirect participation of citizens in government activities, but also an important element of their spirituality. None of these can function in a society whose spirituality is poor or whose development is lagging behind. It follows that democratic values are an important component of spirituality. The development of democratic values in the country is an important factor in sustainable development based on the security of national spirituality and their mutual equality. Although the rule of law and the implementation of democratic values seem to be "far away" from the process of national and spiritual security, in practice they are always harmonious processes. In the face of obstacles to their harmonious development, national and spiritual security is undermined and various political and social dangers arise.

Thus, national and spiritual security is an all-encompassing concept, a process that concerns the nation, the preservation of its spirituality. The breadth of its scope lies in the fact that it is not limited to a narrow circle of 'pure' national spirituality, but is concerned with the sustainable development of all economic, political and social factors involved in its provision. The strength of national and spiritual security is associated with a high level of spiritual and educational development of these factors. Preserving the spirituality of the nation, strengthening national development, economic and political stability will remain an important factor in ensuring national and spiritual security.

PART THREE. THREATS TO THE NATIONAL SPIRIT IN THE CONTEXT OF GLOBALIZATION

In the previous sections of this book, we analysed the concepts of man, nation, national spirituality and security, their interdependence, and noted that in Uzbekistan and most of the CIS countries the concept of "national and spiritual security", its meaning and reasons have not yet been fundamentally studied. With this in mind, today we will focus on the study of "national and spiritual security" as an independent problem, revealing the forms and characteristics of threats to it. At the same time, we have tried to show the reasons for this process, believing that as the intellectual potential of mankind increases, the role of such factors as "spirituality", "national spirituality" increases.

Surprisingly, it is a fact that the very increase in the intellectual potential of humanity should, at first glance, have shown its positive results in real life as an important sign of spiritual progress. Unfortunately, the result is the opposite. Instead of the spiritual upliftment of man, on the contrary, his impoverishment is increasing. There is no limit to its moral impoverishment. In particular, prostitution, human trafficking, the promotion of drugs and the persecution of missionaries in exchange for a meagre amount of money based on ancestral beliefs have gone so far as to change their minds and hearts.

So this spiritual poverty is growing. In this part of our book we will try to reflect on the reasons for its occurrence, the negative changes in national spirituality in the process, and its peculiarities.

FUNDAMENTALS OF THREATS TO NATIONAL SPIRITUALITY

The concept of "national and spiritual security" is generally studied in the system of "national security". Until the end of the twentieth century, the military, political and economic security of the country determined the level of national security. They have not lost their importance even today. Their provision has not lost its relevance in terms of space and time and will remain a priority task. So far, however, ensuring national and spiritual security has risen to the level of priority in the "national security" system. The main reasons for this are: first, ensuring military, border, political and economic security in the national security system ultimately depends on spirituality. In other words, life experience shows that if the majority of the country's population are people with high morality, the chances of ensuring national security will be even higher. Such people understand the destiny of the motherland, its prospects, economic well-being and sustainable development in relation to their own destiny and that of future generations, and they live and act accordingly. Today's development experience shows that it is ultimately possible to make countries completely dependent by capturing the minds and hearts of the people. Secondly, over the years it has become clear that the alienation of peoples from their lands is one of the main causes of spiritual poverty in the world. The fact that this process is being increasingly recognised by many countries, peoples and nations also strengthens their desire to develop on their own land. In general, humanity today is being "forced" to understand that the source of coexistence is not artificial integration, but the natural development of diversity. Thirdly, the spiritual image of the world has changed, the struggle between systems has failed, and instead there is a struggle between uniformity and diversity, which is growing and manifesting itself as a sign of the multipolarity of the world. ... As it grows, it threatens not only the global leadership of each country, but also the well-being of humanity as a whole. The only way to counteract these negative processes is to create a balance between homogeneity and diversity, to create their equilibrium rather than this contradiction. But this is not an easy task, first of all it is necessary to achieve diversity, or rather to preserve national spirituality, to ensure its security, to create conditions for its development on the basis of its objective laws. Any threat to diversity will ultimately lead to the collapse of unity. So, first of all, when the need for "security" arose, what are the manifestations of the various forms of its system, why are the threats to national spirituality growing today more than in other spheres, and what are its prospects? find answers to them by asking very difficult questions.

First of all, it should be noted that the need for security arose at a time when social classes, classes, states and property relations were emerging. The emergence of each of these gave rise to the desire to gain an advantage over the other. In particular, while in the slave-owning society the slave was superior to the slave and the slave was independent of the slave and tried to ensure his safety, in all subsequent societies the struggle for such priority or for a safe life continued, only its forms changed according to the characteristics of development, it can be seen that they have improved.

If we look at history, we will see that security and a free life have been one of the main problems for both the individual and the state, which is one of its pillars. In this sense, the famous Greek thinker Socrates (469-399 BC) said: "Freedom is a wonderful and glorious wealth, both for the individual and for the state"[1].

At the same time, the emergence of the State requires its management, the establishment of justice on its territory, the creation of conditions for the prosperous life of people who have always been exposed to various threats. They have never developed smoothly, but, as we have seen, have been linked to the struggle of one side for domination. This is why, from the emergence of states to the present day, "democracy" has been conceived and accepted as the "ideal" factor to ensure that the government does not "oppress" the people. But this "ideal" is still an "ideal". While some thinkers advocated ways to balance the relationship between government and the people, others advocated the rule of law, others the power of a just king or monarch, and still others the spiritual and moral education of the people. In particular, the ancient Chinese thinker Confucius (Kun-Tszi, 551-479 BC) put forward the idea of governing society by law. He wrote: "If you rule by law, if order is maintained by punishment, people will try to avoid punishment. But they do not feel honour in themselves; if it is regulated by DE (spiritual and moral means), if order is provided by values, people will feel worthy, honest and clean"[2]. From this point of view of Confucius, we can see that he insisted that people follow the harmony of law and morality in order to be safe.

Plato (427-347 BC), a student of Socrates, the leader of the great philosophers, reflected on the benefits of a society governed by law, emphasising that such a governed state could only be bestowed by the gods. He wrote: "I see the destruction of the state where the law has no force, where someone is in power. Where the law rules the rulers, where the rulers are the weapons of the law, the future of such a state is bright, I see that the people are well off. But only the gods can give such a state."3xxviii.

It is worth noting Plato's view that securing human freedom is an important opportunity for the stability and security of society. He puts it this way: "The Persians in the time of Cyrus were in the middle between slavery and freedom, and at first they were free, and then they became masters over many others. But while they were in power, they distributed their share of freedom to their subjects and treated them as equals. Such warriors were close friends of the warlords and marched with full zeal against danger. If someone was wise and could give advice, the king would not be jealous, would allow them to express their opinions openly, and would be grateful for those who could be an advisor. He allowed them to show that they were wise (conscious) in front of a large crowd. That is why the Persians achieved everything at that time - freedom, friendship and the exchange of ideas."4xxix.

From these provisions, it is clear that Plato put forward the idea of a carefree life for people and the sustainable development of a society based on the equality of parties. Freedom (will) can only be realised in conditions of a balance of interests between the parties. But it remained an ideal of humanity, so other thinkers put it forward and made efforts to achieve it.

Another Greek philosopher, Aristotle (384-322 BC), emphasised truth: "The search for truth is both easy and difficult, because no one can fully attain it. At the same time, it is impossible for anyone to know it. But everyone makes at least a small contribution to our understanding of nature, and the sum of these contributions creates a magnificent landscape."5xxx. If we look at these thoughts of the thinker in the direction of security, a situation arises in which this is absolutely impossible to guarantee. Because of the nature of man as a biosocial being, his needs and interests have no end, they continue as an endless process that follows him like a shadow. Their needs are like a shadow: the further they go, the further they go. The need for security remains the same. Since each stage of historical development generates new needs, mankind is forced to live in new conditions and situations under the influence of changes in this process. Thus, the inability to fully satisfy needs gives rise to various instabilities and threats.

Reflecting on the emergence of national spiritual security, it is advisable to clarify what it is based on and what it is connected with. Because in the scientific literature available in Uzbekistan today, we can see that the threats to national spirituality are largely limited to the period of Russian occupation of Central Asia and then the dependence of the Bolsheviks on this country. In our view, it is necessary to take a broader view of the emergence of threats to national spirituality. If we look at the historical data, we can generally see that threats to spirituality existed even before people came together as a nation. The history of the emergence of threats to our national spirituality can be divided into six periods. These are: 1) the period before the spread of Islam in Central Asia; 2) the conquest of Central Asia by the Arabs and the beginning of the practice of Islam in Central Asia; 3) the period associated with the conquest of Central Asia by the Mongols (Genghis Khan); 4) the period associated with the conquest of Central Asia by Tsarism; 5) the period associated with the rise of the Bolsheviks to the top of the Russian state and the establishment of Soviet power; 6) the current period associated with the escalation of the globalisation process.

Although each of them has its own characteristics, each of them is aimed at the conquest of territories, at the acquisition of the material wealth that is available on them, during the implementation of which genocidal wars were first waged, and after the victory, in order to "perpetuate" its rule in the minds and hearts of the people, we see that it has begun to dominate its worldview and thus ensure the dominance of its spirituality.

Consider, for example, the actions of the first period - Alexander the Great - aimed at burning and destroying the Avesto, which today has become part of the spiritual heritage of the peoples of the world. Although this is the oldest written source of the peoples of Central Asia and Iran, dating from the 7th-6th centuries BC, we see that at that time there were attempts to destroy them completely, although the nation had not yet formed as an ethnic unit. ... Abu Raikhan al-Biruni writes: "In the treasury of King Darius there was a copy of the Avesto engraved in gold on the skins of twelve thousand cattle. Alexander destroyed the chimneys and burned them, killing the servants in them. Since then, the Avesto has lost three-fifths (that is, eighteen naskhi). Avesto consisted of thirty naskhi (parts). About twelve thousand remained in the hands of the pagans"[6]. The holy book of Zoroastrianism "Avesto" was created by Zoroaster and reflects the unique spirituality, morality and way of life of the people of that time. The most amazing thing is that Alexander the Great needed this book, why did he burn it? Because it describes the world, man, the creation of mankind, the struggle between good and evil, the victory of good over evil, the definition of justice, the sacredness of the homeland, its soil, water and all its riches, their use. The path of goodness reflects the ideas of fighting evil, such values as moral purity, family, children. Alexander was well aware that these ideas were an important source for people to live freely in the future, to have their own state and spirituality. He was also aware that a nation deprived of them would not be able to stand on its own feet in the future. Therefore, in order to perpetuate his power over the entire people, he burned them. Scientists from all over the world have expressed their admiration for the fact that Avesto is a great source of people's spirituality, and today works of art and science are being created about it. One of the authors of such works is the English Avesta researcher Lawrence Mills. He wrote: "If human thought is an epic and its dignity is mentioned, then we must consider the Avesta as the highest point of this epic. Avesta is the oldest promoter of spirituality.

If we take into account the enormous influence of Avesto on Jewish and Christian theology, we see that he had a dramatic and influential impact on the creation of religion and the destiny of mankind. No one in any language has ever denied that the fragments that have come down to us from Avesto (Gotlar) are surprisingly high. Where can one find such greatness and splendour in the human mind?"[7] [xxxi].

Recognising the same aspects of Avesto, Alexander tried to deprive people of their spirituality by burning it and forcing them to follow in his footsteps.

It can be seen that this process is reflected in the Avesto. In particular, Zoroaster expressed his hope for the triumph of excitement, fear and goodness in life:

"Hey Mazda! In which countries shall I apply? I have been separated from my relatives and friends. I am insulted by colleagues who are far away from me (peasants), as well as by the nobles of the country.

Oh Ahura Mazda! How can I please you?

Hello Mazda! I know why I am poor. It is because I have very little property and very few people.

Oh Ahura! Deep down I regret my low tolerance. Look at my own work. I ask you to help and support me, only this will comfort my heart.

Hello Mazda! When will the dawn come and the day begin when those who want to save the Father (desire and righteousness) will achieve their goal of creating the world of good with wisdom and understanding? Hello Mazda! I have just chosen your teaching.

The corrupt Drukvand (deceiver, liar), notorious for his evil deeds, is misleading the Father's programmers who want to change the lives of the villagers and the country for the better.

Only one who fights Drukvand with all his heart and soul can lead the people of the world on the path of goodness"[8].

It is not by chance that the noble ideas, noble words and noble deeds set forth in the Avesto call for stable peace and prosperity of society and people, because the human world, full of dangers, threats and contradictions, has not lived without them for a moment. Despite the fact that this work was written almost 3000 years ago, we can see that the ideas it contains are becoming more and more important. As history unfolds, the threats to human security and survival are increasing.

The second period of threats to the spirituality of our people is linked to the influx of Arabs into Central Asia. It is known that Islam was born on the Saudi peninsula at the end of the seventh century and first appeared as the main ideological and political force uniting the Arabs, then served to enslave the peoples of the Near and Middle East, and at later stages of its development spread throughout the world and rose to the level of a religion. We see that the processes of its formation, development and spread in the world took place in the form of a fierce struggle, victims of innocent people, robberies, violence, in a word, threats to various stability. The first Arab invasions of Movarounnahr began in 654 in Maimurg and in 667 in Chaganiyan. By the beginning of the eighth century, they had completely conquered Central Asia. "The Arabs will take all possible measures to increase the spread of Islam among the local population in order to strengthen the political power established in Movarounnahr and ensure its stability. They declared the religions of the fire worshippers, Christianity, monism, Buddhism and Kama, which played an important role in the spiritual life of the local population, to be superstitious false religions. In particular, they fought hard against fire worship, which was the main religion of the people of Movarounnahr. Instead of temples, mosques were built. Muslim law begins to take root in socio-economic life"[9][xxxii].

There is much information about the actions taken against the culture, literature and spirituality of Khorezm with the conquest of Khorezm under the leadership of the Arab commander Kutayba. In particular, the Khorezm scholar Professor Iso Jabborov wrote: 'Kutayba ... exterminated and persecuted the scholars who created and preserved the literature and cultural heritage of the Khorezm people. He quotes the words of Abu Raikhan al-Biruni: "After Qutayba ibn Muslim al-Bahili destroyed the Khorezmian calligraphers, killed their priests and burned their books and writings, the Khorezmians became illiterate and relied only on their memories for what they needed"[10][xxxiii].

From the above, it is clear that the Arabs considered the deprivation of the spirituality of the peoples of the occupied territories as a key factor in maintaining their rule. What impact has the Arab invasion had on the development of our national spirituality today? If you ask, of course, we can say that they were able to exert their influence. After the Arabs conquered this country, they introduced their own alphabet, founded mosques and Koranic schools and succeeded in inculcating not only the Arabic language but also its culture in the minds of the local population. The people of Movaronnahr, who lived for centuries, especially before the creation of the

Avesto and from the time of its creation until the Arab invasion, forming their own language, culture, enlightenment and way of life, were deprived of them. In today's national spirituality, we can say that only some elements of Zoroastrianism survived before the arrival of Islam. From this point of view, we can say that the foundations of our national spirituality are associated with the culture of the Arab invaders, separated from its original formation, that is, the ancient culture of our ancestors. Our great ancestor Abu Raikhan Beruni wrote with regret that before the Arab invasion our people had a unique culture, spirituality and enlightenment which were violated by the Arabs. Professor K.B. Buronov, a late teacher, wrote about the Arab invasion: "The Great Turkish Khanate (Empire), which stretched from the Black Sea to the Yellow Sea, that is, to the northeast of China, was in decline when one of the various scattered tribes sharply opposed the Arabs, while the other took the path of reconciliation. This made it easier for the Arabs to conquer the land of Movarounnahr. It was very difficult for the Arabs to conquer the country and assimilate the new religion and ideology among the local people. They killed their rivals, caused various disasters to those who did not convert to Islam, oppressed and humiliated the indigenous people in various ways, and imposed high taxes. At the same time, Arab rulers created various privileges for those who converted to Islam, including exemption from the juzya, or death tax."[11][xxxiv].

In fact, the spread of Islam has taken the form of a fierce struggle, a process that can be seen in a new phase in the intensification of various threats to stability. In general, all violence is based on anti-spiritual acts. This was manifested above in Alexander's efforts to burn the Avesto and instead popularise his ideas or spread Islam in regions such as Central Asia.

It is known that science and culture developed in Central Asia in the 9th-11th centuries, which in turn laid the foundations for the emergence of a new civilisation on a global scale. In particular, after the death of Khorezm Shah Ali ibn Mamun (1009) during the reign of his brother Abul Abbas II ibn Mamun, great opportunities were created for the development of science in the region. During this period, there was the Mamun Academy in Khorezm, led by Abu Raikhan Beruni, and the Mamun

Academy in Baghdad, led by Yahya ibn Abu Mansur and Muhammad Musa al-Khorezmi ('House of the Sages'). In these academies, great research was carried out in various fields of science and great discoveries of world importance were made. The most amazing thing is that the scientists of the academies made their discoveries on the basis of in-depth research, experiments and various expeditions. In particular, Muhammad Musa al-Khorezmi went to India to learn about the Indian numbers and the decimal system of counting and collected the necessary information, creating a new direction in the development of mathematical knowledge based on their study. The discoveries made by Muhammad Khorezmi, Abu Raikhan Beruni, Ahmad Fergani, Abu Ali ibn Sino and a number of other famous scientists working in these academies, with their true meaning and significance, reflect the period of the First Awakening in Central Asia.

On the contrary, the growing scientific and cultural prestige of Khorezm attracted the attention of many politicians and statesmen, and as time went on, efforts to conquer the region intensified. "During this period," writes Khorezm historian Professor I. Jabborov, "Khorezm became completely dependent on Mahmud Ghaznavi, a terrible invader, feudal lord, founder of a great empire." He demands that all scientists living and working in the palace of the Khorezm king be transferred to him. As a result, Beruni was sent to Ghazni along with other scientists."[12][xxxv]. In 1017, Mamun's academy was completed. The saddest thing is that the teacher said that the dictator Mahmoud Ghaznavi gathered writers, poets and scientists around him to gain respect. But in practice, he did not understand or appreciate the importance of the work of these scientists and demanded unconditional obedience from them. According to sources, Mahmud Ghaznavi told Beruni: "If you want to be happy in my presence, speak according to my wishes and not according to your science"[13][xxxvi]. Thus, science became a victim of ignorance, evil and arrogance. Another negative consequence was that Abu Raikhan al-Biruni wrote 152 works, of which only a few survived, Abu Ali ibn Sina wrote 450 works, of which only 240 survived, and Abu Nasr al-Farabi wrote 160 works, of which only about 40 survived. This was the fate of the works of the scientists who worked with them. Their deeds, which have come down to us, still serve the whole of humanity. No one knows how many other discoveries in the work of those thinkers, which have not reached us as a result of ignorance, violence and threats to spirituality, can serve all of humanity.

Take Farobi, for example. It is known that Farobi, like other thinkers of the East, was a versatile scientist, and more than 40 of his works that have come down to us have not yet been translated into Uzbek. However, the vast majority of them have been transferred to many countries of the world and have become popular among other peoples. The very fact that his work "The City of the Noble People", with its scientific value, has methodological significance in the formation of our national statehood, shows that it can be one of the great sources of enrichment of the spirituality and thinking of our people in his works that have not yet reached the USA.

Farobi's role in the development of scientific thought was such that he thoroughly studied and translated Aristotle's works "Metaphysics", "Rhetoric", "Poetics", "Categories", "Analytics", "Ethics", etc.. He made a great contribution to harmonious development. ... His work was highly regarded and during his lifetime he was known as the "second teacher" and "Aristotle of the East" after Aristotle. Farabi's ideas about the state, society, government, community and a number of other institutions in his work "The City of Noble People" are of great theoretical and political importance today. In his views on a noble community, he emphasises that such a community can only emerge if it is based on knowledge and high morality14. Such a scientific conclusion could only be reached by a person with a high level of knowledge and thinking, who was able to foresee the problems of development. At the time he lived, a world that was ideally formed and whose positive aspects were exemplary for all had not yet come to an end. In such circumstances, the promotion of such a perfect understanding of the state shows that Farubi was a highly educated person. His following views on society and human relations are noteworthy. "Every man is organised by nature in such a way that he needs a lot to live and to reach a high level of maturity, and he cannot achieve these things alone. Therefore, in order to have them, a community of people is necessary ... so that only through the unification of the multitude of people who are necessary for survival, who unite people and help each other, can a person reach the maturity he strives for by nature. The activities of the members of such a community as a whole provide each one with what he needs for life and maturation"[15]. It is clear from these ideas of Farobi that he portrays a person and society in harmony and puts forward the idea that human interests in the relations between them can only be realised if they are organised in a certain community.

Thus, in the 9th-12th centuries, in the Central Asian region, as a result of the thinking of Al-Khorezmi, Abu Raikhan Beruni, Ibn Sino, Ahmad Fergani, Farobi and a number of other thinkers, a civilisation (civilization) belonging to humanity was formed. Their discoveries in the fields of science and spirituality later had a positive influence on the development of these fields in Europe. However, a new dangerous situation in the region that created this civilisation, which became the common heritage of mankind as a result of mutual struggle, negatively affected the development of science and spirituality.

The third period is associated with the formation of the Uzbeks as an ethnic unit and the conquest of Movarounnahr by Genghis Khan in the 13th century. It is known that the unification of the Uzbeks into an ethnos began at the end of the 8th - beginning of the 9th century. This also means that they formed their national culture, spirituality and enlightenment. But even during this period, the threat to their culture and spirituality did not pass. In particular, as a result of the conquest of this land by Genghis Khan at the beginning of the 13th century, the national culture formed in the region suffered heavy losses. Not only did the invaders kill civilians, but they also destroyed entire towns with their material monuments. In particular, "at the beginning of 1220, the Mongol conquerors first conquered Otrar on the Syr Darya, then Bukhara and Samarkand. The invaders sacked towns and villages, massacred most of the population and condemned some to slavery. The defenders of Holy Bukhara were completely annihilated, the fortifications destroyed and the city set on fire. Samarkand also heroically defended its city, but only a quarter of its population survived. The people of Urgench, under the leadership of Sultan Humar-Tegin, were forced to surrender after seven months of valiant fighting. The Mongols, who had never before encountered such resistance, massacred the entire population (sending 100,000 craftsmen to Mongolia), young and old. According to historians, each of the 50,000 besieging Mongol troops killed 24 Urgench. The capital was ordered to be completely demolished and wiped off the face of the earth, and when the savage invaders had completely wiped out the population, they destroyed the Amu Darya dam and flooded the capital. As a result, beautiful historical monuments and libraries with thousands of unique books were destroyed"[16]. Naturally, as a result of the evil of the occupiers, who aimed at exterminating the people, destroying their culture and enlightenment, the national culture formed during that period suffered greatly, and the process of uniting the people of the country as a nation went backwards. Of course, the people fought bravely against the Mongols, but the fragmentation of the provincial population, the disunity, led to the victory of the enemy. Jaloliddin Manguberdi, the great son of the Uzbek people, who grew up in Khorezm, fought against the invaders like Genghis Khan and showed great courage as a defender of the motherland. Many works have been written about them. Among them, the work of Shahobiddin Muhammad al-Nasawi "Sultan Jalaliddin Manguberdi" is particularly valuable[17][xxxvii]. For in his work he recounts the events he witnessed. The author was with Jalaliddin and, as his secretary, recorded all the events that took place. The work is based on this exact information.

The reason why we think about the work written about Jalaliddin Manguberdi and its author is that the heroes of every nation will have children who will introduce them to the world. With their dedication and devotion to their homeland and people, they bring their people to the world stage. One of these children of the Uzbek people is Jaloliddin. Today we are proud of his heroism and courage, we receive spiritual and moral strength, his courage in defending our motherland and our people from the aggression of any evil forces will accompany him. National spirituality is enriched by the devotion of patriotic, nationalist and patriotic children who grow up among the representatives of the nation. In this sense, Jaloliddin Manguberdi is not only a great patriot, but also a person who has given a unique "image" to our national spirituality.

We can say that he is a child of our nation who managed to fight an invader as powerful as Genghis Khan, raise the level of the Uzbek nation and show what his children are capable of. Although he died at the hands of the enemy and all our material and spiritual wealth was destroyed at that time, thanks to Jalaliddin's courage it was revived and became an important source of unification of the Uzbeks as a nation.

But there are still major obstacles to overcome. The actions of the state of Genghis Khan, which was born in Mongolia and aimed at invading Central Asia, did not allow the development of this country. On the contrary, the cities, which had been the centres of science and culture that had developed in this country for centuries, were destroyed. The Arab historian Ibn al-Athir (1160-1233) wrote about the actions of the Mongol invaders in Central Asia: "They spared no one, killing women, old people, children... They crossed the country without leaving a single town"[18][xxxviii].

It is known from historical sources that the people fought stubbornly against these invaders, and among them were patriotic boys such as Jaloliddin Manguberdi, Najmiddin Kubro, Temur Malik, who showed heroism in the fight against the evil enemy. But as a result of the invaders' vicious actions, civilians died, property was looted, and the threat to the people and the region increased. Movarounnahr was forced to endure these invasions until Amir Temur came to power. It was only after he came to power (1370) that the Mongol atrocities against Central Asia and the threats to the people's consciousness and lives were eliminated. He created a vast empire by completely defeating the Mongol invaders.

When Amir Temur came to power, his first task was to rebuild the country, restore order and ensure the peace of the people. To accomplish this task, he enlisted the help of some of the most eminent scientists of the time. Nizamiddin Shami, an eminent writer and historian, describes it as follows If any oppressed person is oppressed or any weak person is mistreated, let him pluck the thorns from the feet of the oppressed people and give them back from the treasury. on the other hand, if it can be proved that something has been taken from them by force, let them take it back."[19][xxxix].

The Temur Code books contain special views on Amir Temur's activities in the field of public administration and public security. Our great ancestor, who founded such a great empire and led it skilfully, took into account that there are always threats and dangers to the country and its people. He said: "I have given this order to ministers who are trustworthy and influential people in the Sultanate. Even if they have betrayed the state during their tenure with the intention of overthrowing the kingdom, do not rush to kill them, but first expose the informers themselves, the truth and lies of their sermons. This is because in many cases, envious people and gossips who are out of sight or out of greed fabricate lies, falsify them and achieve their (false) goals. There are many vile and evil people in the state who improve the enemies of the state and destroy its supporters with various tricks. Their aim is to break into the fortress of the kingdom."[20][xl].

Amir Temur not only created a great empire, but also laid the foundation for a new Timurid era in the East, especially in Central Asia, in the development of science, culture, spirituality, literature and art. This period not only restored the scientific potential of Central Asia in the 9th-12th centuries, but also raised it to a new level. The source of the rise and development of spiritual and educational life of this period, the beginning of which dates back to the 9th-12th centuries. The cultural, spiritual and educational maturity of Central Asia in the second half of the fourteenth and fifteenth centuries is a continuation of the culture, spirituality and enlightenment of the ninth to twelfth centuries. At the same time, a whole generation of great thinkers grew up among the peoples of Central Asia. World famous historians - Sharofiddin Ali Yazdi, Mirhand, Khandamir, Davlatshah Samarkandi, great scientists - Ulugbek, Ali Kushchi, Kazizoda Rumi; philosophical poets - Abdurahmon Jami, Alisher Navoi, Lutfi, Sakkoki, Atoi; artists - Kamoliddin Behzod, Kasim Ali, Mirak Nakkosh; calligraphers - Sultan Ali Mashhadi, Sultan Muhammad Khandan Muhammad bin Nur and others. According to the late academician Ibragim Muminov, a devoted son of the Uzbek people: "Among the scientists serving in Timur's palace are Mavlono Abdujabbor Khorezmi, Mavlono Shamsuddin Munshi, Mavlono Abdulla Lison, Mavlono Badriddin Ahmad, Mavlono Khorizuglonidjan, and others. Olow et al. It was. "Temur paid special attention to the development of such sciences as mathematics, mathematics, geometry, handicrafts, architecture, research, astronomy, literature, history, music, and he communicated with great interest with the masters of his profession. It is known from their historical, scientific, spiritual and material heritage that they were all great personalities who mastered all spheres of human spirituality, enlightenment and culture of that time and earlier, who conquered the heights of their chosen fields. possessing encyclopaedic knowledge, intelligence, spirituality.

That is why their rich and diverse creations, their unique and inimitable scientific, philosophical, artistic and historical works have been handed down from century to century, from era to era, surviving all threats and difficulties.

In the history of the peoples of the world, great discoveries have been made in science, culture, spirituality, literature, art and other fields, many of which continue to serve humanity. If we look at the problem from this point of view, we will see that the Temurid period, founded by our ancestor Amir Temur, occupies a special place. In the same way, the warriors who created states, politicians and empires in the world died, but many of them were left with inhuman historical data, such as destruction, plundering, evil, destruction of material and spiritual wealth, and not the legacy inherited from them. serve humanity. But first of all, all the riches inherited from our ancestor Amir Temur, Central Asia and all mankind amaze people with their power and value and enrich their spirituality.

One of the important cultural and spiritual values of the Timurid period is that during this period Islam developed in harmony with science, culture and spirituality. Much attention was paid to the importance of religion in ensuring the stability of the country and the spiritual enrichment of the people.

The pictorial art created during the Timurid period manifested itself as a kind of stage of spiritual development. The art of Kamoliddin Behzod and his students rose to the level of the achievements of the Eastern Renaissance. Behzod left an indelible mark not only in the East but throughout the world with his unique creations, wonderful miniature art and amazing craftsmanship. Respected as "Second

Money" and "Eastern Raphael", Bekhzod is a man of high spirituality who created images of famous artists - Jami, Hussein Boykaro, Shaybanikhan and others.

The development of science, culture and education in the Timurid period is closely connected with the name of Mirzo Ulugbek (1394-1449). He was a statesman, a scientist, a patron of enlightenment, a great scientist and astrologer. In the observatory and scientific and educational centre he built, he gathered more than 100 scientists working in various fields and conducted a wide range of scientific observations. These were the great scientists of the time, such as Kazizada Rumi, Giyosiddin Jamshid, Ali Kushchi, Mawlana Ahmad Muhammad Khawafi, Abul Ali Birjandi, Mirim Chalaboy, Muiniddin Kishi.

On this basis, Mirzo Ulugbek founded the Samarkand Academy - Ulugbek Academy in Samarkand. He was a great scientist who created the works "Ziji Jadidi Koragonii" ("New Astronomical Table of Koragonii") and "History of Four Nations". Ulugbek was famous for his scientific potential, especially in the field of astronomy. His discoveries in this field still serve people all over the world.

The role of Mir Alisher Navoi (1441-1501) in the spirituality and enlightenment of the Timurid period was enormous. He was a great son of the Uzbek people, a thinker, a statesman, the founder of Uzbek literature and language. He created more than forty works in various fields of art and literature. Among them are Chor Devon, Khamsa, Makhbubul-kulub, Muhokamtul-lughatayn, Majolisun-nafois, Lisonut-tair and others.

Navoi understood the contradictions of the times, that ordinary people always live under the threat of time, and reflected this process in his works. All his life he sang and glorified humanity. Caring for people, doing good deeds, showing kindness became the meaning of Navoi's life.

All material and spiritual riches, literary and artistic works created during the reign of the Temurids became a new stage in strengthening the global prestige of the Uzbek people, their worthy contribution to the world civilisation. They are still one of the most important sources of spiritual enrichment for our people[22][xli].

The first president of Uzbekistan, Islam Karimov, wrote about the "Code of Temur" of our ancestor Amir Temur: In my own work I have repeatedly referred to this book and have often been convinced of the vitality of the wise ideas it contains, which will never become obsolete and still nourish human spirituality today. For example: "I know from experience that one determined, enterprising, vigilant, brave and courageous person is better than a thousand careless, indifferent people."[23][xlii].

Unfortunately, much of the material and spiritual wealth created during the reign of the Timurids has not survived to the present day as a result of the struggle for power, violence, evil and various upheavals. This struggle led not only to spirituality and enlightenment, but also to a crisis in the Timurid Empire. After the death of Amir Temur, the struggle for power in the country, the tragic death of Ulugbek, the end of the academy founded by him, the emigration of world-famous scientists from Samarkand to other countries showed the manifestation of this crisis.

After Jaloliddin Manguberdi, Amir Temur is one of those who presented the glory of our people to the world and made a great turn in the development of our national spirituality. He not only rebuilt the destroyed Movarounnahr, but also built a centralised state in which he created magnificent hordes of our national spirituality. He raised Samarkand to the level of the most beautiful, cultural and spiritual city in the world. The way of life of our ancestor Amir Temur, the way of governing the state based on the principle of justice, is also of special importance for the development of our national spirituality. Because the spirit and spiritual image of our nation shines in the buildings, mosques and madrasahs he built, in the gardens he created. Creativity, science, culture and education initiated by Amir Temur, as a special stage in the development of culture and education of our people in XIV-XV centuries, took a worthy place in the world civilisation. Unfortunately, after the death of Amir Temur, as a result of the crisis of the Timurid dynasty, the centralised state created by them was divided. As a result, culture and education lagged behind those of the Timurids.

It can be seen that the internal conflicts that led to the crisis of the Timurid period, the threats to the country's security, did not stop for a minute. Along with these internal threats, the emergence of external threats to the region led to an increase in cultural and spiritual depression.

In particular, the emergence of three independent states in Central Asia - Bukhara, Khiva and Kokand Emirates - led on the one hand to the disintegration of the Uzbek nation, which had not yet fully formed, and on the other hand to its strengthening. through the efforts of countries such as Great Britain and Russia. Under various pretexts, they sent their spies to this country and began to implement their plans for a thorough investigation and seizure of the country. Under these circumstances, the fourth period of threats to our national spirituality began. The characteristic feature of this period was that the process of Uzbek nation-building intensified, and at the same time the evil actions of the opposing forces intensified.

In 1714, the Russian Tsar Peter I (1672-1725) sent a military expedition to Khiva under the command of Bekovich-Cherkassky. Although the expedition was thwarted by the Khiva Khan Shergozikhan (1715-1727), the expeditions did not end there; on the contrary, Russia did not retreat from its plan to conquer Central Asia. From 1865 to 1873, it conquered three independent states in the territory of the whole oasis: Kokand Khanate (1865), Bukhara Emirate (1868), Khiva Khanate (1873). The administration and control of the whole country passed into the hands of governors appointed by the Russian emperor.

Under these conditions, the population of the country began to be largely exploited by bi-national, local wealthy officials and Russian occupiers. All material values, manuscripts, cultural and educational treasures left by our ancestors were taken to Russia. Our national spirituality began to fall under the influence of the Russian invaders as a result of their strict control. This process negatively affected the superficiality of our national spirituality. From the tsarist soldiers sent to Turkestan to the representatives of other spheres, they worked hard to destroy the religion, customs, traditions and values of our people. In particular, an evil, spiritually poor man named V. Vereshchagin wrote: "I threw the mullah from the tower."24 In fact, the mullah is a symbol of the preservation of our sacred religion and national spirituality. Vereshchagin was proud of what he had done. This man, who ate Uzbek bread, salt, drank water and spat on its salt, was proud of his cruelty to our people and our spirituality. Another invader, the military governor of Turkestan, General A.N. Kuropatkin, wrote in 1916: "For 50 years we have kept the native population from development, from school and from Russian life"[25][xliii]. There is no need to explain how such actions influenced the development of our national spirituality. For this is the confession of an invader, not of a man on the brink.

Russia's aim in conquering Central Asia was not limited to the material wealth of the peoples of this land, but at the same time they began to show their spiritual dominance in the country. This is reflected in the following statements by Russian generals

"The school must play an important role in the implementation of the plan for the Russification of the country" (General Rosenbach).

"A thousand sarts are not worth the heel of a Russian soldier" (P. Ivanov - Governor General of Fergana).

"Central Asia is the most expensive place in the Russian crown" (Minister of Finance of the Russian Empire).

"The future of Russia in Central Asia" (Minister of Interior of Russia).

The above need no comment. It is clear from them that the peoples of Central Asia have always experienced threats, violence, discrimination and similar inhuman humiliations after the occupation of Tsarist Russia. Such evil was, of course, condemned by the progressive Russian intelligentsia. In particular, one of the greatest poets of the Russian people, F.M. Dostoevsky, wrote: "Truth is greater than Russia"[27][xliv].

Roy Medvedev, People's Deputy of the USSR, Doctor of Historical Sciences: «As a historian, I must say that we, Soviet historians, are not afraid to admit that Russia invaded Central Asia or even occupied the North Caucasus»[28][xlv].

The idea behind this was the oppression inflicted by tsarism on the people of Central Asia after its conquest. Some intellectuals also attempted to conceal the aims of tsarism in invading Central Asia. At the beginning of the century, D. Logofet, a full member of the Imperial Geographical Society, organized several trips to the cities and villages of Kazakhstan and Central Asia. In his works 'On the Borders of Central Asia', 'In the Land of Lawlessness', 'Russian-Afghan Border', 'Bukhara Mountains and Plains', and 'Bukhara-Afghan Border', the author addresses the violence that occurred during the occupation of Central Asia and Kazakhstan.[29] The occupation resulted in the destruction of villages and cities, leaving behind a barren wasteland and countless innocent lives lost. This tragic reality is a recurring theme throughout the author's works.[xlvi].

This is how the struggle of the country's people against oppression began. The largest of these battles occurred in 1898 under the leadership of 42-year-old Muhammad Ali Khalifa (Madali Eshan), known as the 'Duke of Eshan', and the second in 1916 in Jizzakh against the Russian emperor's recruitment of men aged 19 to 43. Both uprisings resulted in significant bloodshed. However, the uprisings against the violence of tsarism persisted without pause.

Due to the national policy of tsarism in our country, there is an increased risk of our national spirituality becoming separated from our lands. However, even during this period, nationalists and patriots who grew up among our people fought for the independence of our nation and its national identity, even giving their lives for this cause. These individuals are celebrated in the history of our nation's fight for independence in the name of the Jadids. They effectively raised awareness and united people against violence. However, due to the overwhelming material and military power of tsarism, the Jadids were unable to fully achieve their goals. Nevertheless, their struggle for independence was not in vain. On one hand, they contributed to the self-realisation of our people and mobilised the struggle for independence. On the other hand, they demonstrated that our national spirituality surpasses that of the invaders. They acted as representatives of our nation, maintaining the purity of our national spirituality and protecting it from foreign influences, despite the violence of tsarism, in order to perpetuate their domination in the country. The invaders acknowledged the significant material, spiritual, and cultural potential of the Uzbek people. This strengthened the possibilities of safeguarding our national spirituality against the threats of tsarism.

The fifth period of threats to our national spirituality began with the collapse of the Russian Empire and the ascent of the Bolsheviks to power in Russia. During this period, the state policy was to destroy our national spirituality and instead introduce Russian culture and enlightenment to all the peoples of the region. To implement this policy, the Bolsheviks began by physically destroying the Jadids, who were prominent figures in the Uzbek nation and fought for self-realization and independence. The Jadid movement in Turkestan began in the 1990s, and their physical extermination continued from the 1920s until the outbreak of World War II. One of the leaders of the Jadids, Mahmudhoja Behbudi, was arrested on March 25, 1919, in Shakhrisabz and executed in Karshi under mysterious circumstances. The other leader was Munavvarkori. In 1929, an investigation was launched into the 'Munavvarkori gang', which resulted in 87 people being investigated. In April 1931, the OGPU sentenced 15 of them to death, 31 to 10 years, 19 to five years, 14 to three years in prison, one to exile in Omsk for a year, and three to deportation.

On May 23, 1931, Munavvarkori Salimhon Tillakhonov, Said Akhroriy Tangrikul Khoji Maksudov, and Najmiddin Shermukhamedov were executed by firing squad in Moscow's Butyrka prison. Their bodies were buried in secret at Vagankovskoye cemetery. The Russian press reported on this event on May 25, 1992, exactly 61 years later [30][xlvii].

Even after the coup d'état in Russia in October 1917, the peoples of Central Asia remained in a precarious situation, as the Leninist strategy of forced Sovietization and the suppression of non-national socialist statehood was implemented. Even after the coup d'état in Russia in October 1917, the peoples of Central Asia remained in a precarious situation, as the Leninist strategy of forced Sovietization and the suppression of non-national socialist statehood was implemented. This was noted by Professors D.A. Alimova and A.A. Golovanov, who stated that the policy was actively enforced and widely used in Uzbekistan. The Bolshevik government proclaimed the possibility of national development of the peoples of the region, but in practice, they hindered these processes [31][xlviii].

The Bolsheviks fought against national spirituality in several ways. Firstly, they physically exterminated the country's most prominent intellectuals, accusing them of 'nationalism'. Secondly, they eradicated traditional education, including non-religious networks, under various pretexts and replaced them with Russian education through the introduction of a new education system. Upon the Bolsheviks' rise to power, they began to methodically dismantle the interdisciplinary education system and establish a singular Soviet education system. The new rulers utilised the state's economic and military power to exert strict control over state formation. In an attempt to promote a communist worldview among young people, they aimed to increase the number of Soviet-style schools through force. As of 1920, there were already 2,080 'socialist' schools in the TASSR, with a total of 174,820 students. As of 1920, there were already 2,080 'socialist' schools in the TASSR, with a total of 174,820 students [32][xlix].

The number of such schools increased annually, leading to the creation of a uniform education system in the region. Unfortunately, this resulted in the destruction of not only the traditional education system but also the values based on national foundations. It can be argued that the abandonment of these values began during the same period as the failure of the traditional education system. The aim of the policy was to integrate education with education. To achieve this, by the end of 1920, Turkestan had 177 'socialist' libraries, 97 clubs, 76 red tea houses, 172 reading rooms and other institutions. However, locals rarely visited them [33][l].

This is how the local residents perceived the true intentions of the Bolsheviks [34]. However, they faced strong pressure from malefactors and attempted to change the education and training system calmly.

The Bolsheviks were considered enemies of the Soviet regime. According to official data, from 1937 to 1953, 100,000 people were persecuted in the republic, and 13,000 of them were sentenced to death.[li]. Representatives from all levels of society, including ordinary citizens, scientists, literary and artistic workers, and leaders of nationalist states, were among them. These individuals made great sacrifices for the development of Uzbekistan. The majority of those who fell victim to these massacres were members of the national intelligentsia. Tsarism and the Russian Bolsheviks aimed to conquer the nation by eliminating them. The experience of countries that have committed acts of aggression around the world shows that the most effective way to implement their colonial policy is through the physical destruction of prominent intellectuals, nationalists, patriots, and public figures.

Intellectual national consciousness, understanding of national identity, expression of the nation's own rights, and the formation of ideas of free and independent development are the leading force in their popularization. The national intelligentsia plays a crucial role in preserving, developing, and popularising national spirituality. Their activities are essential for the growth and improvement of national spirituality. A developed national intelligentsia is vital for a nation's future. The great sons of our nation, who put into practice the ideas and actions of Jadidism, sacrificed their lives for the liberation and independence of our country from tsarism and the Bolsheviks.

Mahmudhoja Behbudi, Munavvar Qori Abdurashidkhon oglu, Abdurauf Fitrat, Usman Nasir, Abdullah Avloni, Muhammadsharif Sofizoda, and several other Jadids have been working since the late 19th century. They considered enlightenment as the only way to save the country and people from national oppression and backwardness. These selfless individuals fought against the tyrannical regime, ignorance, spiritual slavery, and oppression with all their might. These enlightened ancestors travelled the world, familiarised themselves with the science and culture of different peoples, and believed that colonialism and its shackles could be dismantled through the power of science. They set an example of practical and theoretical courage in developing education, which forms the foundation of spirituality and culture in our country.

The Jadid movement highlights the perilous state of the future of national spirituality and culture under both tsarism and the Bolsheviks. Their efforts to cultivate national identity and spirituality through educational reform were crucial. Professor Begali Kasimov, a renowned scientist who extensively studied the Jadid movement and dedicated his fundamental works to revealing its activities and ideas, stated that the term 'Jadid' forms the basis of Jadidism. 'Jadid' means 'new', not only in terms of innovation but also in the sense of 'new thinking', 'new man', and 'new generation' [35][lii].

The Jadids implemented a two-pronged reform in education. The first direction was to abandon the old teaching methods in Turkestan and introduce a new 'serious method'. The second direction was to send talented youth from Turkestan to study at leading European universities. In the summer of 1922, more than 60 students were sent to study in Germany by the decision of the Collegium of the Central Executive Committee of Turkestan and the Government of Bukhara. In 1923, there were 11 students from Turkestan and 51 students from Bukhara studying in Germany [36][liii].

The Jadids established innovative schools, prioritised the growth of the press, literature, and art, and worked tirelessly to advance them. Their efforts were aimed at fostering national identity, self-awareness, and spirituality. It is evident that their work was not in vain. Throughout the world and in our nation, the potential for achieving national development, preserving spirituality, and educating a harmoniously developed person has been confirmed at all stages of development.

However, during the years of dependence, actions were taken against the national and spiritual heritage of the Uzbek people, resulting in the physical

destruction of the Jadids by the Bolsheviks. The representatives of our nation have played a crucial role in modern education, self-expression, and preparation for national independence. They have initiated a new stage in the development of national spirituality that meets modern requirements. This includes the establishment of a new era press, the creation of a theatre, and the formation of Uzbek novels (such as A. Kadiri's novels) and drama. The Bolsheviks labelled the Jadids as 'nationalists' because they believed in developing national spirituality as an integral part of the consciousness and worldview of their nation. The Bolsheviks understood that a nation that understands itself will never become dependent on others and can fight for its independence. They accused the Jadids of 'nationalism' and physically destroyed them.

The Bolsheviks' suppression of our national spirituality did not end with the physical extermination of the Jadids. It continued until we achieved our national independence. This was reflected in the development and implementation of an unscientific theory of the formation of a 'national', which in reality was a 'socialist' spirituality. This form served to standardise the national spirituality developed under Soviet rule. They aimed to turn this theory into reality by taking away our national land and making Russian the state language. This has caused a disconnect between the population, especially young people, and their national spirituality. It can be said that they have had some success. Twenty years after gaining independence, some of our compatriots still retain elements of the Soviet era in their consciousness and worldview. Additionally, works of art that ideally reflect our national history and independence are lagging behind the level of daily need.

There is much information available about efforts to capture the spirituality, consciousness, and heart of the nation, as well as the consequences of these efforts in preventing their development. It is important to take necessary measures to prevent a repetition of this process and to warn the population about it, as this remains an urgent task today. This activity is crucial in preventing threats to our national spirituality.

Considering the significance of these matters, let us examine the approach towards our national and spiritual legacy in the former Soviet Union.

It is widely acknowledged that the oral traditions of our ancestors form the foundation of the spirituality of every nation. In times when writing did not yet exist, they conveyed their aspirations, experiences, and visions orally, and played a crucial role in linking past and future generations. Separating people from their heritage, history, and roots is equivalent to stripping them of their identity. It is important to consider these works objectively and in their historical context. The ancient values of our people during the totalitarian regime, such as myths, legends, fairy tales, and proverbs, as well as epics like 'Ravshankhan', 'Alpomish', 'Gorogly', 'Rustam', 'Avazkhan', were evaluated one-sidedly from the perspective of modernity, class, and partisanship. The assessment of each piece of Uzbek folklore was based on two cultural theories that were deemed suitable from the perspective of communist ideology. However, these theories ignored national and universal values and ideas.

For instance, in the epic 'Alpomish', khans and beys were praised, aggression and violence were promoted, and non-Muslims were accused. The protagonist of the epic, Alpomish, did not embody the noble qualities and aspirations of the people, but instead portrayed himself as a ruler, butcher, and typical tyrant. This attitude represents a threat to the foundation of national spirituality.

A similar disregard was shown towards national languages and literature. Under various pretexts, national records were periodically promoted, with the main emphasis on the development of the Russian language instead of other national languages. It is true that knowledge of different languages is of great importance for personal growth and development. The more languages a person knows, the more their worldview expands and is enriched by different cultures, perspectives, and values. To achieve this, it is important for individuals to have a strong foundation in their ancestral language. This will enable them to learn other languages more effectively.

Language plays a crucial role in the development of national identity, thinking, and spirituality. It has evolved alongside the nation over centuries, reflecting all of its unique characteristics. The lack of a national language could result in the assimilation of the nation into other cultures. The lack of a national language could result in the assimilation of the nation into other cultures. Therefore, it is important to consider that limiting or reducing national forms in the acquisition or popularization of any other language may have negative consequences for national development.

In summary, there is a significant need for tireless and selfless work to eliminate remnants of the worldview formed during the Soviet Union era, enrich our national spirituality based on our lands, and make them an integral part of the mindset and worldview of our youth.

The ongoing globalization of the world today is associated with the sixth period of threats to our national spirituality. This period is characterised by three key factors. Firstly, we have achieved national independence, which is a necessary condition for the development of our national spirituality. Secondly, the possibility of using force to destroy our nation and our spirituality has disappeared. Finally, the erosion of national spirituality is not due to military weapons, but rather to the factors driving the process of globalization. It is evident that this process, with its immense power and strength, is more hazardous than any attempt to force a nation towards self-sufficiency. The main direction of this process involves dangerous ideas and practices, such as the conquest of the mind, worldview, and soul, which can lead to the destruction of a nation. When a nation's mind, worldview, and heart are stripped away from their national identity, it becomes easy for them to lose their sense of self and assimilate into other cultures. Today, there are two tasks at hand: ensuring the security of our national identity and enriching our national consciousness and worldview through our spiritual heritage. Additionally, we must promote globalization.

Over the years of independence, significant efforts have been made towards our national and spiritual revival, the development of our national heritage, the establishment of our national identity, and the restoration of the Uzbek language as the state language. Despite these efforts, the threats to our national spirituality have not been completely eliminated. Threats today are not manifested through direct force and violence, but rather through the erosion of national spirituality. This erosion captures the minds and hearts of people, particularly young people, with the 'charm' and 'modernity' of these threats. Further elaboration on this topic will be provided in the following sections.

The desire of a nation to preserve its identity will continue as long as the nation exists. However, preserving national spirituality and its place in world civilization, as well as prioritising it in national development, is a complex process.

Throughout history, there have been attempts to use national spirituality to claim ownership of a nation's riches. The six periods mentioned occurred at different levels. In five of these periods, conquest and subjugation were achieved through violent means, including destructive wars, followed by the imposition of a spiritual deprivation to maintain control. In the current period, however, highly developed countries have abandoned this approach and instead use their capabilities to first influence the minds and worldviews of nations, before taking complete control and ownership of their resources. This is a new trend in global dominance in the 21st century. If people do not understand its implications and the potential tragedies it can bring, it will inevitably accelerate the disintegration of national identity. When ensuring national and spiritual security, it is important to consider that the adoption or blocking of any regulatory document will not have the desired effect unless its potential for dominance exceeds that of any foreign nation.

Preserving national identity and utilizing the educational potential of the mind, spirit, heart, and thinking are crucial for achieving expected results in ensuring national and spiritual security. The principle of relying on force and violence based on national and spiritual security is ineffective. It is important to avoid biased language and employ a formal register. The text should adhere to conventional structure and use precise word choice. Causal connections between statements are necessary for a clear and logical flow of information. One of its defining characteristics is the use of force or coercion, which can have violent repercussions and lead to unexpected negative actions. This behaviour can also lead to an increase in interest and imitation in the national and public consciousness, not for personal gain, but for others. It is important to note that this is a sensitive issue.

The distinction between national and spiritual security, as opposed to other forms of security, lies in its association with the human mind, heart, and thinking. This protection is essential for achieving the desired practical outcomes. Therefore, the theoretical concept of providing spiritual security reflects the need to protect these faculties from external influences and the 'mass spirituality' of society.

Threats to national spirituality arise from the desire of other parties to achieve material and spiritual superiority. Such threats have not always been a priority issue. To eliminate them, it is necessary to assess their impact, warn the population, introduce modern education, and promote the growth of national spirituality, particularly among representatives of the nation and the world.

In this process, the First President noted that if there is a gap in nature or society, someone will try to fill it. Therefore, we must follow the conceptual idea.

3.2. EXTERNAL THREATS AFFECTING NATIONAL SPIRITUALITY

The acceleration of globalization, a result of human intelligence, poses a growing threat to peaceful coexistence. Risks take on various forms and manifestations, and their impact may not be immediately apparent to the public. However, over time, their influence increases and can become a mass threat. It is crucial to address these risks objectively and comprehensively. Today's developments confirm that forming 'immunity' to withstand such situations requires significant effort, resources, and time.

In the present day, humanity faces a multitude of growing dangers that pose a threat. This highlights the importance of uniting to combat emerging threats. Before delving into the topic, let us first consider the meaning of the term 'threat'.

Scientists worldwide analyse various aspects of the political and philosophical essence of the concept of 'threat'. Since the beginning of conscious human activity, 'threat' has coexisted with humans, growing in power to become what it is today. It is crucial for humanity to understand its content, essence, and negative impact and take steps to curb it. Failure to do so will result in a catastrophic future. There is a growing interest in studying the meaning, content, basis, impact, and containment of the concept worldwide, including Uzbekistan. It is worth noting that the book 'Uzbekistan on the Threshold of the XXI Century: A Threat to Security, Conditions of Stability, and Guarantees of Development' by the First President Islam Karimov holds significant structural importance.

The significance of this work lies in its methodological, theoretical, and practical aspects. It is important to note that while the former Soviet republics were celebrating their newfound independence, the President of Uzbekistan highlighted the need for awareness of potential threats not only for the people of Uzbekistan but also for those of the CIS. The ideas, dangers, and threats presented in this work have been relevant since 1997 when it was first announced.

"One of the most difficult questions," he warned, "is whether we are aware of the challenges that threaten our stability and security."[1][liv].

Maintaining and strengthening our independence becomes increasingly challenging as we develop.

The First President's threats are a destructive force for the entire country, and their forms and manifestations were also highlighted.

In brief, this fundamental work provides a theoretical basis for examining the characteristics and impact of threats on our development at every stage of history.

Doctor of Political Sciences, Professor Sh. Pakhrutdinov studied the concept of 'threat', its content, and influence on our development for the first time in our country, based on this fundamental work. He defined the concept of threat as follows: A threat is a socio-political situation with a specific goal in a certain historical period. Its aim is to weaken and destroy the political foundations of the state as a social system, as well as to undermine human life in general. This is often due to the influence of global factors^{2} [lv].

The author describes the socio-political situation as a 'threat'. In the following section of the book, they elaborate on this point, stating that this threat has a negative impact on human and social life. Furthermore, it destroys the constitutional foundations of the state and is a characteristic event with clear boundaries in space and time. It complicates life, destabilises it, and undermines its stability, development, and security. Furthermore, it destroys the constitutional foundations of the state and is a characteristic event with clear boundaries in space and time. Furthermore, it destroys the constitutional foundations of the state and is a characteristic event with clear boundaries in space and time^{3} [lvi]. The author aims to reveal the political aspects of the 'threat' and suggests that it is large-scale.

It is worth noting that the concept of 'threat' is included in Spirituality: A Glossary of Basic Concepts, published in 2009, and defined as follows: A threat is a situation that arises from negative factors, whether local, regional, or global, with the aim of achieving a specific goal that affects the life and activities of individuals, society, and the state over a certain period of time. It is important to maintain a stable political, social, and historical situation^{4} [lvii].

There is a growing interest in studying the concept of this 'threat' and its content, essence, and possibilities of interaction. This is because it poses an increasing danger to the development and safety of countries and peoples, as well as the development of national spirituality. Therefore, it is urgent to identify the causes and develop appropriate measures.

We focus on threats to national spirituality rather than the broader concept, meaning, and potential of influence. It is important to note that this issue is also extensively discussed in President Islam Karimov's book 'High Spirituality is an Invincible Force', which outlines a program for the development of our spirituality. The article includes a section titled 'Threat to Spirituality - A Threat to Our Self and Our Future', which outlines the potential dangers to our spiritual well-being.[5][lviii]. Studying threats in depth can help us comprehend their nature and develop a robust spiritual immunity in our society.

Threats come in various forms, such as human, individual, civil, national, state, societal, regional, global, and others, depending on their origin, manifestation, and impact on development. Regardless of their form, they hinder progress and aim to cause failure. Where applicable, a 'threat' refers to a force, event, factor, or process. This is distinct from 'risk', which is the likelihood of a negative outcome occurring. In this text, we will attempt to answer several questions regarding the concept of a threat.

Firstly, it is challenging to provide an unambiguous definition of this term, as it is often intangible and gradual in its development. It can be thought of as a weapon in some cases, but in most instances, it is invisible, abstract, and hidden, gradually impacting stability and development. The manifestation of this effect as a material being is the only way it can be felt, perceived and seen. However, this is a lengthy process. Understanding the nature and impact of threats to spirituality quickly is challenging because it involves consciousness and worldview. Removing negative influences from the mind and worldview is a difficult and time-consuming task that requires sacrifice.

It can be argued that a threat is a material force, factor, or theoretical process. When a threat takes a material form, such as a weapon or a vehicle, it becomes a manifestation of power. Threats that arise in the form of spirituality, ideas, and ideologies gradually become material as they take root in consciousness and worldview. This is known as the theoretical process of a threat. The appearance of threats in any form is extremely dangerous for development.

Why consider a theoretical view of threat as a process? Spiritual, ideological, and ideological threats are difficult to perceive and comprehend. Reason is the only means to represent them, understand their meaning, and exert influence. As a result, they manifest as abstract, long-term processes that operate as an 'invisible' force and vary in content and essence. Strength is a material property that can cause instability in an object, but its impact may vary. When measuring threat, the factor's propensity to act is passive compared to the force. A factor can be present in events and processes, but it cannot always be an influencing force. In the event of a power increase, he may only participate if his intervention is necessary to restore balance. Power, as a force with its own inner strength, is always actively involved in events and processes and exerts its influence. It should also be noted that threats can be detrimental to development at the factor level. If the subject does not pose a threat, they are considered passive in relation to force. However, even this passive state can negatively impact the smoothness of development. It is important to note that the factor causing this impact is not the force itself, but rather its source and basis. Therefore, power cannot exist without a factor. Initially, factors associated with events, processes, interests, purposes, and events are formed. The level of strength of 'factors' depends on the direction of the event, process, interest, and purpose. The influence of 'factors' and 'strength' on goals, interests, and processes can be positive or negative, depending on their nature and direction. If a 'factor' has a negative direction, it becomes a threat and rises to the level of power. This implies that the 'threat' does not emerge instantly, but rather in the form of the 'factor' reaching the level of 'strength' and exerting its influence.

When considering spirituality, it is important to recognise that threats to it can occur gradually rather than suddenly. Factors associated with these threats may silently form over time, eventually becoming a force with expanding possibilities of influence. This can lead to the process of spiritual decay. On the contrary, its strengthening arises from the depths and indicates a decline in spirituality, not only from within but also from external factors. Therefore, it is more accurate to view threats to spirituality as a long-term process rather than a short-term one. These are complex concepts and processes that require further political and philosophical analysis. This text discusses the concepts of 'force' and 'factor' in the context of a threat.

The 'process' of the threat is said to operate in spiritual, ideological, and ideological 'appearance'. The text has been improved to adhere to the following characteristics: objectivity, comprehensibility and logical structure, conventional structure, clear and objective language, format, formal register, structure, balance, precise word choice, and grammatical correctness. The concept of 'process' is associated with continuous events and phenomena that occur in space and on Earth. Therefore, threats to 'appearance' from a spiritual or ideological perspective are not short-term, but rather long-term and permanent. Military, economic, and political threats can be felt, seen, and prevented, but the impact and consequences of threats to spirituality are difficult to quickly realize. As it does not immediately attack, but first weakens the mind and worldview, achieving the main goal becomes easier. This process is difficult to understand and poses a dangerous threat to spiritual, ideological, and ideological aspects. This process is difficult to understand and poses a dangerous threat to spiritual, ideological, and ideological aspects. This process is difficult to understand and poses a dangerous threat to spiritual, ideological, and ideological aspects. It captures the consciousness of individuals and nations, depriving them of their sense of self.

Threats emerge from conflicting interests and aim to prioritise one side. They have existed since the beginning of human consciousness, but their expression has varied in form, size, force, and interaction. They have existed since the beginning of human consciousness, but their expression has varied in form, size, force, and interaction. As human intellect and needs grow, so does aggression. Today's threats cannot be equated with those of the past. They are extremely aggressive and pose a danger to the development of people, nations, and societies. These threats not only endanger individuals and communities but also the entire civilization created by mankind. Unfortunately, some entrepreneurs are actively contributing to the escalation of this catastrophe instead of uniting to prevent it. It is worth noting that those who make up 'mass spirituality' are acting without realizing that they will become its victims in the future. Their actions are threatening the civilizations that humanity has acquired today. Later, we will discuss the threat to humanity posed by the destruction of national spirituality.

It is important to note the difference between the concepts of 'threat' and 'risk'. Risk arises from the escalation of threats due to objective and subjective reasons, leading to negative situations such as limitation, myopia, and indifference. Failure to notice or acknowledge threats can lead to their deepening and the creation of danger. Failure to notice or acknowledge threats can lead to their deepening and the creation of danger. Risks arise as a result of threats to goals and interests. Therefore, it is important to identify and address threats in a timely manner. The process can be considered a 'factor', but its rise to power poses a threat. Threats are a force that creates danger, and there is no risk before the threat.

Therefore, preventing threats to sustainable development requires efforts to prevent their emergence in practice. This can yield expected results, but it requires a solid foundation to mitigate the threat. In this analysis, we will examine the threats to national spirituality related to our theme without delving too deeply into their analysis.

Why are threats to national spirituality increasing more than ever? According to the First President, the answer is clear: '...a thousand years of human experience shows that if the brutal and aggressive forces of the world want to subjugate a people or a country, they first disarm it, that is, they seek to deprive it of its greatest wealth, its national values, history and spirituality.'[6 lix].

A nation without spirituality has no future. Spirituality is a subtle and complex human wealth, and a nation deprived of it will inevitably lose its identity. A society with completely impoverished spirituality can be compared to a dead tree, which no matter how tall, can easily catch fire. An individual, nation, or society that lacks spirituality is destined to fail, just as a plant cannot grow without taking root and sprouting. An individual, nation, or society that lacks spirituality is destined to fail, just as a plant cannot grow without taking root and sprouting. It is important to maintain self-esteem, even if one is economically strong. Spirituality is a powerful force that can lead to the flourishing of human values such as consciousness, peace, joy, tolerance, pride, and honour. The language used should be clear, objective, and value-neutral, avoiding biased, emotional, figurative, or ornamental language. The text should also adhere to conventional structure, using common academic sections and maintaining regular author and institution formatting. Finally, the text should be free from grammatical errors, spelling mistakes, and punctuation errors. However, it is important to note that subjective evaluations should be excluded unless clearly marked as such. Furthermore, the weapons amassed on our planet have reached a critical point where they can obliterate humanity multiple times over. It is now a fact that anyone who chooses to use these weapons for malicious purposes will not survive.

Stripping individuals, nations, and societies of their spirituality can lead to the capture of their minds and hearts. In such circumstances, they are left obedient. The 21st century is significant for its role in developing global consciousness and shaping national spirituality. It is crucial for the peoples of the world to cooperate in preventing the rejection of spirituality, as it may lead to an economic crisis and political disruption, ultimately threatening the survival of mankind on the planet. It is crucial for the peoples of the world to cooperate in preventing the rejection of spirituality, as it may lead to an economic crisis and political disruption, ultimately threatening the survival of mankind on the planet.

In the context of our topic, threats to spirituality can be divided into two groups: external and internal. This division helps us to clearly understand the meaning of threats to national spirituality and to clarify the possibilities of their impact. It is important to identify and address these threats in order to protect our spirituality. External and internal threats manifest themselves in certain ways and have a specific scope. The following chapter will analyse internal threats to national spirituality, while this chapter will reveal the nature of external threats.

Today, globalization, ideological attacks, drug trafficking, and human trafficking are external threats to national spirituality. The forces behind these threats are increasingly using cunning methods and means to fight against national spirituality, utilizing their material, technical, and technological capabilities. Analysis of this process shows that it is difficult to control them. National spirituality is reflected in the minds, worldviews, hearts, bodies, and blood of a nation, although it is invisible from the outside. It takes the inner and outer image of the entire nation.

Globalization is an objective process that affects all sectors and its achievements are the product of human thinking. It should serve the interests of humanity and its development. However, throughout the history of human development, it is evident that not all advancements in thinking have been beneficial. Specifically, nuclear and thermonuclear weapons are a result of human innovation, but unfortunately, they have been used to sacrifice innocent lives or have been wielded by countries that prioritize their own interests over others, perpetuating a spirit of great state chauvinism. It is important to note that globalization is not exempt from these issues. It is a well-known fact that countries with advanced military, technical, and scientific capabilities often use these resources to influence the beliefs and attitudes of less developed nations. The negative impact of globalization on national spirituality has been extensively discussed in the author's previous book, 'Globalization and the Nation.'[7][lx].

Globalization is often compared to an ocean that attracts nations with its scale, power, and economic means. However, it also has a negative impact on national identity. This is particularly true for countries with high intellectual and economic potential, who are often the creators and owners of this 'ocean'. Less developed countries are often attracted to this 'ocean', but its unique nature also poses a risk of losing their customs, traditions, and values.

It is noteworthy that no nation or people who have not reached a high level of development can bypass it, as it effectively utilizes the economic factor to serve its own interests. The danger of this 'ocean' lies in its ability to impact the economy, modern media, television, computers, the internet, mobile phones, and other means of communication. This can have an effect on people, especially the youth, their nationality, thinking, and worldview. It is evident that developed countries are utilising these same opportunities and tools to propagate the 'mass culture' they have created in five strategic directions of the policy of developing culture and spirituality.

The monograph presents several conceptual ideas regarding the adverse effects of globalization on national life.

However, the increasing trend of globalization indicates that it is not only eroding national values but also universal human values. The text appears to be a list of universal values, including peace, stability, humanity, human dignity, nationalism, preservation of the nation, equality, justice, creativity, democracy, preservation and transmission of civilization created by the peoples of the world, human rights, individual freedom, liberalism, religious tolerance, and interethnic harmony. The language used is clear and objective, and the sentence structure is simple and concise. The author notes that these values are declining, and it is important to uphold them. Currently, the world is experiencing instability, with innocent people being killed due to the interests of malevolent forces. Additionally, smaller nations are being assimilated by larger ones, and conflicts between religions and nations are escalating. It can be argued that globalization is contributing to these issues. In fact, some countries that are leading the globalization charge are actively disregarding universal values in favor of their own material and spiritual interests. Although they present themselves as defenders of these values, in practice they violate them. Their actions may lead to the destruction of these values and the establishment of their dominance over the planet. Their actions may lead to the destruction of these values and the establishment of their dominance over the planet. Such an outcome could lead to the demise of humanity.

What is included in our national spirituality through globalization? If these concepts are not named accurately, globalization can become an abstract idea.

National and universal values develop over time and space, absorbing specific aspects of historical, national, and human development, and enriching values in the process. However, it is important to consider that not all aspects of national and regional morality, spirituality, culture, and life, which have been elevated to the level of values, can be considered universal values. Today, we are witnessing the collapse of national spirituality. This is due to the formation of new moral norms in advanced countries and the influence of their economic, socio-political, spiritual, and educational development. Additionally, globalization has created opportunities for the promotion of spiritual and cultural achievements. It is important to note that this statement is presented objectively without any subjective evaluations. A precise approach to the question reveals that developed countries and their inhabitants benefit more from globalization than developing countries and their inhabitants. A precise approach to the question reveals that developed countries and their inhabitants benefit more from globalization than developing countries and their inhabitants. The logical flow of information is maintained with causal connections between statements. A precise approach to the question reveals that developed countries and their inhabitants benefit more from globalization than developing countries and their inhabitants. It is important to note that this is an objective evaluation and not a subjective one. The language used is clear, concise, and value-neutral, with a formal register and precise word choice. The text adheres to conventional structure and formatting features, with consistent citation and footnote style. The text is free from grammatical errors, spelling mistakes, and punctuation errors. No changes in content have been made. Considering globalization as an objective process, let us examine its effects. Developed countries' achievements in science, technology, and other fields are now accessible to developing countries, which can accelerate their development by purchasing and utilizing them. Developed countries' achievements in science, technology, and other fields are now accessible to developing countries, which can accelerate their development by purchasing and utilizing them. However, it is important to recognize that economic, socio-political, and educational interests may be driving this process. In the context of globalization, the primary challenge for national development is understanding and addressing its underlying issues objectively. It is often overlooked that the acquisition of new equipment, technologies, and scientific advancements can create dependencies between developing countries and their more developed counterparts.

Today, with the proliferation of science, technology, and communication in their countries, people may struggle to form an objective opinion about the potential negative consequences of globalization. It is important to recognize that individuals may unknowingly develop a biased perspective, or even an addiction, towards certain ideas. It is becoming increasingly clear that these processes are causing a growing dependence on developed countries, which may threaten their national independence in the future. Only time will tell what the future holds," he said.

It is evident that the inclination towards 'ready-made cunning' and dependence will hinder the development of the national intelligentsia, thus eroding the identity of the nation and replacing it with that of others. Globalization can be viewed as an opportunity for developed countries to become reliant on developing countries and their inhabitants in the 21st century.

Globalization has a negative impact on national spirituality due to the influx and popularization of the lives, traditions, and values of developed countries, alongside their technical, technological, and scientific achievements. The erosion of national spirituality occurs due to the growing desire of nations and peoples to emulate the technological and scientific achievements of other countries and peoples. This process leads to a decline in universal human values, which are formed through the most advanced aspects of national values. In this process, countries with ample opportunities are effectively promoting their morals, way of life, traditions, and values. It cannot be assumed that all peoples and cultures will accept them, as some may choose not to participate.

From the above, it is evident that globalization is not merely a process, but rather a means for developed countries and their citizens to impart their moral norms, customs, traditions, and values, along with technical, technological, and scientific advancements, to developing countries and their citizens. This can have an impact on the erosion of national spiritual identity. The impact of globalisation on the national spirituality of developing countries and their inhabitants, as demonstrated by the practices of countries and peoples that are effectively utilising this factor, can result in spiritual poverty, selfishness, interpersonal alienation, and the legalisation of same-sex marriages, which can affect the relationships between parents, families, children, blood relatives, and others. This is due to the introduction of Western 'values' that are considered 'modern' but contradict a number of universal values. They represent external spiritual threats that infiltrate our national spirituality through the process of globalization. In the future, they are expected to reach the level of universal value, but they also pose a danger to national development due to the same factors that contribute to their growth.

Spiritual poverty is a negative state that results in the loss of human, national, and spiritual values such as honor, shame, purity, modesty, religion, faith, conscience, and tolerance. It affects individuals, nations, and societies. When situations like this arise in spirituality, is there a contribution from someone or something, particularly achievements in the field of economic and social life, influenced by humanity's intellectual potential? Or is it the contribution of the West that has become the prevailing tradition of criticism? It is time to ask this question and find an answer. However, the answer to this question remains somewhat complex. Both factors contribute to the lack of spiritual development in individuals, nations, and societies. It is important to note that this is an objective evaluation and not a subjective opinion. Western countries have achieved a high level of intellectual potential and have a model for development, which has allowed them to surpass other nations and exert economic, socio-political, spiritual, and educational influence. As mentioned earlier, our national spirituality is influenced by various factors such as modernity and originality, which are elevated to the level of 'value'. It is important to acknowledge this reality. However, it is worth questioning why our national spirituality accepts these influences despite being far superior to the spirituality of the West. Additionally, a question can also be raised.

The main issue identified is the impact of the post-Soviet era on our worldview, which has resulted in a sense of 'obedience' within our nation. Additionally, the economic challenges faced during the transition period have contributed to the problem. It is important to address the growing wealth gap and ensure that everyone has the opportunity to express themselves and reach their full potential. The popularization of Western traditions, customs, and values as 'novelty' and 'modernity' is inevitable, despite efforts to preserve the originality and charm of our national spirituality. This acceptance comes at a great cost and puts pressure on our compatriots, ultimately affecting our national spirituality.

The need to enhance unity and cooperation among all members of our society in preventing such negative processes is increasing. When considering the impact of these processes, it is worth acknowledging the experiences of peoples such as the Japanese, South Koreans, and Indians who overcame the spiritual tyranny of the West and became dependent on a mere three hundred British individuals. The main idea presented is that Western traditions, customs, and values are being spread through globalization and are influencing our national spirituality. This influence is being promoted by the West and is even being imposed on the minds of our youth. As a result, young people have a growing need to increase their absorption of these values. To achieve this, it is recommended to utilise the opportunities presented by our independence and recognise the importance of promoting the traditions, customs, and values of our nation. It is crucial to focus on the 'new Uzbeks' who are making significant progress in terms of material well-being. This approach should be avoided as it creates a sense of superiority and undermines the unity of our nation. However, there is a growing trend among them to differentiate themselves from their fellow citizens and present themselves as more civilised and innovative. Failure to do so may result in national and spiritual disintegration, as well as internal disunity.

Under the influence of globalization, it is increasingly important to make full use of the opportunities available to prevent threats to national spirituality and work actively towards this goal. Therefore, it is crucial to maintain a balanced approach and avoid biased language when discussing these issues.

When considering globalization, it is important to acknowledge its impact on the survival of humanity, not only in terms of material resources but also national and spiritual resources. Globalization is often seen as a result of human development and thinking, and can serve as a factor in accelerating survival. However, the search for opportunities that do not endanger human life will inevitably become one of the most pressing problems in the future. The depletion of material and national-spiritual resources for their development could lead to the extinction of all human life. Considering potential tragedies that can affect humanity, it is important to recognise the increasing significance of globalization in conserving material, national, and spiritual resources, as well as extending human life on their land. This has become a primary objective and responsibility for global intellectuals and humanity as a whole.

An external threat to our national spirituality is ideological attack. It is widely acknowledged that human and social development cannot exist without ideology. However, the purpose and benefit of ideology must be considered. If used for the development of people and nations, it can have a positive impact. If used for evil and disgusting goals, it can create crises in all areas.

Ideology can be used to manipulate people, change their beliefs, and create divisions in society. It can also have a negative impact on development, especially during times of crisis. Additionally, it can lead to heinous acts, such as turning friends into enemies.

With the use of this tool, it is possible to gain global dominance and promote abhorrent ideas. The danger of ideological aggression against national identity lies in the ability to implant negative traits that contradict the nation's identity, leading to loss of land and ultimately, loss of identity.

Another important aspect is that the actions taken as a result of a long process of ideological interaction can deeply influence the consciousness of individuals and nations. Therefore, eliminating stereotypes, prejudices, and values that contradict national spirituality can be a challenging task. Ideology has the power to transform various views and ideas into beliefs in the minds of people and nations. Preventing the formation of Akiki is a more appropriate approach to ending ideological attacks, rather than getting rid of it.

Ideological aggression is often driven by selfish goals and interests, which may include weakening a particular nation, society, or state, subordinating them, or acquiring their material resources. To comprehend them, it is necessary to foster national self-awareness, identity, unity, political consciousness, and culture, while maintaining social stability. Failure to do so may result in vulnerability to their influence. Ideological attacks are often carried out covertly, making it challenging to defend against them. Ideological attacks are often carried out covertly, making it challenging to defend against them. Although this is one aspect of the issue, ideological sensitivity is also linked to an attempt to influence one's mindset, worldview, and beliefs. Furthermore, such occupation undermines national development, leads to societal instability, and enables those who implement it to easily achieve their basic goals.

Today, various forms of ideological aggression are carried out through modern media. These can be divided into two groups: promotion and propaganda of ideas such as global culture, lifestyle, art, and values; and distortion of national identity in the development of democracy. These can be divided into two groups: promotion and propaganda of ideas such as global culture, lifestyle, art, and values; and distortion of national identity in the development of democracy. These can be divided into two groups: promotion and propaganda of ideas such as global culture, lifestyle, art, and values; and distortion of national identity in the development of democracy. The first group promotes global ideas, while the second group distorts national identity. The reasons for this

are related to human curiosity. For individuals, the way of life of other cultures, their accomplishments and shortcomings, is often a novelty. One notable feature is that no one can live in isolation from the rest of the world, its developments, and processes. People strive for innovation, draw positive aspects from other cultures, and learn from their negative aspects. In this sense, people's interest in foreign films can be viewed as a natural inclination. Secondly, most of the films produced in Uzbekistan depict carefree events that are far from reality. They mainly focus on love, existing problems, and their solutions, while ignoring real issues. Even when real problems are portrayed, they are often presented in a way that does not meet the needs of modern society. Our people yearn for a way of life depicted in the novel 'The Last Days' by the great Uzbek writer Abdullah Kodiri, which portrays love, fatherhood, children, and family relationships. There is a growing demand for foreign films in Uzbekistan as local films do not cover this genre. However, this trend poses a great danger to our national spirituality and may lead to a crisis. It is important to maintain a balanced approach and avoid biased language.

Today, many people in our country are becoming aware that foreign media often publish content that contradicts our national values. For instance, there is a concern about the impact of foreign television programs on our national spirituality. It is important to objectively evaluate the influence of such programs and their potential effects. 44% of the population, 37% of workers, 11% of the community, and 9% of the local population. Among students, 41% are part of the population, 10% are part of the community, and 30% are part of the staff. Among staff, 23% are students, 13% are part of the community, and 13% are employees. The percentages are as follows: 44% of the population, 37% of workers, 11% of the community, and 9% of the local population. Additionally, 6% of workers and 21 people are part of the statistics.

In summary, the survey results indicate that, on average, 88% of respondents believe that foreign television has a negative impact on our national spirituality. However, it is important to note that not all members of the population share this sentiment. For instance, 36% of respondents reported watching DTV, which broadcasts controversial footage of Russia, despite 57% of respondents expressing negative views towards it. It is noteworthy that our population shows an increasing interest in watching films and TV programs filmed in foreign countries, despite the potential negative impact on our national spirituality. However, the main challenge lies in our inability to provide films and screenings that cater to the growing demand of our population in this area. Foreign countries, with their vast material, scientific, technical, and technological potential, not only spread their culture to other nations but also use their skills to influence the beliefs of others. This poses a threat to our national spirituality through ideological factors.

The first ideological attack suggests that national peculiarities in culture, lifestyle, art, and values are losing significance and moving towards expressing unity. The first ideological attack suggests that national peculiarities in culture, lifestyle, art, and values are losing significance and moving towards expressing unity. However, they still share commonalities and express national identity. However, this commonality does not completely erode national identity. Instead, it has a positive effect on mutual enrichment and spiritual growth of people worldwide based on diversity.

It is widely acknowledged that the promotion of a 'cultural' lifestyle and global values in Western media is driven by a desire for global dominance. While these ideas and actions may be concerning, it is premature to dismiss the importance of preserving national spirituality that benefits humanity. Positive aspects of national culture contribute to the formation of universal values. It is impossible to completely eradicate universal ideas, as the fight against them will always intensify as long as there are people. This struggle is a crucial aspect of self-awareness and protection against selfish ideas. The views of the cultural expert U. Saidov are worth noting in this regard. According to the author, the notion of a unified culture is purely imaginary. While there may be shared characteristics, values, and forms of expression among different peoples, as well as a common perception of the world and interaction with reality, there are also significant differences in basic concepts. In particular, each culture - both Eastern and Western - has its own genotype and, accordingly, a unique logic of internal development [8][lxi].

However, ideas that go against the unity of culture, lifestyle, art, and values pose an ideological threat to national spirituality and can weaken its development according to its national identity. These ideas, which are promoted through the media and modern technology, can arouse the interest of people who do not believe in the nation. This can lead to their inclination to accept these ideas and ultimately turn them into participants in the 'popularization' of these ideas. Unfortunately, we still see this happening today, although it is rare in life. This can be observed in the case of individuals who currently distrust religious leaders, reject traditional religious values, adopt alternative religions, and promote them to younger generations.

It is important to remember that even though ideological attacks, mainly from the West, may be powerful and have modern technical capabilities, their ideas will eventually reach their peak. It is crucial for humanity to strengthen its own vision of development, otherwise, the civilization that has been created over centuries may be destroyed by its own intellect and hand. It is believed that the strength of humanity lies in its consciousness, which allows for an understanding of positive and negative aspects. This consciousness has enabled the creation of civilization, which continues to thrive and promote goodness. Throughout history, there have been various forms and levels of ideological attacks on national spirituality, and it is likely that this will continue in the future. The threat of their appearance today reflects the level and 'needs' of the period and human development. However, it does not completely destroy national spirituality.

Alongside threats to national spirituality through ideology, attempts to undermine the democratic process in our country are also a concern.

At first glance, the question is how much national spirituality is connected with the democratic process. On closer inspection, it becomes clear that they are closely intertwined. Specifically, their interdependence is reflected in the following: firstly, democracy, no matter how universal, cannot have a standard that applies to all nations worldwide. Each nation must work hard and utilise its intellectual potential to develop its unique aspects.

The formation of a democracy takes time and requires material, political, spiritual, and educational conditions. The formation of a democracy takes time and requires material, political, spiritual, and educational conditions. It is important to avoid subjective evaluations and biased language. Democracy requires not only political power's inclination towards it, but also citizens' desire to be active in forming it.

The experience of the most developed countries in the world has tested these aspects. The mentality, lifestyle, worldview, customs, traditions, and values of a nation are all associated with democracy.

It is important to distinguish between the universal values of democracy and values that reflect national characteristics. Some scientific literature published in Uzbekistan divides these values into 'western' and 'eastern' criteria, which is a result of a lack of clarity

in the definitions of 'criteria' and 'national characteristics'. The criteria of democracy are universal and not specific to any particular region or culture. It is unscientific to divide them into criteria characteristic of the peoples of the 'West' or 'East'. While no country has fully formed all the criteria, some have made progress in developing them at their current level of development. Another perspective is that the criteria for democracy are constantly evolving, and the generally accepted criteria should not be considered final for the future of humanity. Democracy is an endless and continuous process. In this sense, 'pure' democracy, which can fully meet the needs of all people, will continue to evolve towards its ideal.

Now, let us consider the problem of expressing national characteristics in democracy. This reflection encompasses not only the traits of 'Western' and 'Eastern' peoples, but also those of nations, regions, and humanity as a whole. The concept encompasses not only the national mentality, customs, traditions, and values but also the temperament of the nation, including moderation, curiosity, indifference, and restraint. Additionally, it considers the factors that connect the peoples living in the region, such as material, political, spiritual, regional, and natural aspects. Furthermore, it takes into account the factors that unite people globally, such as global problems, concerns about the future, and responsibility for the future. Democracy is not an end in itself, but rather a means of achieving freedom, peace, and prosperity for people. Therefore, it cannot be used as a criterion. Instead, it may be more appropriate to consider the unique characteristics of a nation, region, or humanity as a whole and study them as independent issues.

The reason for the detailed discussion of democracy is that certain media outlets and foreign politicians and scientists are attempting to distort the democratic process in Uzbekistan. They believe that the democratic process in Uzbekistan is lagging behind other countries and should follow the example of 'developing democracies' in the CIS. The attempts of these individuals to influence Uzbekistan's democratic process are concerning. Additionally, it is important to note that these ideas are not founded on the interests of the Uzbek people, but rather on the objective of creating political instability in Uzbekistan and fulfilling the malicious intentions of certain politicians.

By working against these objectives, they not only undermine democratic values but also the cultural and traditional values of our nation and people. Revealing the true nature and purpose of external threats to our national spirituality and democratic processes is crucial in the fight against ideological aggression. It is important to preserve the identity of our people while doing so.

One external threat to our national well-being is the increasing prevalence of drug addiction and the spread of drugs.

The consumption of drugs poses a threat to our society in several ways: a) it endangers our national heritage and the development of

a healthy and spiritually sound generation; b) it contributes to family breakdown and the loss of children without parents; c) it leads to the incidence and spread of various chronic diseases, including AIDS, throughout our country. According to experts, the most challenging aspect of addiction is treating individuals who have become accustomed to it. The consequences of addiction on society are significant, particularly in the spiritual, moral, and emotional domains. The consequences of addiction on society are significant, particularly in the spiritual, moral, and emotional domains. The consequences of addiction on society are significant, particularly in the spiritual, moral, and emotional domains. Addiction's influence on these areas contributes to the country's spiritual and moral impoverishment. It is especially concerning that addiction is spreading among young people. Drug addiction can lead individuals to sell their wealth, honor, and even their lives to sustain their habit, resulting in an incurable disease. The fight against drug addiction has become a universal task due to the negative impact it has on young people's spiritual and physical well-being, competence, and future prospects. However, despite efforts to curb drug addiction, entrepreneurs continue to profit greatly from it.

Uzbekistan has not been immune to the issue of drug trafficking. Currently, drugs enter the country through various channels, and unfortunately, some of our own citizens are involved in their distribution. For instance, on July 4, 2008, during an inspection of a Nexia car in the Tashkent region, authorities discovered 3,565 kilograms of heroin and 6,160 kilograms of opium concealed in a secret compartment. On 24th July, during a search of an Uzbek citizen's house in the Surkhandarya region, 133.2 kg of opium imported from Tajikistan by horses was found and seized.

On 27th June, an Uzbek citizen was detained in the Bukhara region for smuggling 14.4 kg of heroin.

Afghan citizens are actively involved in drug smuggling into Uzbekistan. In 2008, about 470 kilograms of drugs were seized from Afghan citizens. The increasing spread of drugs poses a threat to our national stability and spiritual well-being. Drug use and distribution are becoming more prevalent, leading to spiritual impoverishment and instability. In 2008, there were 10,200 drug-related crimes detected in the country, up from 9,435 in 2007 [9].

The influx of drugs into the country is increasing. While law enforcement agencies are working to prevent this, it is important for all those who love Uzbekistan to actively engage in educating the younger generation about the harmful consequences of drug abuse, in order to promote spiritual and moral health. There is a growing need to actively identify and uncover drug distributors among us. If we unite and participate in this effort, we can maintain the stability of our national and spiritual life. It is crucial that we work together to address this issue. It is important to note that the import of medicines into our country by citizens of foreign countries would be significantly reduced if these individuals did not participate in this process. Preventing drug use, particularly among young people, can help reduce external threats to our national spirituality.

These threats include globalization, ideological attacks, distortion of democratic values, and the popularization of drug abuse. It is important to note that these threats are considered external because they are the main sources of all other threats, both large and small. Although they may appear to be disconnected from national spirituality, in reality they pose a significant threat. They aim to undermine our spirituality both internally and externally.

The danger they pose to our progress is that they are all designed to first impoverish the mind, worldview, and soul, and then enslave the representatives of our people and nation. They achieve their goals by using the spirit of obedience that they have instilled in their victims. It is important to protect the mind, worldview, and heart of a nation from external threats to preserve its prospects. The potential of national spirituality as a unique wealth remains relevant today and in the future.

3.3. INTERNAL THREATS OF NATIONAL SPIRIT AND THE PROCESS OF REALIZATION

Above, we considered the processes by which external threats to our national identity become dangerous. Based on the presented data and opinions, it is evident that external threats are a significant factor in the increasing globalization of the threat. Additionally, the negligence of our population also contributes to this process. Sociological polls have shown that, as external threats increase, our population's political consciousness, cultural and spiritual development, and education still lag behind the level of globalization. Despite the vast opportunities for promoting our national spirituality, it still falls behind that of foreign countries. Consequently, external threats are growing, and their negative impact on our national spirituality is increasing. This convergence of external and internal threats is particularly evident in cases where the challenges of transitioning to a market-based economy have led some members of our society to uncritically adopt foreign values and promote them among our people. This has resulted in the emergence of new 'values' that are at odds with our national and spiritual character. It is concerning that these negative habits are influencing the younger generation. As the former President Islam Karimov stated, 'When discussing the protection of our youth from spiritual aggression, we must openly address not only the positive qualities that bring glory to our people, but also the negative habits of the past that continue to impact us.' Firstly, we need to consider liberating our society from negative traits such as selfishness, indifference, nepotism, parochialism, corruption, and neglect of others [1 lxii].

It is a fact that we take pride in the unique spiritual wealth of our people, which elevates our status and brings glory to Uzbekistan. This legacy has become the main source of our development since gaining independence. However, in addition to our current achievements, the unprecedented acceleration of global development demands that we recognize the need to overcome challenges to our national spirituality.

The increasing demand for this arises from two factors. Firstly, the escalating magnitude of various global threats, particularly their capacity to influence the minds and perspectives of young individuals. Secondly, the lack of comprehension of these processes. It is important to acknowledge that during this perilous time, neglecting the study of our national and spiritual heritage in favour of other pursuits poses a significant challenge. External forces often employ insidious methods to influence the minds and worldviews of young people, making it difficult for them to recognise the danger. To protect our youth from these dangers, it is important to develop a culture of choice and ability in their consciousness and worldview. This task is of practical importance for national and spiritual security.

Internal threats that undermine national spirituality are becoming increasingly serious. When we refer to something as a threat, we are describing the process of the decline of national morale. This process is currently ongoing, but not everyone comprehends it fully. However, the magnitude of this process is increasing rapidly. In particular, they have not existed for a long time in the internal life of the country. However, they have a preference for modern spirituality, music, and art, as well as a tendency towards imitation. Additionally, there is a concerning trend of drug popularisation, particularly among young people, and human trafficking. The text discusses internal threats to our nations, including social stratification, corruption, tribalism, and other negative factors. The text should be revised to adhere to the desired characteristics, including objectivity, comprehensibility, conventional structure, clear and objective language, format, formal register, structure, balance, precise word choice, and grammatical correctness.

It is important to note that these issues have been recently covered in our press. It is important to acknowledge that these threats are not decreasing, but rather increasing. Each threat will be discussed separately, beginning with the impact of music,

songs, theatre, and TV shows on the human mind and psyche, and their effect on our national spirituality.

Several psychologists have noted that music has a powerful effect on the human psyche. Whether happy or depressed, a human child longs to listen to music and sing, receiving spiritual nourishment and celebrating joy, while trying to alleviate pain and sorrow. It is a fact that music is a means of spiritual accompaniment for a person from birth to the last breath. The benefits of music are well-established and do not require further proof.

The increasing popularity of using music and singing in education and healthcare is a well-known fact. This is evidenced by the extensive coverage in the press about the integration of music therapy in medicine.

Music and singing have the ability to shape the character of young people, including their attitudes towards their environment, homeland, nation, people, spirit of humanity, tolerance, and joy of life. Classical music and songs can have a profound impact on the human psyche. They are often imbued with a sense of national identity and cultural heritage, shaped over centuries.

Efforts have been made to revive these art forms and promote them to our youth, thanks to our independence. The popularity of classical music, singing, lapar, dombra, and other traditional forms of art among our people has great practical value for the development of our national spirituality. This is especially evident during the annual celebrations of our independence. It is important to note that these art forms have been passed down from generation to generation for centuries. The popularity of classical music, singing, lapar, dombra, and other traditional forms of art among our people has great practical value for the development of our national spirituality. The popularization of cultural practices enriches our national heritage and positively impacts the preservation of our national identity. These changes have practical significance in restoring opportunities lost during the Soviet era. There are numerous examples of our achievements in this area, which need not be quoted. Today, we are witnessing the revival and popularisation of [something]. It is important to note that this trend is gaining attention in our country, and [something] are returning to our people. This process reflects the character, aspirations, and high spirits of our people.

The independence of our people is a developing characteristic in modern times. Throughout history, there has been a wealth of information and archaeological finds that have preserved the unique development of music, singing, and dance in our country. Music, songs, and dances have been praised for their ability to enhance the beauty and meaning of life. Looking at our national development history, it is evident that art was highly valued and respected by both great statesmen and ordinary citizens. Unfortunately, during Soviet times, our people were exposed to art that was not unique to them, which led to a shallowing of their appreciation. However, our independence has allowed us to restore the legacy left by our ancestors.

Classical music, singing, and lapar have experienced a revival in popularity. However, they are currently lagging behind in protecting our national spirituality from external threats.

It is important to note that in the modern world, the predominance of classical music in the competition between modernity and classicism is reflected in our national music and singing. This process has been practiced in the arts and other fields. However, its current manifestation has the peculiarity of not enriching the spirituality of today's youth, but rather making it more superficial. The increasing value placed on 'pop music' in the West poses a threat to our national spirituality. Many songs in this genre, now considered modern, promote a carefree lifestyle for young people. However, some argue that these songs may also contribute to negative behaviours such as drug addiction, prostitution, and immorality. These negative influences can have a detrimental effect on the development of our national spirituality. As the first president said, if a person becomes accustomed to light and muted tones, their artistic taste and musical culture will gradually decline, and their spiritual world will be captured by false ideas. In the end, such a person will find it difficult to appreciate the unique masterpieces of our national heritage, such as Shashmakom, as well as the works of world-famous composers like Mozart, Beethoven, Bach, and Tchaikovsky [2,lxiii].

Unfortunately, in reality, this process occurs during the current development of our national spirituality. Specifically, the music, songs, and dances in the 'modern' pop genre that are broadcast on television are actually far from 'modern' in terms of meeting the needs and requirements of national and spiritual development. They influence the formation of popular views and the emergence of 'fluidity', which is not inherent in our mentality. Of course, it is not suggested that the pop genre should be excluded from our national culture. However, it should be developed at a generally recognized level, drawing on our national heritage rather than relying on superficial Western content that undermines our national spirit and promotes negative traits such as immorality and greed. It is important to reiterate that the content of modern pop songs, which are currently broadcast on television, is often superficial and outdated. The lyrics can be spiritually and mentally draining for listeners. As noted by the renowned scientist Shukhrat Rizo, a careful analysis of the videos reveals a number of negative aspects that have unfortunately become a tradition. For instance, the author discusses the superficial and awkward nature of the song's theme, lyrics, music, and performance. The song even includes references to mundane objects such as 'mini skirt', 'car', 'tea', and 'cigarette'. The author's views on the current state of affairs are significant. Today, our daily press lacks reviews of modernity that negatively affect the development of our national spirituality.

This negative situation is known to profile experts and officials of our television, but they do not acknowledge it. Sometimes, TV companies have to work for themselves in a market economy and prioritize profit over artistic expression. It is important to avoid subjective evaluations and instead present a balanced view of the situation. Television and other mass media are not owned by individuals and should not be used solely for profit. They belong to the people of Uzbekistan and play a crucial role in their education and development. However, it is evident that they are currently not meeting this important responsibility to the required standard.

The behaviour of some 'artists' who sing about love, affection, fidelity, and devotion in their songs is insincere and deceitful. They do not truly feel these emotions in their hearts. In contrast, great ancestors such as Alisher Navoi, Hafiz Khorezmi, and Abdullah Kodiri sang and dreamed about love and devotion in a sincere and genuine manner. The question arises as to why our national art is so disconnected from its roots. If this trend persists, will our national spirituality be able to withstand future threats? It is imperative that we find answers to these questions today. When considering the risks to the development of our national spirituality, we must examine the role of television.

It is widely acknowledged that today, not only city dwellers but also those in the most remote villages have access to not only Uzbek television but also dozens of foreign channels, thanks to the installation of special antennas. This allows people to gain a better understanding of the world and its inhabitants. In particular, these channels play a positive role in introducing viewers to the customs, traditions, and values of people from around the world, as well as their way of life, nature, and pleasures. At the same time, some of these media sources contain explicit content such as obscene films, TV series, and indecent behavior. The main characters are often dressed in revealing clothing and even use inappropriate language in Uzbek (for example, the word for sex). These elements have become normalized in our society, but it is important to recognize their negative impact on our spiritual well-being.

In recent years, Uzbek television has shown a number of serials from Korea, Japan, China, and Turkey that promote patriotism and love for the people's past. Examples include 'Jumong', 'Sheryurak', 'Bakhor ifori', and 'Sevgi tumi', which have all garnered significant interest and viewership in Uzbekistan. They can be remembered for a long time with their charm, depth of events, spiritual wealth and nationality, as well as their name.

However, the series «Shelter», «Punishment», «Revenge» and others, filmed by their own filmmakers, do not meet the needs of the development of our spirituality today, even taking into account the essence of events, superficiality of content. and even the disgrace of the name.

Love is an inner state of mind of every person, it is a very subtle feeling. Our ancestors attempted to make it visible to everyone, but they did not dare to reveal it. Their loyalty to their beliefs was unwavering. Numerous historical and artistic works have been created about them. By comparing the love, affection, and devotion celebrated by our ancestors with the contemporary songs of love, devotion, and worship, it is evident that today's expressions lack depth and are merely for entertainment purposes.

When comparing the two situations in the series, it is important to note that there is a growing need for our filmmakers to create series at the level of cinematographers in the aforementioned countries.

This would help to reduce the viewing of seductive films and series from Western countries, albeit only slightly. It is important to recognise that watching obscene films and TV series with family members can erode the boundaries of family shame, honour and dignity, which are integral to our national identity.

Furthermore, a nation that has been deprived of its lands will inevitably lose the ability to develop independently. It is crucial that we build our own spiritual foundations rather than relying on those of others for progress on the path of independent development. Although a nation's development may be advanced, it cannot be considered a resource due to the fact that national spirituality arises and develops as a product of the nation's consciousness, spiritual world, and worldview.

When referring to a nation, it is important to consider the factors that define its identity. When referring to a nation, it is important to consider the factors that define its identity. Preserving a nation's heritage is crucial in maintaining its spiritual identity, providing strength, and ensuring modernity when necessary. The negative impact on our spirituality is growing due to the disconnection from our national spiritual heritage in all genres of art, the development of imitation of the West, and the prioritization of creating works that are in demand.

It is important to note that this is a subjective opinion and further analysis is necessary. It is important to consider what actions can be taken to address these negative influences rather than assigning blame. Answers to these questions can be found through open discussions, meetings, scientific conferences, and dialogues. It is important to create partnerships between experts in the field, artists, and the general public. Indifference, irresponsibility, and attempts to avoid the problem contribute to the collapse of our national spirituality. The security of our national spirituality is currently under threat due to this attitude.

It is important to address this issue. Human trafficking is a threat to our national morality, unity, and mutual trust between citizens, which ultimately leads to instability in our society. One of the most tragic aspects of human trafficking is that it involves not only the sale of individuals for profit, but also the sale of their own family members for very little gain. The following data confirms the severity of this issue. Gavkhar Obiddinova, a resident of Samarkand, entered into an agreement with E. Ibragimov and F. Aliyev, at the suggestion of her sister Gulnoza Obiddinova, who was in Thailand, with the aim of hiring prostitutes. The criminal group was detained at Tashkent International Airport when they attempted to persuade several girls to work in a Thai restaurant and engage in prostitution, according to a pre-agreed plan [4][lxiv].

M. Esimbetov deported 34 people, claiming that he would find work abroad at a brick factory for 25,000 tenge a month. However, after 7 months, none of the deportees had received any payment. Additionally, Esimbetov had previously deceived 20 villagers, resulting in a total of 31,322,000 soums in cash. Additionally,

Esimbetov had previously deceived 20 villagers, resulting in a total of 31,322,000 soums in cash. Additionally, Esimbetov had previously deceived 20 villagers, resulting in a total of 31,322,000 soums in cash. This behaviour constitutes a shameful betrayal of his compatriots [5][lxv]. Approximately 2.7 million people worldwide are reportedly victims of serious crimes, such as human trafficking, each year[6][lxvi]. According to official data, 1,449 people fell victim to human trafficking in the country during the first nine months of this year. Of these, 1,283 were men, 166 were women, and 28 were minors. The victims were forced to work or serve in various countries, including the United Arab Emirates, Kazakhstan, Russia, Thailand, Turkey, India, Israel, Malaysia, South Korea, Japan, and Costa Rica. Prosecutor General Rashijon Kadyrov reported that some of these victims were taken to Russia to engage in prostitution.

In 2008-S.O., law enforcement agencies of the republic initiated 436 criminal cases on the facts of human trafficking, resulting in 339 people being brought to justice. Of those prosecuted, 203 were men and 136 were women. For instance, M. Dzhuraeva and Z. Saidova, who lived in Kattakurgan, colluded with accomplices and deceived several girls into being sent to Dubai, United Arab Emirates, via the Kyrgyz Republic. In the city, a man named 'Shohista' confiscated the girls' passports and forced them into prostitution for a year[7][lxvii].

Many of the examples above can be cited. It is difficult to find an answer to why our national values, such as human shame, modesty, honor, and femininity, are so violated. The fact that people who sell female chastity for money live among us is a terrible threat to the development of our national spirituality. To what extent is the spiritual depravity of some representatives of the current generation of the nation, whose ancestors made a significant contribution to world civilization, associated with material needs? It is important to avoid associating the foundation of spirituality with material needs.

Additionally, it is important to consider the extent to which human trafficking affects the security of our national spirituality. It can be confidently stated that there is a direct correlation. If national representatives engage in selling their compatriots, they betray the nation, destroy its spiritual values, and ultimately contribute to the disappearance of their own nation by joining others. This path is terrible and cannot be rebuilt with any amount of money, leading the nation to tragedy.

During the transition to market relations, some individuals may resort to compromising the dignity and chastity of women in order to improve their financial situation. This not only deprives these women of their identity but also leads to spiritual impoverishment. Similarly, those who violate the honor of their family, parents, relatives, nation, and homeland are also morally and spiritually crippled. Women are individuals who stand alongside those who deceive them into selling their bodies, as well as those who willingly sell their honour and chastity. They do not consider obeying the law or feeling ashamed in front of others. However, can those who betray their nation and degrade themselves spiritually by selling their chastity for material gain truly experience the warmth, tenderness, and aroma of human connection through their eyes, heart, and soul? It is akin to the deprivation of humanity.

Those who have chosen this path should not be judged differently. It is concerning that the number of people entering this path is increasing rather than decreasing, which poses a danger to the spiritual progress of the nation. These occurrences are happening within our national life, with representatives of our compatriots taking part in their implementation. Therefore, it poses a significant threat to our national spirituality.

The missionary movement is considered a threat to the development of our national spirituality. It is important to clarify the meaning of this concept, which has been present in scientific literature worldwide but has only recently entered Uzbek scientific literature in the last 10-15 years. Thus, the term 'missionary' is used to refer to an order, while 'mubashshir' refers to the spread of one religion among nations. It is important to note that missionary work is largely associated with Christianity and first appeared in the 4th century. During the 13th and 14th centuries, Christian missionary work spread to India, China, and Japan. The Catholic Church's missionary activity intensified after the formation of the Spanish and Portuguese Empires in the

15th and 16th centuries. In 1662, Pope Gregory XV established the Congregation for Religious Propaganda to lead the Catholic mission. Missionary activity became more active in the 19th century, especially when Christian missionaries intensified their activities in Africa and helped shape the policies of their countries[8][lxviii].

Missionary activity is often perceived as an external threat, as it involves individuals from one religion abandoning their faith and encouraging others to do the same. This can lead to the undermining of national spirituality. It is important to avoid such actions and respect the beliefs of others.

Following the gaining of independence and the establishment of a society based on democratic values, our country removed all restrictions imposed by the former Soviet rule. The law now guarantees freedom of conscience to all. However, a missionary movement has arisen in Uzbekistan with the support of external forces seeking to achieve their own selfish goals. Initially, the leaders of this movement took advantage of the inexperience of legislation in our country and even infiltrated the Ministry of Justice. They constructed new churches and recruited a small number of local believers.

While the established churches operated publicly, the missionaries themselves worked covertly and employed underhanded tactics. Various training centres for language teaching, computer skills, and specialist training, as well as charitable organisations, have established themselves in our country. For instance, in Uzbekistan, the non-governmental organisation 'Global Participation through Education' (USA) has been discovered. The organisation is involved in teaching English and Korean in lyceums and colleges, and its activities in the country will be restricted[9][lxix].

The main objective of missionary work is to gain support for their cause. Missionaries rely on financial backing to win over people, particularly young individuals who may lack life experience and a strong faith. This can create instability in the country and incite religious conflicts, potentially leading to a power grab. Therefore, it can be argued that the missionary movement poses a threat to the development of our national spirituality.

National spirituality and religious values are closely intertwined, as they both represent the inner wealth of a person and a nation. It is important to note that disbelief in either of these values can lead to spiritual poverty.

Additionally, it is worth mentioning that a person who has abandoned the religion of their ancestors may also struggle to believe in their parents, family, homeland, nation, or people as a whole. The fact that an unbeliever is in danger does not necessarily indicate a threat to national spirituality.

Additionally, missionaries' primary objective is often to gain political power, which they pursue by creating political instability and conflicts between religious groups. This approach limits the potential for the development of national spirituality.

Fourthly, individuals engage in activities aimed at undermining the nation from within by exploiting those who are not steadfast in their beliefs or who are willing to compromise their faith for a small sum of money. This, in turn, has a detrimental effect on the nation's integrity, leading to internal conflicts. Under such circumstances, the cultivation of national spirituality becomes more challenging.

Returning to the topic of the missionary movement, it is important to note that there are concerns about its impact on our national spirituality. The unity of the youth and adults within the movement is seen by some as a potential threat. Although the initial threat came from abroad, the presence of some compatriots promoting these ideas among our people, particularly the youth, means that the threat has become internal. Internal threats are more dangerous than external ones because external threats tend to unite the nation and create a spirit of resistance against them. The internal threat caused alienation within the nation and its people. Therefore, the proverb 'Where to go to heal your own trouble' has become a call to awareness in our lives and has risen to the level of a value for our people.

Although freedom of conscience and religion are guaranteed by law, it is not acceptable to encourage others to renounce their religious beliefs in exchange for material gain. It is important to respect both conscience and religious convictions as they are fundamental values for everyone and a sign of humanity. The act of selling one's conscience for personal gain or abandoning a religion inherited from ancestors and converting to another religion is often seen as a manifestation of poverty. It is natural to question whether such individuals truly believe in the religion they have adopted. A person of true character does not compromise their beliefs for material wealth, but instead sees them as a sign of their greatest wealth: their humanity. In this sense, despite the extent to which human rights are guaranteed by laws and regulations, their unwritten humanity, conscience, convictions, and spiritual and moral responsibility are of greater importance than written laws. These are sacred feelings for all and without them, a person cannot be fully understood. If there are individuals among the representatives of our nation who possess these qualities, then there is reason to believe that there is a growing internal threat to our national spirituality. It is of practical importance to strengthen our national unity in order to limit these threats.

The transition of our country to market relations poses a threat to the development of our national spirituality due to the stratification that occurs. It is important to note that stratification is an objective condition that arises in the context of the formation of market relations. Market relations allow individuals to live off their own strengths, intelligence, abilities, and entrepreneurship, which can lead to stratification. Under such circumstances, those who possess strength will thrive and attain a favourable economic, social, and spiritual status. It is widely acknowledged that artificial entrepreneurship and easy money are unattainable. The market is unforgiving towards those who are indolent, uneducated, and lack sensibility.

However, despite the market's ruthlessness, it should not result in a significant stratification of society or a widening gap between the affluent and the impoverished. Instability in society can lead to the disappearance of cherished values such as love, sincerity, trust, and mutual respect, ultimately resulting in economic, socio-political, and spiritual and educational crises. To prevent such negative situations, Uzbekistan pursues a consistent policy based on the principle of social protection, which helps prevent sharp social stratification to some extent. However, no country can achieve this process alone. It relies solely on the growth of the country's economic potential and the increasing activity of the population to overcome the overwhelming power of the market.

Unfortunately, in today's market-driven society, we are witnessing the negative impact of certain 'values' on morality, behavior, and attitudes towards different values among some members of our nation, which is hindering the development of our national spirituality. In particular, it is concerning that individuals who rely on their honest work and intellectual abilities are often left behind in the development of market relations, while those who are already wealthy tend to benefit the most. Additionally, the practice of appointing officials based on personal connections can have a negative impact on our national values and sense of community.

It has become customary to separate the 'elite' of new Uzbeks, formed in the conditions of market relations, from ordinary people at weddings and funerals. They are often seated in a separate room and at a separate table. Such premises are present in all the magnificent weddings being held today, designed to distinguish between the simple and the elite guests.

It is difficult to determine whether this process should be considered a new stage in the development of spirituality or a practice aimed at consciously impoverishing morality, which is the foundation of ancient and national spirituality. Objective evaluation is necessary to answer such questions. At weddings, celebrations, and other public events, the division of society into classes poses an internal threat that can ultimately lead to national disintegration and the collapse of values such as sincerity and mutual trust. It is unfortunate that the district, which is responsible for bringing people together in such dire situations, does not respond adequately.

In contemporary society, the primary strategic task is to raise an ideal person. However, instilling the idea of perfection in young people who see and adopt these new 'traditions' may not have a positive effect.

Additionally, the inconsistency of related values poses a threat to the development of our national spirituality. After the death of their parents, the siblings filed a lawsuit against each other, each claiming their 'rights'. Our elderly grandparents, who witnessed this scene, were appalled. They reminisced about the time when 30-40 family members, including parents, brothers, and sisters, lived together and shared meals from the same pot. The love between them was strong. Although times have changed and some siblings have better living conditions, it is important to remember the value of family unity. However, the older generation is concerned about the reality of inheritance and property lawsuits, as well as insults becoming more common. This concern is not unfounded. For instance, during last year's month of fasting in 2008, I overheard a conversation between two young people on a bus that caught the attention of both myself and an elderly man sitting next to me. During the conversation, one of the individuals mentioned attending his uncle's iftar the previous night and helping with the cleanup afterwards, causing him to arrive home late and miss the phone call. When asked why, he explained that none of them have jobs and therefore do not have a need to socialize. Another individual expressed unfamiliarity with the man's family members due to a lack of interaction. When asked why, he explained that none of them have jobs and therefore do not have a need to socialize.

An elderly man sitting next to me was taken aback by this conversation and looked at me in surprise, saying: 'Repent, repent'. I didn't know how to respond, so I simply said, 'Father, they are still young and will learn with time'.

This conversation can be interpreted as a reflection of the relationship between a young man and his family, whether positive or negative. Limiting ourselves to such an answer would not fully address the negative situation developing in our national spirituality.

While it is true that cold relations between relatives can form in a child's psyche, it is important to consider why a spirit of linking everything to necessity is being formed today. Is it due to the legitimacy of the market or a collapse in our national spirituality?

The response 'we don't need them' is a subjective evaluation and should be excluded. The statement suggests a decline in national and spiritual values due to market relations and a lack of education among young people. To improve clarity and objectivity, it is recommended to rephrase the statement to reflect a more balanced view.

When considering the unfortunate state of our national spirituality, I am reminded of a speech I heard at the scientific-theoretical conference 'National Development and Interethnic Relations' in October 1988 at the Polytechnic Museum in Moscow. During the conference, a professor from Yerevan University in Armenia (whose name I cannot recall) made a statement about the Uzbeks: 'Armenians have a more liberal national upbringing, and the tradition of kinship is weakening.' Many Uzbek people believe it is a great tragedy to take their parents to a nursing home when they have children who could care for them. This is due to the fact that they may not be invited to weddings, celebrations, and other events, and their neighbours may not visit them. When considering this process, it is important to note the strong values of kinship in Uzbekistan. The interviewee stated that this is likely why the values of kinship are so strong in the country.

In fact, the interviewee had a strong family and parenting relationship. Today, it has been reported that they have already been hacked. Nursing homes have been established in each province, accommodating approximately four thousand parents. Many of these parents have children who are financially stable, but unfortunately, they were left in the care of underprivileged children who lacked spiritual wealth. It is a national challenge to identify the factors underlying the conversation between the aforementioned students and eliminate them with the active participation of all nationalists. The upbringing of children in nursing homes and the weakening of love and kinship between relatives can lead to the collapse of national spirituality and the nation from both internal and external factors.

From a theoretical perspective, this can be considered a paradox that arises in spiritual life when faced with great opportunities for independence. From a practical standpoint, Uzbeks can be seen as a manifestation of enrichment at the expense of 'mass spirituality'. The weakening of our national values in the face of violent aggression and the opportunities created by independence to preserve our people under Soviet dependence raise the question of whether these negative processes are related to the market. The weakening of our national values in the face of violent aggression and the opportunities created by independence to preserve our people under Soviet dependence raise the question of whether these negative processes are related to the market. It is important to examine this issue more deeply rather than providing a simplistic answer.

Tying regulations to the market and imposing them is not necessarily the solution to the problem. This is supported by the experience of the most economically developed countries in the world. While they have achieved high levels of economic growth, they have also experienced a decline in traditional values such as fatherhood, children, and kinship. The principle of 'know yourself, leave others' has become the essence of life, leading to spiritual impoverishment in society. Today, leading politicians and heads of state acknowledge this process and express concern about its negative impact on society. The same factors that cause instability and undermine national unity are also responsible for destroying society from within. Overcoming this challenge requires economic progress and the efficient use of available resources.

Negative situations can also be viewed as opportunities for personal growth and development. It is important to consider the changes in consciousness, worldview, and mentality that occur over time. Are these changes a result of the age we live in or are they self-discovered? These are important questions that need to be addressed. In our opinion, these questions are related to the disconnection between material well-being and spirituality. The preservation of our national spirituality is a national challenge that can ensure political and social stability, interethnic friendship, interreligious tolerance, and economic development in our country. The preservation of our national spirituality is a national challenge that can ensure political and social stability, interethnic friendship, interreligious tolerance, and economic development in our country. The preservation of our national spirituality is a national challenge that can ensure political and social stability, interethnic friendship, interreligious tolerance, and economic development in our country. Therefore, it is important to make nationwide efforts to preserve national spirituality.

One negative aspect of our national and spiritual life concerns the scheduling of weddings. Those wishing to get married in Tashkent are required to set their wedding date based on their free time, rather than a mutually convenient time for both parties. This is due to the fact that wedding venues in the city are always fully booked, with no days off. These venues host weddings, receptions, birthdays, and even iftar events on a daily basis. While it is positive that our economic situation is improving, we must also consider the development of our national spirituality. However, it is unfortunate that certain individuals at weddings can negatively impact our spirituality, as seen with the 'hangover' effect. It is important to address this issue. In particular, there is a concerning trend in our national art and entertainment industry where famous artists are deceiving wedding guests. This is especially evident with the young performers invited to perform at weddings.

Many of these performers heavily rely on microphones and sound amplifiers to sing. Some performers at weddings lip-sync to pre-recorded songs. They may arrive with their hosts to avoid drawing attention to their appearance or skill, but instead to briefly entertain guests with their singing. They may also try to collect additional money from guests beyond their agreed fee. It is not uncommon for them to falsely claim to be popular artists or favourites of the people, such as Farhod, who is known for his interpretations of mountain music. If they are genuine artists, it is evident that they will not exhibit such crude behaviour and conceit.

The wedding ring has a second issue related to sound amplification. At weddings, many 'artists' use loudspeakers to encourage guests to leave faster, as they do not have a natural voice. This can cause discomfort for guests who may feel rushed or anxious. I have personally witnessed this and found it to be unpleasant. Last year, I read articles in the Khalk Sozi newspaper by Professor Maksud Asadullayev, a neurology professor at the Tashkent Medical Academy, and Abdushukur Abdullayev, a candidate of technical sciences, about the harmful effects of noise on human health. Professor Asadullaev specifically stated that noise can cause increased blood pressure. Candidate of Technical Sciences Abdushukur Abdullaev states that loud music is harmful to humans, as it is one of the main factors leading to a decrease in blood flow to the brain, coronary heart disease, and the rapid development of angina pectoris (Abdullaev, 10). Candidate of Technical Sciences Abdushukur Abdullaev states that loud music is harmful to humans, as it is one of the main factors leading to a decrease in blood flow to the brain, coronary heart disease, and the rapid development of angina pectoris (Abdullaev, 10). It is important to avoid listening to loud music to prevent these negative health effects. For instance, according to a study, 20% of young people who enjoy contemporary music have the same level of hearing as 85-year-olds. It is evident that loudness and inappropriate behaviour, which go against our national traditions, not only jeopardise the development of a national character among young people but also pose a threat to human health in general.

Additionally, weddings are attended by people from diverse backgrounds, and it is reasonable to assume that they will have the opportunity to unwind and show respect to the host. This text requires significant improvement to meet the desired characteristics. The following is an improved version: The issue at hand has multiple perspectives, and it is important to consider all sides. Additionally, it is crucial to recognise that certain cultural practices, such as excessive drinking at weddings, can have

a negative impact on our national spirituality. For instance, in Japan, noise pollution is a major concern for the population, as highlighted in the national report. Similarly, according to British doctors, a significant proportion of the population suffers from mental illness due to noise exposure. It is important to address these issues and work towards a better future for all. French psychiatrists found that 20% of patients in psychiatric hospitals developed mental illness as a result of exposure to loud noise[12].

Despite the potential dangers of noise pollution, the use of loud devices at weddings is becoming increasingly common. Talat Shamsiev, an elder of the Uzbekiston mahalla in Tashkent, expressed concern that the loud music makes it difficult for guests to socialise and converse[13 lxx].

The occurrence of negative situations at weddings can be viewed from two perspectives. Firstly, as the author of the aforementioned article points out, 'self-promotion' can be seen as a sign of arrogance by those who believe they are throwing a party to show off. Secondly, a lavish wedding can be attributed to a decline in spiritual, intellectual, and moral values. Some individuals may not consider that hosting a loud wedding goes against our national ethics. When reflecting on these unfortunate events, it is important to remember the traditional wedding customs of our youth, which emphasised proper behaviour and respect for others. Notably, the esteemed Uzbek artist Komiljon Otaniyozov would sing throughout the wedding circle using a microphone, rather than remaining in one place. Thus, he was not only an artist but also a skilled teacher who could connect with people during this period. Many artists during this time embodied this ideal. It is important to note that artists should also be educators. Although they have passed away, their legacy lives on in the hearts and minds of our people. The participation of some artists in today's weddings, whose songs are incomprehensible, and the excessive noise levels, which can be harmful to human health, are examples of how our 'greats' are contributing to the impoverishment of our ancient national spirituality. It is important to address this alarming situation now before it is too late. There is a growing danger of the collapse of our national spirituality and its replacement by 'mass spirituality' from the West.

Weddings are not just about individuals, but they represent beauty, prosperity, and spiritual wealth, as well as the spiritual potential of a nation. Weddings help to popularise and pass on national customs, traditions, values, rituals, and ceremonies to future generations. It is important to ensure that these practices enrich our national spirituality and do not contribute to its destruction.

Another internal threat to our national spirituality is associated with the dress code among our youth. We must be vigilant against the spread of 'mass spirituality' in the dress, behavior, and attitudes of some girls in schools, colleges, and universities. It is regrettable that some children end up in orphanages in a state of undress and exhibit rude behavior. It is important to avoid dictating how individuals should dress. However, it is also important to recognize that indifference towards our national values can develop if we do not pay attention to the clothing choices that are being promoted through various media channels such as television and the internet. This can become a significant issue. It is possible that family relationships play a role in this development. It is possible that family relationships play a role in this development. It is important to remember that the threat to our national values can also come from clothing and the impact it has on our spirituality.

Some parents may even contribute to this issue, while others may struggle to prevent it. Therefore, it is crucial to address this matter objectively and without bias. If we do not address this situation, it may become a problem for instilling love for our national values. Clothing and behaviour reflect a person's inner world and influence their character and attitude towards the environment. The prevalence of negative attitudes towards national spirituality can lead to internal threats.

Today, we are witnessing that development has a negative impact on the increasing number of internal threats to our national spirituality. These threats are dangerous because they lead our compatriots to develop a spirit of indifference towards them, and a growing tendency to assimilate elements of 'mass spirituality' that occur in family ties, various weddings, and events. There is an increasing need to remain impartial towards these threats, to actively seek and utilise opportunities to prevent them, and to recognise that eliminating internal threats to our national spirituality is an urgent task.

Most importantly, we fail to understand that prioritizing internal threats over external threats to our national spirituality is crucial. For a nation to be spiritually strong, it must first be free from internal threats. A country free from them will have an enhanced ability to prevent and understand external threats. From this perspective, to combat the persistent spiritual poverty in the modern world, it becomes a universal task to address internal threats arising within each nation. A nation that can develop its morality, heart, soul, and psyche on the basis of its national lands and adapt them to modern requirements can protect itself from such dangers.

Today, some argue that deeply understanding and popularizing our ancestors' spiritual heritage, especially among young people, is crucial for preserving national spirituality. This heritage is truly an inexhaustible source of spiritual strength for the nation. No other factors can replace it. Just as the roots of a maple tree support and nourish its height, warning of dangers, so too does a nation's heritage and historical memory.

As a nation recovers its historical memory and assimilates its heritage, it becomes spiritually strong, inspired, and enriched. It strives for independence, and its activity naturally increases. However, neglecting aspirations for independence creates conditions and opportunities for both internal and external threats to national spirituality to grow. Only by recognizing this can we truly save our national spirituality from danger.

PART FOUR. FACTORS OF ENSURING NATIONAL AND SPIRITUAL SECURITY

The main factor that defines a nation's "I" is its spirituality, customs, traditions, and values, which express its uniqueness. Therefore, preserving the nation, likened to a flower of human beauty, and its diverse spirituality, the main source of self-realization, requires its development in accordance with universal development processes.

However, experience shows that national development is not smooth. The main issue lies in the process of increasing humanity's intellectual potential. While there is a growing desire to understand one's national identity, develop on one's own land, assimilate one's heritage, and protect one's "I," the risk also increases. Some "great" nations (countries) exploit this in their insidious efforts to achieve world domination.

The dangerous aspect of this process is that they escalate conflict through the "nation" factor. In this context, preventing the misuse of the national factor for abhorrent purposes, searching for factors that positively impact interethnic harmony, effectively utilizing them, and preserving the nation – which has become one of humanity's great values – are becoming global problems. Today's problems confirm the impossibility of saving humanity without solving this issue.

In this part of the book, we present our views and opinions on the possibility, factors, and effects of using external and internal threats against growing globalization in the context of its actualization.

4.1. DEVELOPMENT OF NATIONAL IDENTITY IN THE PROCESS OF GLOBALIZATION TRENDS

The protection of a nation from various dangers depends on how developed its consciousness is. Especially in the context of globalization, a high level of development of national self-awareness is becoming one of the factors of its self-preservation.

Before proceeding to analyze the issue of the connection between globalization and national consciousness, let's delve into the concept of national consciousness, its essence, the process of formation, and the peculiarities of its manifestation.

First, it's important to note that this concept was a "closed" issue for researchers in the former Soviet republics during the Soviet era. Researchers at the "former center" only "secretly" studied it, providing information to relevant organizations in their own interests. The main goal of such studies was to attract the attention of peoples with a developing national identity who demanded the observance of their rights and freedoms. Therefore, this issue was not openly and fundamentally studied in a scientific way. Even the definition of this concept was missing from dictionaries published during the Soviet era.

It surprised many heads of state that the inability to objectively study national consciousness led to significant problems in this area and seriously impacted the collapse of the Soviet state. Over the past years, the rights and freedoms of peoples living in the former Soviet republics have been violated. The process of reconstruction and democratization of the country, which began in the mid-1980s, generated latent national consciousness and national aspirations. ... This, in turn, hastened the collapse of a crumbling society. The failure of the former Soviet regime showed that national consciousness can only be temporarily suppressed with violence, but it cannot be eradicated from the worldview, mind, and heart. For this reason, the fundamental study of national identity began only after the fall of the Soviet regime. In particular, in Uzbekistan, we have the opportunity to study this issue only after gaining independence.

Today in Uzbekistan, there are different views on the concept of "national consciousness." Each author tries to reveal their own unique perspectives. In particular, our late teacher, academician Erkin Yusupov, offered the following definition of national consciousness: "National consciousness is not simply an emotion but a belief based on certain moral, legal, scientific, and ideological values."[1]

[lxxi]. According to another late teacher, academician Zhondor Tulanov, "national identity is an integral part of national culture, the pinnacle of national culture. National consciousness is the expression in the consciousness of a person of problems related to the national interests of national culture, the future of the nation, and development."[2] [lxxii]. According to psychologist Zukhra Abdurakhmanova, "... national consciousness is an understanding of the unity of our history and destiny, that we are children of one parent"[3] [lxxiii].

Doctoral M. Khodzhieva analyzes various forms of consciousness and defines national consciousness as follows: "National consciousness encompasses understanding a nation's history and identity, its goals and interests. It involves understanding these interests in dialogue with other nations, their development challenges, and the proximity of views and ideas in decision-making."[4] [lxxiv].

So, there are different views on the concept of national identity. The most important of them is that all [problem] problems see it as an important factor in national development. Because without faith (E. Yusupov), a nation cannot develop, and only if it develops at a high level as an integral part of the nation's spirituality (J. Tulanov) will it lead the nation to development. Additionally, understanding the parent-child relationship (Z. Abdurakhmanova) also has practical significance for the future of the nation. Finally, understanding the goal, the presence of interests, understanding the problems, and the unity of views and opinions in their solution (M. Khodzhieva) is also of practical importance for the nation's development.

These ideas reflect one or another aspect of national identity. At the same time, there is a growing need for a fundamental study of the nature and content of this complex factor.

Indeed, national consciousness is a complex concept that can include all aspects of the nation's factors. National consciousness is associated with the existence of a nation, its historical development, and prospects. It ensures the formation, development, and stability of the nation. National consciousness is formed by the nation itself. Only the formation of its own interests and goals, different from others, is relevant to its emergence. Consequently, national consciousness, in proportion to the nation, is formed over a long historical period as a result of the influence of its way of life, economic, socio-political, and broad spiritual and educational potential. In this sense, national consciousness is a system of ideas and thoughts related to the history, fate, and prospects of the nation, representing the interests and problems of the nation, setting the direction of the activities of the nation's representatives.

When defining national identity, it is necessary not only to give primary attention to the intellectual potential of the nation but also to take into account the level of its activity. That is, if a nation has a consciousness that expresses its interests and goals but does not try to realize them, the nation's consciousness cannot find its expression. In this sense, national consciousness is also a level of activity in realizing the interests and goals of each nation.

National consciousness as a factor reflecting national interests is formed in the process of production of material and spiritual wealth of the nation, interacting with other peoples. It is in this process that the characteristics, customs, traditions, and values of each nation are formed. They distinguish a nation from other nations and become a leading factor in the formation of national interests and goals. Thus, the socio-political, economic, spiritual, and educational maturity of the nation in all historical periods is reflected in the national consciousness.

Without national identity, not only national customs, traditions, and values but also the nation itself as a real subject, social, and ethnic institution, cannot exist. Only national consciousness and its development are key factors in ensuring the rise of the masses to the level of the nation. Because national unity is formed only on the basis of mature national consciousness. Only then will the nation be able to enter the field of history as a single force.

National consciousness creates national interests and goals. On this basis, such negative vices as national fragmentation, tribalism, parochialism, and banditry, dangerous for the future of the nation, will be eliminated. The development of national identity is one of the factors that ensure the sustainable development of the state. Because a nation with a developed consciousness will be free from chauvinism, nationalism, disregard for the nations and peoples living next to it, or from vices and cripples, such as evil, violence, and ignorance. It never puts its interests and goals in conflict with the interests of others, but tries to unite around it representatives of other nations. That is why the development of national identity plays a leading role in a democratic state.

The existing social system, the internal spiritual and educational potential of the nation, and its activities play an important role in the development of national identity. In the process of its formation, a nation develops its integrity and all the factors inherent in it. In turn, these factors also influence the development of national identity. That is, each nation creates its own unique potential that contributes to the development of national identity. More precisely, the development of national self-awareness involves a cyclical process of "impact" and "reverse effect." It is this dynamic process that ensures the nation's continued existence. Unfortunately, these crucial processes, which, like other national development challenges, are vital for a nation's longevity, are not comprehensively studied, not only in Uzbekistan but also in the Commonwealth of Independent States.

The period following the collapse of the totalitarian Soviet dictatorship and the global experience of national development demonstrate that national consciousness, mentality, and psyche are enduring elements stemming from the conscious life of every individual. They are integral parts of the beauty of the Universe and humanity itself. In this context, the role and significance of the spiritual and educational potential, in the broadest sense, are paramount in the formation of national self-awareness. The bedrock of a nation's identity is formed by its language, heritage, historical memory, customs, traditions, values, and the education system. These factors provide the spiritual nourishment that enables individuals and the nation to understand themselves and their place in the world.

In order to fully understand the processes of national consciousness development:

a) We need to understand the factors that influence its formation and development.

b) We need to identify what it affects.

To achieve this, we must find answers to specific questions. By doing so, we can gain insight into the development of national consciousness in today's globalized world, including the causes of potential crises and possible prevention strategies.

Let's start by addressing the first question. It would be helpful to seek an answer in the following definition of a nation:

A nation is characterized by a unique language spoken by its people, a strong sense of national identity, spirituality (in its broadest sense), shared customs, traditions, and values. It also involves the ethnic unity of its creators.

It's important to remember that the concept of "nation" has been defined in various ways by different authors, reflecting their individual perspectives. While we have extensively explored these viewpoints in our previous works, here we will focus on the factors that influence the formation of national identity, based on our own definition of a nation.

This definition emphasizes the importance of a shared language. Examining the foundations of language development, we see that it arises from the interaction of people and their essential needs. In this sense, language emerged first and became a crucial factor in nation formation. People living in a specific territory facing shared needs like food, clothing, shelter, and protection naturally utilized language as a means of communication and understanding. Over time, the language evolved through this same interaction, further strengthening the bonds between people within the same area. Thus, language played a critical role in fostering human relationships and grew increasingly complex. This extended historical process facilitated the spiritual and emotional connection of people through their shared tongue. Other characteristics of a nation also developed under the influence of this ongoing process.

So, we can say that language is one of the most influential factors in the formation of a nation. Because with the help of language, people living in a particular area have formed their own way of life, traditions, customs, and values. Since language is the main means of expressing one's identity, and a nation is often considered a material entity consisting of an association of people sharing a common language, its development leads to the formation of the first associations of tribes, clans, and nations.

Language connects a person with their environment. It allows them to learn the secrets of the Universe, experience it firsthand, and use it to their advantage. Through language, a person's consciousness grows, and they communicate with others. This communication is an important factor in mutual spiritual and educational enrichment. Just as the eyes and ears are important for a person to see the environment and hear events, language is equally important for "materializing" them. As Professor Kh. Khonazarov correctly noted: "We cannot imagine the world without language. The world we know consists of the world expressed in our language. The universe, expressed in language, is infinite in time and space. Unknown parts of it, not yet studied by humans, are also included in the language, which has a certain name, 'a set of events and processes that have not yet been studied.' This definition mobilizes our consciousness for cognition, encourages our thinking to work, stimulates and emphasizes our imagination, and draws our attention to the process of cognition."[5][lxxv].

So, it is impossible to imagine humanity without language. Thanks to this tool, humanity has reached the level of civilization we see today, and continues to use its potential to solve the most difficult problems facing our future.

Just as language plays a crucial role in human life and development, it will also play a critical role in the formation, development, and improvement of a nation. A nation that lacks its own national language cannot rise to the level of a fully-fledged nation. This is because language creates national unity, bringing together people who communicate in the same language, both spiritually and intellectually. It fosters a sense of shared national interests among them.

In this sense, knowing the language of one's nation is of great importance for truly understanding its soul and heart. The diversity of languages also reflects the unique qualities of different peoples. Therefore, in the description of a nation above, we have identified language as one of its key characteristics.

It is also important to note that the decline of a nation, or one of the factors leading to its assimilation into other cultures, often begins with the decline of its language. This is because the heritage of ancestors, their life experiences, psyche, and mentality are passed down from generation to generation through language and find expression in the minds of those who speak it.

The understanding of national identity also develops in a mutually reinforcing way with language. Therefore, the definition of a nation is shaped by this understanding. It is noteworthy that, in all the definitions of nation given in the scientific literature during the Soviet era, two factors were not included: the understanding of national identity and the presence of a national state. When the author was a doctoral student at the FA Institute of Philosophy in the Soviet Union (1988-1990), there was much debate among scholars about whether to include national identity as an important characteristic of a nation. Kamina was also a valuable contributor to this discussion, and the author included her work in their doctoral dissertation, analyzing the existing views and attempting to justify its importance as a feature of nationhood and express their own perspective on its role in the life of a nation.

The author's supervisor, Professor Askold Ivanovich Doronchenkov, was a man of deep thought and a highly democratic figure in the scientific world. He said: "At a time when this issue is being seriously discussed at the Institute of Philosophy, I do not mind if you are not afraid to substantiate your opinion." Thanks to his support, the author was able to include "national identity" as an important feature in their definition of nation in the dissertation. This concept subsequently gained popularity among scholars at the center when studying issues related to nations.

Of course, the inclusion of this concept and its widespread adoption in research was also due to the fact that interethnic conflicts were erupting as a result of the "reconstruction" that began in the former Soviet Union, conflicts that had been silently simmering under the oppressive Soviet regime. At that time, it was not possible to include "the existence of a nation-state" as an important feature in the author's definition of a nation (this will be discussed later).

So, why is the understanding of national identity an important characteristic of a nation, and yet it is not included in the definitions given in the scientific literature in the context of the former Soviet rule? There were several reasons for this: firstly, scientists and specialists did not have the opportunity to maintain the old system or go beyond the tasks and instructions set within it. They were forced to obey the orders of the current politicians. Secondly, while some scholars recognized that understanding national identity was an important feature of a nation, they were also alarmed by the idea that its suppression or recognition could affect national movements. Thirdly, only scientists from the former center could engage in the study of the "nation," the creation and publication of scientific works dedicated to it. Although some (not all) of them were aware that there would be negative developments in the future of national relations, they did not subscribe to the notion that "in the future, of course, all the peoples of the former Soviet Union will come closer and eventually merge into a single Soviet nation." Some firmly believed in the emergence of a single Soviet (communist) nation and constantly put forward new "theories" about the effective use of methods, opportunities, and means to "accelerate" this process. Fourthly, scholars from former Soviet republics such as the Baltic republics, Georgia, and Armenia consistently published articles on the need to improve interethnic relations and advocated for these views in their speeches at scientific conferences in the former center. Scientists from other union republics, including Uzbekistan, conducted research on national issues based on the ideas of the twentieth century (their views are set forth in our book, published jointly with Sarvar Otamuratov)[lxxvi].

In particular, Kamina initially considered the internationalization of national cultures as a leading process in scientific research, envisioning a future communist culture. However, the influence of the former center limited his ideas. Studying interethnic issues objectively was challenging due to the politicized socio-philosophical landscape, where straying from the approved narrative was forbidden.

Returning to the views of Uzbek scientists on national development, it's important to acknowledge the historical trauma. Nationalists in the 1920s-1940s faced physical persecution, leaving a lasting fear of repetition among scholars. While concerned about this "bitter" precedent, they also recognized that studying interethnic issues was reserved for scholars of the former center, who controlled topics and research directions. This aimed to suppress the development of national consciousness and identity in the republics.

Despite these limitations, efforts to integrate nations did not hinder the growth of national self-awareness and identity. It continued to develop and gain strength, ultimately playing a role in the collapse of the previous regime in the 1990s. This historical experience demonstrates that attempts to suppress national identity, even through violence and physical destruction, cannot permanently erase it. New generations emerge, carrying the inherited psyche and transmitting it through mother's milk, paternal genes, and education. While external factors can influence and "enrich" national consciousness, they cannot completely eradicate it.

At a certain point, the "national psyche" embedded within individuals compels them to return to their roots. This inherent human characteristic, bestowed by Allah, sets limits on the acceptance of other cultures, no matter how appealing they may seem. When these limits are reached, feelings of boredom, even hatred, towards the adopted culture can arise. Similarly, members of a nation enriched by external influences eventually yearn for their own land, where their identity is naturally ingrained and resistant to external manipulation. While external "spiritual wealth" can play a role, it cannot replace the importance of national lands as a source of identity and self-preservation.

Based on these ideas, we define national identity as a crucial element of a nation. (We will explore its development processes further in the next chapter.)

In our definition of a nation, we propose the idea that "spirituality is the inner potential of a nation." Internal potential is a broad concept expressed in a nation's consciousness, worldview, heart, creation and appreciation of beauty, mentality, life, actions, self-preservation, protection, and relations with other nations and peoples. ... National spirituality manifests in the unique customs, traditions, and values of each nation. This peculiar inner world is distinct from others, and it's through this that nations express their beauty and charm.

Since we discussed specific aspects of national spirituality earlier, we won't repeat them here. The main point is that, to become a full-fledged nation, a nation must possess its own unique spirituality. It expresses itself through this very spirituality, which is formed and developed through the nation's activities. Ultimately, the impoverishment of spirituality leads to the demise of the nation. Thus, spirituality, as one of a nation's important features, holds not only theoretical but also practical significance.

Our definition of a nation also includes the unity of customs, traditions, and values. The importance of these as symbols of a nation has been demonstrably proven by many scientists and teachers. However, their perspectives raise a crucial contemporary question: how can we develop new ideas that determine the future of these elements in the face of globalization? Whether they will remain (or continue to be) important indicators of a nation's survival as a tangible entity requires further scientific exploration.

Customs, traditions, and values are not static; they evolve. In the era of globalization, this evolution is accelerating significantly. While efforts might be made to resist these changes, completely restoring the customs, traditions, and values of our ancestors exactly as they existed is not feasible. Instead, we can adapt them to a rapidly changing world. The effectiveness of this process depends on the nation's inclination. If it readily adapts to the flow of change, customs, traditions, and values will adapt accordingly. Conversely, if a strong conservative spirit prevails, change will be slower and rooted in the nation's land and specific characteristics. Can be protected and developed within its own national core. Regardless of the approach, national customs, traditions, and values, as significant symbols of a nation, will not vanish entirely; they will evolve. Their demise would signal the demise of the nation itself.

Another important feature of a nation is its territory. This region is where the people's ancestors lived, forming their customs, traditions, and values. Here, they created various material and spiritual wealth, which they inherited and passed down through generations. Within this region, certain stages and manifestations of various groupings, such as tribes, clans, and ethnic groups, emerged and developed, ultimately leading to the formation of the nation. Without this specific territory, scattered across different regions, a nation could never coalesce and develop its unique identity.

Another crucial aspect of this region is its connection to the ancestors. It is not just a geographical space but also a spiritual resting place for them. This land holds a deep emotional and spiritual significance for the nation, offering a sense of belonging and identity. While individuals belonging to a nation can live in other regions, they may not fully express their national identity there. They may live as citizens of different countries or as individual representatives of their nation, but they may not experience the full cultural and spiritual connection they find within their ancestral territory. This "reserve zone" serves as a space for spiritual and cultural sustenance, reminding them of their heritage and fostering a sense of unity.

However, in multiethnic countries, this "reserve zone" concept necessitates careful consideration regarding interethnic relations. It is crucial to strive for continuous improvement in these relations, ensuring everyone feels respected and included within their shared territory. This ongoing effort of fostering positive interethnic relations remains an urgent and ever-present task. After all, the inherent sacredness of one's homeland extends beyond a single nation, encompassing the diverse populations that share it.

Different legends from different nations are told about this region. One such legend describes a great war between two countries. In this battle, one side emerged victorious, but their king refused to end the war, willing to sacrifice countless lives.

The defeated king, deeply valuing his people's ancestral land, was ready to give his life for it and sought ways to end the war, even if it meant sacrificing all his wealth. However, his pleas were ignored. He then sent an envoy to the victor, expressing his consent to any conditions they set.

The victorious king demanded the defeated king surrender his prized flying horse as a condition for ending the war. The defeated king refused, unwilling to part with such a symbol of his power and prestige. After some time, the war resumed, and the victorious king demanded the king's beautiful daughter as a new condition. Driven by his love for his people and homeland, the defeated king fulfilled this condition as well.

Despite these sacrifices, the war continued. The defeated king, unable to understand the victor's relentless pursuit, sent another envoy to question his motives. The victor's new demand was a fertile border province within the defeated king's territory.

Infuriated by this blatant disregard for his people's heritage, the defeated king declared, "You asked for my horse, which I did not give to anyone in the world, and I gave you my only child, my daughter, and I gave you all my treasures. The land on the territory of my country does not belong to me, it is not my property, I have no right to give it away. This is a place inherited from people, their ancestors, a place where they now rest. You have found the most intimate feelings for a person, for people. Now we will fight with you until you become the last child of my country!"

A fierce war broke out once more. The defeated king and his people, united by their refusal to yield an inch of their homeland, finally defeated the enemy and achieved a just victory.

This legend emphasizes the sacredness of the land, inherited from ancestors and passed down to future generations. It is considered an unforgivable betrayal to give it away for personal gain. As long as humanity exists, the land, the Motherland, will remain a cherished symbol, a source of inspiration and immortality. It is equally sacred to all, from the tsar to the beggar, for it is the resting place of ancestors and the cradle of future generations. The land, the Motherland, glorifies a person, a nation, and their existence, representing an incomparable material and spiritual wealth.

In the definition of nation, the state is often presented as one of its key characteristics. However, there's some debate about whether it truly acts as a symbol of the nation. While most scientific literature doesn't address this question directly, there seems to be an implicit acceptance of the state's symbolic role.

One argument for this inclusion stems from the modern reality of multi-ethnic countries. With citizens forming a single nation, dividing them into smaller nations might be seen as detrimental, reflecting "spiritual poverty and ignorance." However, the existence of "titular" nations, comprising the majority of a country's population and often giving their name to the state, introduces complexity. These nations face crucial tasks like maintaining territorial integrity and representing diverse nationalities within their borders. Additionally, the "titular" nation arguably cannot fully realize its national identity outside its own state. Therefore, as long as nations exist, the need for a nation-state may persist, potentially strengthening national unity rather than hindering it.

Despite this perspective, the inclusion of the state as a national symbol remains contested. Several reasons contribute to this debate:

Firstly, as mentioned previously, the former Soviet Union housed over 250 nationalities and ethnic groups, none of which had their own nation-state. Even former union republics and autonomous regions lacked the status of nation-states, ultimately controlled by the central authority and unable to advocate for their national rights. This totalitarian policy influenced scientific research, making it difficult to consider the state as a national symbol within the context of the Soviet Union. However, this policy didn't necessarily erase the desire for national statehood among the diverse populations. In fact, it arguably fueled aspirations for independence and self-determination.

Secondly, developed countries increasingly emphasize the concept of citizenship over nationhood. For example, the idea of being "American" – regardless of individual nationality, race, religion, or gender – holds significant value for citizens living within the United States. Similarly, while European nations like England, France, and Germany haven't traditionally prioritized the concept of nation, they haven't entirely suppressed the sense of belonging among non-titular nationalities residing within their borders. It appears that while these countries prioritize civil or human aspects over national identity, completely erasing the sense of belonging hasn't proven achievable.

The text continues with examples of how individuals belonging to non-titular nations living in various countries might react to being told they have no nationality and belong solely to their adopted nation.

Moreover, the peoples of the world today speak 6,809 languages[7], they live in about 280 countries of the world, and only more than 2,500 of these 6809 speaking people have achieved the status of a nation or people. Moreover, there is a danger that 80% of these languages we use to communicate today will gradually disappear. This is why the United Nations Educational, Scientific and Cultural Organization (UNESCO) is working, at least, to save them. However, this does not mean that all ethnic groups speaking different languages should have their own states. It is neither feasible nor desirable. The fact is that their sense of belonging to their nation has been preserved in their national consciousness in all conditions and cannot be completely eradicated.

Thirdly, the world today is changing rapidly, and great changes are taking place in the minds of people. Naturally, these changes also affect national consciousness. With regard to non-titular nations and peoples living in the modern world, it cannot be ignored that if the titular nation tends to be suppressed in national or state policy, or if this suppression becomes common practice, then these groups might try to create their own state based on national symbols. In particular, the idea of great nationalism and aggressive chauvinism was central to the rise and disintegration of the former union, and its implementation played a key role in its failure. As a result, independent states with their titular nations arose. It is worth noting that Abkhazia and South Ossetia separated from Georgia and declared their independence. Although their independence is not recognized by the vast majority of the world community, it remains a factual situation. Additionally, the collapse of the former union coincided with the collapse of the world socialist system. Subsequently, the policy of violence in interethnic relations within former socialist countries led to significant changes even in countries that had embarked on their own path of independent development. For example, Czechoslovakia was divided into two independent states, Czech Republic and Slovakia, and Yugoslavia disintegrated into states like Serbia and Croatia.

Today, in a number of countries around the world, the number of attempts to create new national states is growing. Five to six years ago, the concept of titular (dominant) and non-titular nations was not widely discussed in countries like the US and Europe. However, today, not only titular nations themselves, but also migrants, immigrants, and ethnic groups, are pushing for recognition at the level of heads of state. This local emphasis suggests an understanding that migrants and immigrants must respect the language, customs, traditions, and values of the titular nation, assimilate, and become an integral part of its society. The main reason for this focus is the declining population of titular nations due to low birth rates.

It is clear that the feeling of belonging to one's nation and the desire to preserve it exist not only in developing countries but also in highly developed ones. Denying this reality is no longer productive. While developed countries previously did not prioritize ethnicity, leaders now recognize that focusing solely on employment and well-being of migrants does not lead to assimilation. In practice, the opposite has occurred. As migrants strive for material well-being in their new countries, they also develop a longing for their homeland. Today, in developed countries, people of other nationalities and ethnic groups unite in communities based on their shared language, customs, traditions, and values, and actively work to preserve them.

It is clear that the feeling of preserving national identity cannot be eradicated from the national consciousness. In countries where repression against non-titular nations and ethnic groups occurs, there are attempts to separate from the titular nation and create an independent state or emigrate to their homeland.

Since the historical development of nations shows that the number of countries named after nations is not decreasing but increasing, this trend is likely to continue in the future. However, it is uncertain whether such movements will eventually stop.

(The answer to this question can only be determined by time, ongoing global processes, changes in national consciousness, and the overall direction of development trends.)

Based on these ideas, we studied the issues of national identity and its formative processes. Our definition of a nation includes the state as an important symbol.

If we consider the aforementioned theoretical and empirical material, along with the growing desire of nations to fight for their rights and freedoms, it is reasonable to define the state as an important symbol of the nation. However, this does not imply that all peoples and ethnic groups residing in the present-day territory of Kurrai, who currently lack their own state, will necessarily form their own. The need for independent statehood does not automatically arise in every case.

Where there is a balance of interests between the titular nation and non-titular nations and ethnic groups, the sense of a shared homeland within the minds of the population strengthens. In such environments, representatives of each nation and ethnic group can freely develop their traditions, customs, and values.

This opportunity ensures peaceful and prosperous lives for these populations. Under such conditions, representatives of non-titular nations and ethnic groups harmonize their national identity with the titular nation within the framework of a shared homeland. This very process allows us to preserve the civilization achieved by humanity today, and reinforces the individual's sense of belonging to their nation.

Another sign of a nation's identity is the presence of economic ties. In today's world, where integration between countries is crucial for development, the economic factor cannot be solely confined within national borders. However, this doesn't negate the existence of a national economy.

Each nation possesses unique characteristics, including mentality, local conditions, resources, labor force, and traditions, all of which influence its production system and integration into the global economy. These aspects define the functioning of a nation's economy. Each country and its people, guided by their national interests, determine their own economic development path and integration strategies. If a nation's interests aren't reflected in its economic system, it will seek alternative, effective development models.

Common economic interests unite a nation's people. Even in the context of emerging global economic spaces, the connection to economic ties remains vital in defining a nation. In fact, this characteristic persists in most definitions of a nation proposed to this day.

The key question is whether a nation's identity will survive or vanish in the face of a single economic space. We believe that a nation's state will persevere as long as the nation itself exists, and it will retain its own national economy.

This national economy acts as a crucial symbol, uniting the nation's representatives and the entire population. The formation, development, and improvement of national identity are intertwined with various elements: a shared language, cultural identity, shared psyche, customs, traditions, values, territory, statehood, and economic ties.

As the consciousness of each nation evolves, the influence of these elements on the nation's stability strengthens. However, the development of national identity should not lead to isolation, disregard for other peoples' interests, or the emergence of extreme nationalism. These tendencies are particularly detrimental in multi-ethnic states, where they can deeply embed themselves in the dominant group's national consciousness.

The development of national identity is reflected in the fact that in such countries, the leader unites the nation, first and foremost, by making all peoples recognize themselves as citizens of the same homeland and respect each other's customs, traditions, and values. If these feelings are not cultivated and instilled in the minds of the dominant populations, the leader will be unable to escape the quagmire of interethnic conflicts and ultimately fall behind in development. Therefore, fostering a strong sense of tolerance towards other nations within the dominant population is recognized as one of the crucial conditions for a country's progress.

A glaring example of this is the historical practice of national policy in the former Soviet Union. The Russian people were designated as the largest and most developed nation, considered an "elder brother," and other peoples were expected to unite around them. The most unfortunate aspect of this approach was that it cultivated a "nationalist" mentality among the so-called "titular" nations in the union republics. As a result, educating them in the spirit of internationalism became the main objective. However, it was the representatives of Russian-speaking nationalities living among the local populations who were designated as the "internationalists," unofficially granting them the authority to educate and control the entire local population in this spirit. This condemned the indigenous peoples to live in their own homeland at the behest of their "big brother," a nation without a "title." Similar sentiments were planted in the minds of the indigenous peoples of the union republics, fostering a hidden, and sometimes open, hatred that ultimately played a significant role in accelerating the collapse of the former union.

We can still witness the vestiges of this bitter experience today in some CIS countries. In some cases, politicians from developed countries have made promises to help independent states achieve their geopolitical goals. It is no secret that the infiltration of nationalist sentiment and the abhorrent practice of pitting peoples against each other leads to contradictory development in the consciousness of the people inhabiting these countries today. They are acutely aware that national consciousness is fragile and emotionally volatile, susceptible to external influences that may run counter to national interests or be completely ignored. It is a complex spiritual factor that can unite a nation against violence. Countries aiming for global dominance have exploited these vulnerabilities in the past, and some politicians and "democrats" continue to attempt to do so even today. The process, unfortunately, persists.

If national consciousness is one of the factors leading a nation to development, then its development fosters in the nation's representatives feelings like national pride, honor, and responsibility. These are the spiritual potential of the nation and the main sources of strengthening its identity. We are trying to understand the essence of their content and their role in the development of national identity.

National pride is a feeling inherent in all nations that consider themselves independent. It manifests as pride in the achievements of a nation's ancestors and descendants, its prestige in the eyes of other peoples, and the joy of its potential and greatness in the minds and hearts of every member.

National pride is based on the heritage of our ancestors, the achievements of generations, the nation's progress, and the viability of future opportunities. However, it goes beyond mere pride in our heritage or disdain for other peoples. It involves a deep study of this heritage to feel its freshness and make it an integral part of our spirituality, actively contributing to our nation's development while respecting others. National pride is an expression of the development of national identity, as well as the spirituality and spirit of the nation, which inspires, strengthens, and contributes to its development. Its material manifestation can be seen in the attitude of the nation's representatives towards their ancestors' heritage and their actions in the interests of their people. Only a nation with pride has firm faith not only in the present but also in the future, and is able to show dedication to its cause on the path of creativity.

National honor is a concept that expresses the spiritual, emotional, and moral feelings of members of a nation. It arises from the rise of national pride to a higher level. National honor is a manifestation of spiritual uplift, formed in the consciousness of the nation's representatives through deep assimilation of the material and spiritual wealth created and left behind by their ancestors. If national pride is a feeling of pride in the minds of the nation, then national honor is the enjoyment of the ancestors' heritage and the emotional rise of inspiration from today's achievements. In this sense, if national pride in the consciousness of a nation is the emergence of a sense of pride in its achievements, we can say that national honor is their "material" expression. They develop in harmony with each other. A proud nation will feel true honor, and its members will be able to express themselves with confidence in front of other nations. National honor means that representatives of a nation can not only be proud of their achievements, past and present, but also act selflessly with confidence in their nation's path of development today and in the future.

The feeling of pride can be a great spiritual blessing, contributing to the development of national self-awareness. However, a nation cannot be solely built on national pride; it also requires the unification of people, which often starts at the community level.

Honor is one of the most delicate yet potent feelings within a nation's collective consciousness. It serves as a guardian of a nation's dignity, preventing its tarnishing under any circumstance. Honor manifests as the understanding that the nation's integrity surpasses all individual interests. Any perceived humiliation, insult, or neglect towards the nation's representatives is taken as a personal affront, igniting a fierce resistance that prioritizes national pride above all else.

As custodians of their heritage, noble nations strive to keep the memory of their ancestors untarnished and actively overcome obstacles to ensure they faithfully carry forward the legacy without sullying its honor. Honor, in this context, symbolizes the cherished values of purity, modesty, chastity, and humility. Since a nation is a collective of individuals bound by shared characteristics, these personal values naturally translate into the national consciousness.

Furthermore, the national consciousness develops a protective instinct against sacrificing its dignity for material gain. This sentiment finds voice in the ancestral proverb, "I devote my life not to my stomach, but to my dignity." It stands as a testament to the nation's inner spirit, representing its resilience and its determination to shield itself from hardship. Ultimately, a nation that loses its honor resembles an individual stripped of their cherished values, wandering in a state of despair. In this sense, preserving national honor transcends individual lives and becomes an integral part of the nation's identity and purpose.

National Responsibility:

Understanding national responsibility requires examining various forms of responsibility, including responsibility towards parents, family, nation, homeland, and people. Among these, a unique and crucial role is played by the obligation each nation feels towards its present and future. This feeling stems from the understanding that just as an individual cannot exist without a nation, a nation cannot thrive without its individuals.

National responsibility arises from a strong sense of national identity, pride, and honor. It embodies the internalization of national interests, the preservation of centuries-old material and spiritual treasures, traditions, customs, and values. It manifests in the transmission of these legacies to future generations, instilling in the youth a sense of national identity and purpose. Ultimately, it fosters a spirit of nationalism, civilization, and a willingness to selflessly contribute one's potential and fulfill one's duty as a representative of the nation.

It is noteworthy that the understanding of national responsibility among national representatives evolves and improves based on the challenges encountered at different stages of historical development. Interestingly, the need to preserve national identity grows alongside national development and self-awareness. This stems, in part, from the significant responsibility individual members hold in preventing their nation's assimilation under the "elder brother" during the former Soviet era. Particularly for the Uzbek nation, upholding national independence is now a sacred duty for every citizen, protecting them from globalization's negative impact on their national spirit.

Understanding national responsibility does not equate to national egoism, disrespect for other nations, indifference to their interests, or denying their needs. Instead, it fosters cooperation between one nation and others, cultivating respect for all nations and the people who live alongside them, acknowledging their needs alongside their own. It further entails recognizing their own needs and supporting their collective development. Superficiality in understanding one's indebtedness to their nation and indifference to its future, among national representatives, can lead to national disintegration and ultimately, assimilation with other nations. Therefore, consistently cultivating a spirit of understanding national responsibility within every national representative remains a fundamental task for preserving and developing the nation.

The primary factors shaping and developing national self-awareness include the national language, the spirit of national identity, spirituality, customs, traditions, values, a specific region, state, and economic ties. In contrast, national pride, honor, dignity, and responsibility represent the "spiritual clothing" of a nation. Without these, a nation cannot achieve true independence. They act as an internal force transforming the nation's formative factors into material power.

Returning to the topic of national identity development, its role in understanding identity is paramount. As an outcome of national self-awareness development, the level of understanding among national representatives regarding traditions, customs, values, national interests, and the responsibility to address national challenges and contribute to their solutions reflects the degree of its development. Serving as the primary source of understanding national identity, it provides the nation with a material and spiritual "image" while empowering its representatives with the spiritual strength to defend their identity. In this sense, a nation's stability once again hinges on its collective consciousness.

No matter how independent the national consciousness, its existence and level of development can be understood only through the development of the nation and the actions of its representatives in pursuit of national interests arising from that development. This national identity, however, varies in its level of expression, with two key moments of vivid demonstration:

a) When external threats arise to the nation's interests, pride, honor, and dignity.

b) When the nation becomes aware of critical problems and new challenges, with their resolution being crucial to its future.

Under other circumstances, the understanding of national identity continues to evolve steadily, like a guiding star reflecting the nation's unique character.

Among the factors shaping a nation, national identity stands out for its sensitivity, immediacy, and unifying force against external threats. This strength and inspiration stem from national consciousness. Therefore, it's accurate to say that national identity and national consciousness develop in tandem.

Contrary to popular belief, a strong national identity doesn't lead to interethnic conflicts. In fact, it fosters harmony by promoting cooperation and solidarity with other peoples, which is an integral part of its development. No nation thrives in isolation, and the pursuit of "purity" or seclusion is detrimental.

Many interethnic conflicts arise from a lagging national consciousness, failing to adapt to changing times. Often, aggressive countries with well-developed national consciousness exploit this lag, disregarding other nations' interests in their quest for dominance. Additionally, nations unwilling to cooperate with others due to anxieties about the future or a desire for isolation can contribute to conflict.

The most dangerous factor, however, is the formation of an arrogant nationalist mentality. This mentality harms both individuals and the union of nations, ultimately leading to a crisis within the nation itself. Therefore, sustainable national consciousness development requires strengthening positive aspects, such as stability in interethnic relations.

Understanding this process is crucial for the harmonious coexistence of nations and peoples, especially in diverse societies. In this context, developing national self-awareness is not negative but rather a positive force for free and independent expression. However, any attempt to manipulate this process for harmful purposes, especially if it inflicts suffering on other nations, will destabilize the world.

Thus, national consciousness is a complex factor. Its backwardness leads to the general backwardness of the nation, while attempts to misuse its high level of development for negative purposes can lead to interethnic conflicts and instability. In this sense, ensuring the development of national identity in accordance with the development potential of nations enhances the ability to focus on strengthening interethnic cooperation and jointly solving common problems. However, the possibilities for achieving this crucial task are limited. This is due, on the one hand, to the different levels of development that nations around the world have attained in the economic, social, political, and spiritual spheres. On the other hand, as nations develop and their intellectual potential increases, so do the challenges of borderless access and utilization of this potential, contributing to ongoing issues in interethnic relations. These factors naturally influence the development of national identity.

Now, considering the process of globalization, we will analyze the trends in the development of national consciousness. It is crucial to recognize that national consciousness, along with any other process or event, depends on the development of society and its capabilities. It cannot advance ahead of a society's overall development. National consciousness positively impacts the development of the nation through its unifying, organizing, and goal-oriented functions. We can see this reflected in the formation and development of our own nation.

If we imagine the dark days of our nation, from its formation as an ethnic unit to today's opportunity for independent and free development, we will witness the difficult stages its consciousness and self-awareness have gone through. Its tragic situation, especially during the period of colonialism and dependence, is forever etched in history. Notably, despite possessing great scientific, spiritual, and enlightenment achievements, and contributing to a certain stage of world civilization, our country, whose experience of national statehood is recognized globally, was forced to endure these hardships under colonial and dependent rule.

In fact, our spirituality surpassed the spirituality of the peoples of those countries that colonized and subjugated us. Even the invaders who occupied our country and turned it into a colony were forced to admit that our spirituality and culture were more developed than their own. We have already mentioned the opinion of the orientalist V.V. Bartold on the occupation of Turkestan by Russia and their perceived superiority over this country in the national and spiritual sphere.

This well-known scientist, who was well-acquainted with the people and culture of Turkestan and was recognized in Russian science and culture of that time, raised two key questions. Firstly, he acknowledged the high level of spirituality of the Turkestani people. Secondly, he emphasized the impossibility of subjugating a people without first robbing them of their spirituality. His ideas were sadly borne out after the invasions of Tsarist Russia and the Bolsheviks.

Of course, historical data confirms that the collapse of the Timurid Empire and the emergence of three independent states in Central Asia – the Kokand and Khiva Khanates and the Bukhara Emirate – weakened the people living in this region, ultimately leading to colonization and dependence. However, this process did not even momentarily halt the development of our national identity. The strong spiritual and material foundations of our people have always served as a source of strength, power, and inspiration, ultimately leading to regaining independence and pursuing our chosen path of development. Nevertheless, this does not imply that threats to our national development have vanished entirely.

Especially today, the influence of the rapidly developing process of globalization, a force even powerful nations cannot stop, poses an increasing threat to our national spirituality. The most dangerous aspect of globalization in the 21st century is this: while former empires employed force to colonize nations, today's highly developed countries do not resort to weapons of mass destruction. Instead, they seek to achieve dependence through more "enlightened" means, occupying the minds and hearts of less developed nations now embarking on the path of development.

What changes does this process bring to the consciousness of peoples? Do we fully understand the consequences of this unfolding phenomenon? I believe that under the intense pressure of globalization, national consciousness is not adequately protected, and nations are struggling to understand themselves.

Globalization brings together countries of the world, large and small, highly developed, now following the path of independent development, and less developed countries, as well as the nations and peoples living in them. It is impossible for any nation or people to escape its influence.

Under such conditions, several changes occur in the consciousness of nations under its influence. In our opinion, they are reflected in the following:

First, the development of national identity lags behind the acceleration of globalization. Since globalization draws all nations and peoples into its orbit, nations and peoples now living in developing and underdeveloped countries may not have enough time to realize their strength and essence before their national identity is weakened by joining the global current. In other words, the development of national self-awareness in these nations and peoples is overshadowed by globalization.

This process can be viewed from two sides:

a) Globalization, as a new stage of development, has a certain impact on the development of the intellectual potential of all nations and peoples, including those who are now embarking on the path of development and underdeveloped countries. This is evident in practice today. Naturally, this is reflected in national consciousness as well. In this sense, globalization and the development of national consciousness are interconnected. At the same time, intellectual potential is also a product of a higher development of the mind, which positively impacts national development, whether it be reflected in scientific, technological, or other advancements. In this sense, globalization can be viewed as a process that positively affects the development of national identity.

However, the main problem here is that the national consciousness of all nations and peoples does not develop at the same pace as globalization, especially the consciousness of nations and peoples who are now embarking on the path of development. This is primarily due to their limited material opportunities to achieve great achievements in science, technology, and innovation, which are key drivers of globalization. Therefore, globalization easily draws them into its current, and the inclination towards this process within their national consciousness increases. Thus, the danger that their national consciousness will be lost in the ocean of globalization always remains.

b) One of the most dangerous aspects of the globalization process for nations and peoples that are now on the path of development or lagging behind in development is that those who participate in this process more effectively will reap greater benefits and, unintentionally, widen the gap between themselves and less developed nations and peoples. This can lead to the development of a spirit of domination in the minds of highly developed nations and a tendency to rely on highly developed nations in the national consciousness of less developed nations and peoples embarking on the path of independent development.

So, in both cases, national consciousness cannot develop outside the influence of globalization. While this can positively accelerate the development of one party's national consciousness, it can also lead to a tendency in the other's national consciousness to rely on others (particularly powerful nations). This dependency can cause the national consciousness of underdeveloped and undeveloped nations and peoples to lag behind the process of globalization, gradually decline, and fall behind the level of general development requirements.

Secondly, globalization, despite its many distinctive features, presents a unique challenge to national self-awareness, understanding of national identity, and their practical expression in national development. This is because globalization can sometimes erode national identities, negatively affect the unity of nations, and even lead to interethnic inequality on a global scale. As these processes inevitably influence national consciousness, contradictions between globalization and national consciousness arise.

These contradictions emerge not only from material interests but also from the growing need to protect the national and spiritual potential of national development from the consequences of globalization. The driving force behind these contradictions is not the process of globalization itself, but the advances in science, technology, and information technology that fuel it, along with the highly developed countries that create and benefit from it. As mentioned earlier, globalization acts like a powerful force that attracts nations with its scale, power, and economic opportunities. However, its impact on the economy, politics, public life, and interstate relations carries the potential to negatively affect the consciousness and identity of nations.

Countries with high intellectual and economic potential act as the creators, owners, and main beneficiaries of this "ocean." They naturally try to attract peoples from less developed countries to participate. The problem with this process is that even if contradictions exist today but haven't yet manifested in practice, they may surface later, potentially with significant consequences. These potential conflicts could arise, on the one hand, between nations in highly developed countries that create and benefit from this "ocean" within their national consciousness, and on the other hand, between nations and peoples in less developed countries. As an example, we see this reflected in the growing sentiment in some developed countries towards deporting migrants, even if such initiatives are not yet widely publicized. While these trends may not be currently widespread, there is no guarantee they won't become significant factors in the future. The degree of their development and potential consequences will depend on how relations between these parties evolve and how well the balance of interests is maintained within the process of globalization. However, achieving this balanced development is an immensely challenging task. On the one hand, globalization has its own inherent laws of development that cannot be halted or impeded. On the other hand, the leading countries that benefit from globalization, along with the nations and peoples within them, cannot simply ignore their own interests.

So, the only way to achieve balance is to develop the national consciousness of nations and peoples in less developed countries, aligning it with the current levels of globalization and effectively utilizing available opportunities. This necessitates forming the perception that globalization, while presenting opportunities, also poses the risk of future assimilation with more developed nations for less developed ones. Conversely, highly developed nations and peoples must understand that refusing equal cooperation with less developed counterparts now, regardless of the current situation, will ultimately hinder their own future interests. Recognizing that they too risk becoming dependent on others helps mitigate some of the underlying contradictions forming within interethnic consciousness.

The urgency of the issue is evident in the actions of certain developed nations, including Great Britain, France, Germany, and Russia. Leaders in these countries, through various means, promote hatred towards migrants within their titular nations and advocate for the appropriation of resources from underdeveloped countries. Such openly expressed and implemented policies, based on sources cited herein, represent a dangerous path that could escalate simmering conflicts into major forces. As our proverb states, "There is vomiting of food eaten," implying that developed nations' current attempts to exploit globalization's possibilities for dependent relationships could backfire in the future.

Thirdly, globalization also influences spontaneous alienation among nations. Alienation, referring to indifference and detachment from one's heritage, customs, traditions, and values, arises not spontaneously but due to specific objective or subjective reasons. These include individuals from a nation integrating into more developed societies for multiple generations, colonization leading to the imposition of alien lifestyles, spiritualities, customs, and traditions, and systematic efforts to erase a nation's identity. However, alienation doesn't necessarily imply complete loss of identity. One of humanity's greatest blessings is the sense of belonging to a nation, serving as a spiritual fortress and distinguishing characteristic. We see this exemplified by our own nation, where despite centuries living amongst other peoples, several generations preserved their heritage and passed it on. Similarly, despite forced assimilation policies, our compatriots living abroad maintained their connection, as evidenced by their emotional return to their ancestral homeland. This vital example underscores that alienation, particularly forced alienation, doesn't result in complete assimilation into another nation. History has proven that attempts to forcibly assimilate a nation over time ultimately fail.

Now, let's consider the impact of globalization on the alienation of peoples. Can the current process of alienation ultimately lead to a complete collapse of national consciousness?

As noted earlier, the argument that globalization fosters national alienation hinges on the idea that a person's sense of belonging stems not from political institutions or social organizations, but from their heritage, deeply rooted in their mother tongue, culture, and pre-birth experiences. However, this argument doesn't necessarily lead to complete extinction.

Globalization may indeed prioritize material factors over spiritual aspects of national identity. We can observe a growing tendency for people to prioritize comfort and opportunity over national identity, adopting the principle of "where life is good, that's my homeland." This can raise concerns about the future of national identity. However, the example of the former Soviet Union suggests that this process may not be linear. While a significant portion of the Russian population initially desired restoration, their support diminished considerably over time. This demonstrates that adaptation based on objective reality can occur, even when sentiments of nostalgia exist.

Applying this to the current context, we can consider whether the increasing superficiality of national consciousness, potentially influenced by globalization, might lead to future collapse. Analyzing the interaction between globalization and national consciousness, it's important to avoid absolutes like "impossible to resist" or "continues to destroy." Instead, we should acknowledge a more nuanced reality where globalization presents challenges and opportunities. One key challenge is the potential lag between the pace of globalization and the development of factors that solidify national identity as a "material force." This necessitates finding ways for national consciousness to evolve, keeping pace with globalization while fostering responsibility for national protection and engagement with advancements in science and technology.

4.2. IN THE CONTEXT OF GLOBALIZATION OF NATIONAL IDENTITY FUNCTIONS

The concept of national identity, its functions, problems, and solutions, and its role in national development, are analyzed in a number of works by the author of these lines[1][lxxvii]. With this in mind, we briefly dwell on the concept of national identity and its characteristics, analyzing its development in the context of today's growing threats to national spirituality.

First, it's worth noting that after the collapse of the USSR and the independence of its former republics, the concept of national identity, its development, and its role in national development became one of the most pressing topics of scientific research. There are at least four reasons for this:

1. Forced Assimilation: Under Soviet rule, a violent national policy aimed at merging "smaller" nations into one large "brother" and forming a single Soviet nation prevented them from realizing their identity and developing independently. The imposition of a "singular" Soviet culture led to growing ambiguity in national spirituality, hindering the development of a strong national identity. Soviet policy prioritized the development of national spirituality based on rejecting "old" (national heritage) and forming a one-sided, unified Soviet culture. This not only impoverished national spirituality but also risked severing ties with it entirely. The main problem was maintaining a balance between developing national identity and integrating with global civilization.

2. Resurgence of Identity: Democratic processes in the former USSR's final years ignited anger, pain, and a sense of self in the minds and hearts of "smaller" nations who had suffered under the regime. Titular nations in all former republics gained a renewed understanding of their identity and a desire to restore their traditions, customs, and values. This caused interethnic tensions, leading to tragic loss of life in some regions. Naturally, mutual trust eroded under Soviet rule, and tensions between "non-titular" and "titular" peoples intensified. In regions with diverse populations, fear, indecision, and insecurity about the future arose. This process demonstrably showed that forced annexation of nations can lead to significant tragedies. The key challenge today is developing and implementing mechanisms that ensure peaceful coexistence among all nations, considering their multi-ethnic nature. The post-Soviet experience highlights the crucial importance of ensuring true equality for nations, not just in theory but in practice, fostering spiritual closeness, tolerance, and community ties. Guaranteeing every nation's right to self-determination is of primary importance.

3. Globalization and Its Impact: Today's globalized world fosters the formation of new values and rapid sharing of scientific and technological advancements. This, in turn, leads to increased integration among the world's peoples. While the previous section discussed both the positive and negative impacts of globalization on countries and peoples, here we focus on conflicts arising from developed countries leveraging

their immense potential to exploit developing countries and their people. This raises concerns about the potential superficiality of national identities in the face of globalization.

Indeed, in the context of growing globalization, two scenarios are possible:

On the one hand, as a product of its universal intellectual potential, it can be a positive factor for overall development, as noted above.

On the other hand, developed countries and their peoples could become more dependent on external styles, especially as the struggle for surface and underground resources intensifies.

In such conditions, the development of self-consciousness among nations and peoples embarking on the path of development should not be influenced by any state and should become a factor in ensuring their independent development. In this context, it is important that the development of national identity serves the principle of equality and mutual benefit in all respects.

The political philosophy of this process is that, given no nation or people can stay away from globalization, they are all now on the path of development. However, they must be able to critically evaluate external influences and implement the strategies that best suit their own needs.

One key problem in this process is the perceived difference between the practice of developed countries of "giving something in return" and the spirit of developing countries of "giving more" and striving for friendship. If the principle of mutual equality is not applied in relationships, and the tendency to accept external influence ("help") in the development of national identity increases, then globalization as a process could lead to the assimilation of many "smaller" nations into "larger" ones.

As difficult as the state of dependence and liberation may be for nations, the process of globalization can also prompt many nations and peoples to become "bait" for others before they fully realize their identity. The need to explore the possibility of avoiding this fate requires close examination of the current and future state of development of national identity.

Fourthly, it is well known that national spirituality often develops in harmony with religion. Religion can be an integral part of it, and their interdependence can influence the development of the nation's internal potential. Consequently, the development of national identity can go hand in hand with religious values. However, when the balance of harmony between them is disturbed, the predominance of one over the other can occur, leading to national or religious bias.

Today, in some countries, attempts are being made to use religion as a factor in developing national identity. This includes introducing religion as the main theme in kindergartens, schools, and other educational systems, as well as in the military. In particular, efforts are focused on ensuring the dominance of religious ideas over national ones.

This approach, to put it mildly, suggests that national ideas are becoming "weaker" than religion. This could lead to a future increase in the perception of religious identity rather than national self-awareness. In a multi-confessional environment, conflicts between religions can lead to even more severe consequences than interethnic conflicts, ultimately threatening the collapse of the entire state and even the civilization humanity has achieved.

In this sense, a comprehensive study of national identity development requires finding factors that combine and balance national and religious values in practice. As highlighted above, this is a very complex and serious issue.

From this perspective, it is necessary to re-examine the concept of "national identity" and its development process. Firstly, it is important to note that during the Soviet Union era, the understanding of national identity was not explored as an independent academic subject within its territory.

The primary reason for this was the central government's policy of suppressing the self-realization of the union's peoples, using brutal force against any national awakening. This "external" suppression served as a practical confirmation of the "absence" of a problem in national development. Additionally, research by scholars in the former Soviet republics about the nation and related issues could have resulted in significant problems for them at the time. Discussing the rise of national identity and its associated issues would have labeled them "nationalists" and subjected them to punishment.

Scholars in the former Soviet Union, including Uzbekistan, focused only on the positive aspects of the nation. All decisions of the ruling Communist Party, the pivotal state authority, mandated "research" on the people's formation. As mentioned earlier, those who did not comply were punished as "nationalists" or enemies of the regime.

An example of this is the movement of the Jadids in Turkestan in the late 19th and early 20th centuries and their activities aimed at awakening our people, as well as their tragic fate.

The late Jadid scientist and renowned scholar Begali Kasimov, who studied their nationalism and patriotism to achieve the country's independence by enhancing the education of our nation, wrote, "The essence of Jadidism is an intense and exciting process, from understanding the nation and the motherland to the struggle for their interests. At the same time, the movement also nurtured the nation, raising it from interpreting every calamity that befell it to the level of seeking a solution."[2][lxxviii].

The process of raising the Jadid educational movement to the level of the struggle for national independence was investigated by my student, Gairatjon Kholmatov. According to his dissertation, the Jadids were selfless individuals who grew up in our nation and called on it to express itself, fight for its rights and freedoms, and unite as a single force for independence.

Their actions were severely punished, first by Tsarism and then by Soviet authorities. Historical records have been preserved showing that the physical extermination of participants in the movement continued until the outbreak of World War II, peaking in the mid-1930s. The Soviets aimed to break the spirit of our nation by destroying the Jadids, depriving them of their lands, and severing their connection to their identity. However, they failed.

Although the lives of the Jadids ended tragically, the light of national awakening they ignited did not extinguish. On the contrary, it continued to burn brightly in the minds and hearts of our nation, keeping them connected to their lands and identities. It can be said that the violent policy directed by the Soviets against our national identity did, to some extent, slow down its growth during their rule. We will explore this further in more detail later.

Furthermore, the existence of the former union and the policies pursued by its central authority towards its constituent nations led not only to scientific research in this area but also to the risk of these nations being cut off from their lands. However, the collapse of the union and the subsequent desire of the titular nations within it to understand their identities demonstrated that when a nation's foundations are deep and rich, it is incredibly difficult, if not impossible, to fully deprive it of its identity.

The development process of our nation confirms that this process is not merely open for a limited period but rather develops continuously, even when seemingly hidden, and resists attempts to suppress its national identity. The possibility of scientific study and objective analysis of this process only became possible after our country gained independence.

Today, several researchers are conducting valuable research in this area. However, even greater tasks lie ahead in studying this critical issue. As a nation exists, it becomes necessary to examine the process of national identity growth. This allows the nation to contribute to the greatness of humanity and continue to evolve over time. Therefore, another challenge in studying national identity lies in its consistent exploration from both historical and contemporary perspectives, considering the new challenges that arise for national development. With these needs in mind, and considering our previously published discussions on the concept of national identity, we will focus here on briefly addressing the issues highlighted above.

Awareness of national identity belongs to the people of a nation and is the outcome of its formation and ongoing development. The main factor contributing to its formation is the development and understanding of the human mind, its growth, and the consequent construction of national identity. After all, just as a nation cannot exist without individuals, an understanding of national identity cannot be formed without the growth of one's own individuality and consciousness. The individual is the most fundamental basis, source, and force that transforms the realization of national identity into a tangible power. It is not formed "outside" of a person and their consciousness, but rather fashioned by the individual and gives them a sense of belonging. At the same time, the individual themself continues to develop through this awareness, which serves as an important marker of self-improvement. In this sense, the more complex a person's self-awareness becomes, the more challenging it is to grasp the dynamic nature of national identity and harness it as a force for interethnic stability.

While the definition of national identity is an important factor in social development, it also ensures the renewal of society and strengthens the needs of the nation. However, it can also become a primary factor in the emergence of "painful" areas within society. By "painful" areas, we mean, first of all, the instability of the population due to the multiethnic composition of the population, discrimination against one nation or another, neglect of spiritual needs, disrespect for honor and pride, and interethnic conflicts.

However, limiting this process to the past and present does not fully express its meaning and significance. Because the future existence of the nation will also depend on the solution of the problems and tasks it faces. As a product of people, a nation is also "alive," and its needs grow alongside the development of time. Based on this, we can define the understanding of national identity as follows:

National identity is the understanding of each nation (ethnos) as a truly existing entity representing specific material and spiritual wealth, a common language, customs, traditions, values, and belonging to the state, as well as shared interests, needs, and future tasks.

The difference between this definition and our previously published works is that it defines the problems the nation faces in protecting itself from the negative consequences of growing globalization and the task of finding solutions as an independent factor. True, this can also be seen as referring to understanding interests and needs. However, the role of the nation in the process of globalization, which has emerged and continues today, may remain overlooked. In the context of globalization, it is not enough for a nation to understand general goals and needs, but also to understand new tasks that arise in terms of practical measures to protect itself from its influence, and the "mechanisms" by which they can be implemented in real life.

National identity is a relatively advanced stage in the formation of a nation. It arises as a result of its unification around a state in a specific region based on the formation of its own customs, traditions, and values.

However, this does not mean that the nation is truly self-aware. It requires understanding not only common interests and needs, but also the need to protect them together. After all, the diversity in the levels of material and spiritual development of the nation's representatives, where it is high in one part and low in another, can hinder their unification into a single whole. In such conditions, the interest in preserving the traditions, customs, and values of the nation, and the need to work to ensure it does not lag behind other nations in development, leads to the unification of the nation's representatives, regardless of their level of material and spiritual development. In other words, the ability of a nation to prioritize national interests and needs over a narrow range of private interests and needs, regardless of who they are and their level of material well-being, is a key indicator of the level of development of national identity.

The perception of national identity is associated with national consciousness, but these are not synonymous concepts. There are certain differences between them. National consciousness manifests as a reflection of the development of a single language, customs, traditions, values, and spirituality of each nation. In other words, they are formed, developed, and improved as a result of the development of national identity. At the same time, national consciousness itself develops through the use of these factors. National self-awareness is formed on the basis of national consciousness as a result of the protection of these factors from external negative influences and the emergence of a need for national development. The development of national self-awareness raises the level of self-awareness of each nation. While national consciousness is an indicator of the development of a nation based on its identity, national self-awareness is a spiritual potential that acts to protect its interests. Only their harmonious development will lead the nation to progress.

At the same time, national consciousness always develops and is formed from the bottom up as a process. This is reflected in the development and improvement of customs, traditions, and values. On the other hand, the development of a sense of national identity manifests itself in two situations. First, national identity manifests itself when the honor, dignity, and prestige of the nation as a real material force are violated by external forces. Second, it manifests itself as a result of violent actions that contradict its material and spiritual interests. Representatives of a nation whose dignity, honor, prestige, and interests have been violated must unite as one common force and defend their identity, regardless of their social status, wealth, or position. In this process, the concept of a person as a representative of a nation plays a role, as described in section 2.1 of our previous book. The dignity, honor, prestige, and interests inherent in an individual are "transferred" to the nation and reflected in it. Thus, representatives of the nation, whose honor, dignity, prestige, and interests have been violated, regardless of their position, wealth, or poverty, unite as a single common force to protect these great values of the national "I." In this process, the understanding of national identity is manifested at the level of material power.

In addition, in this case, understanding national identity as a material force becomes not only a unifying and organizing force, but also a driving force in defending the "self" of the nation. Put another way, it's not just a force protecting the "self" and national interests, but also one that unites and mobilizes the nation to solve problems related to its development. This process cannot be solely based on specific development programs.

The spiritual and educational power of understanding national identity lies in its ability to awaken the inner spiritual potential of individuals (representatives) of the nation, naturally encouraging them to unite and act. Consequently, this understanding cannot be artificially developed through laws and regulations; instead, it manifests itself as a reflection of national development. Laws and regulations are adopted based on the development needs of national progress, taking into account the interests of not only the titular nations, but also the representatives of nations and peoples living alongside them. In other words, we're talking about the connection between the understanding of national identity and the consciousness of national representatives, their internal spiritual potential.

Of course, this doesn't mean that state-led policies have no role in the growth and development of national identity. Rather, state-led national policies play an important role in national development. The state acts as an institution that also coordinates national identity processes. Its inability to understand this process in a timely manner can lead to the emergence of interethnic conflicts and instability in society.

In this sense, understanding national identity does not entirely "depend" on state activities. Just as defining a person's inner world and level of views is a complex process, determining the level of self-awareness of a nation, which is an association of real people, is also a difficult task. It's particularly challenging to make a clear "diagnosis" of this process, especially in conditions of minimal external negative impact on national development.

However, the main indicator of a nation's existence as an independent entity is its self-awareness, its ability to defend its "self." Therefore, self-awareness is the protagonist of any nation. It's one of the leading forces that transforms the nation into a material force, drawing upon its spiritual potential. Without self-awareness, a nation cannot be imagined as an integral being.

So, understanding national identity is a soul that, with its immense potential, supports the heart, soul, blood, and body of the nation, keeping it upright. This understanding is, first and foremost, the divine-spiritual power bestowed upon a person, and then upon a nation, by Allah. That is why any nation that loses its self-awareness or is deprived of it is doomed to spiritual death. A nation that dies spiritually also dies physically, turning into a mere crowd.

Awareness of national identity performs a number of functions that serve the development of the nation. In particular, it is important to note the presence and functioning of the functions of assessment and encouragement, normative coordination (as noted by Russian scientist B.A. Shuvalov), adaptation, protection, self-control, and the influence of responsibility (as emphasized by Russian scientist K.N. Khabibulin). These functions "work" depending on the development tasks and directions facing the state, the level of emerging problems, and the possibility of interaction. From this point of view, the levels of formation and "performance" are also linked to the levels of national development.

In particular, a nation, like other factors, goes through stages of formation, development, maturity, and improvement until it becomes a real material force. The functionality of the functions stems from the need to address the underlying problem in the chain of problems that exist in these processes. For example, in the context of nation dependency, the functions of evaluation, reward, accountability, unification, goal orientation, and mobilization are often excluded. Even in the context in which a nation has gained independence, the educational function serving to bring about national revival may come to the fore, as needed. Function workflows are detailed in your book mentioned above. With this in mind, we will focus on analyzing the state of national identity in the context of globalization.

An analysis of the levels of national development shows that the "peaceful" course of national development is not development that serves to mobilize the nation in response to external negative influences, but rather development that occurs in accordance with the nation's own needs and development processes.

The development of national identity can be divided into a number of stages and indicator levels depending on their levels of mobilization of the nation. In our opinion, these stages are:

Associated with the process of nation formation

Associated with the state of dependence of the nation

Associated with gaining independence

Associated with the conditions of independence and restoration

Associated with the transition to market relations, which is an objective necessity of national development

Associated with the globalization of the world and its impact on national development

During these six stages, the development of national identity manifests itself at different levels.

Let's take the first step. It is associated with the formation of a nation and differs in that it covers the longest period. This is because the nation itself forms over a lengthy historical stage. In some cases, this period can even become stagnant without reaching the level of true formation.

A characteristic feature of this period is the relatively "peaceful" development of a sense of national identity. During this time, the nation itself is undergoing the process of becoming and cannot yet fully express its "I" as a single force. Furthermore, if at this stage the nation becomes dependent on or influenced by external forces, the stage of formation and development of national identity can be extended.

Another characteristic aspect of the first stage of national identity is that it paves the way for the next stage. In simpler terms, the nation in this period creates not only material wealth but also the spiritual wealth necessary for its future. The degree to which it creates these resources determines the nation's future prospects. If a nation can produce not only material but also strong spiritual wealth, its future will be bright. Even if it suffers tragic misfortune, such as aggression or dependence, these material and spiritual foundations act as a source of self-realization in the struggle for awakening and independence.

If a nation fails to create a solid material and spiritual foundation, it may assimilate with other nations before fully forming its national identity. Therefore, strengthening this foundation is crucial for the nation's future.

The second stage in the development of national identity consciousness is associated with the period when the nation falls into a state of dependence. In fact, most countries in the world have experienced this situation. This situation, due to a combination of subjective and objective reasons, can have two primary consequences: Firstly, it can prolong the process of forming the nation as an independent entity, and in some cases, the nation can assimilate into stronger nations without fully realizing its identity. Secondly, if the nation has established strong material and spiritual foundations, an underground process of developing an understanding of national identity will occur. This same process leads to the unification of the nation as a single force to achieve its independence.

The period of struggle for national independence is the most active level of development of national identity consciousness. This is because the nation realizes that it cannot progress without gaining independence. It understands that it faces the risk of "assimilating" with or becoming "dependent" on more developed colonial nations. In response, the nation unites as a new force, not under someone's leadership, but rather as a manifestation of its drive to develop its national identity. Thus, understanding national identity becomes a key factor in the nation's achievement of independence, allowing it to break free from dependence and gain self-rule.

The third stage is associated with the period when the nation gains independence and embarks on independent development. A characteristic feature of this stage includes: a) restoring the national language, customs, traditions, and values that were compromised during the period of dependence; b) celebrating its pride, honor, dignity, and interests; and c) achieving equality on an equal footing becoming the main goal. During this period, the heightened awareness of national identity will be no less than during the struggle for independence, but it will rise to a new level. This is because this period witnesses the quenching of the thirst for national and spiritual fulfillment that arose during the state of dependence. The experience of national revival shows that fulfilling this national and spiritual thirst is also a complex process. Notably, the experience of national restoration reflects the emergence of both positive and negative aspects in the understanding of national identity.

In our opinion, achieving independence and enjoying its benefits fosters both a sense of satisfaction in understanding national identity and a simultaneous weakening of some aspects of it. This doesn't imply complete vulnerability, but rather a state of transformation. During this period, however, the understanding of national identity continues to evolve, particularly among the leading force realizing its status as a powerful national factor and in its vigilant response to external threats. However, the development of national identity during this period can be marked by contrasting approaches: succumbing to emotions, seeking quick wins, or prioritizing calmness, stability, and consistency.

In this sense, national independence marks the beginning of a new era in the development of national identity. Most importantly, it should always inspire the nation, keeping it vigilant against various negative influences.

The development of national identity in the context of transitioning to market relations presents unique challenges. On one hand, each state striving for development fosters free competition within the market, which in turn drives the country's progress. On the other hand, market conditions create an environment where individuals are free to function and pursue opportunities. In a market economy, individual well-being is directly tied to personal effort, with the state providing the necessary framework for this freedom.

The market operates under an "iron law" based on merit, not factors like nationality, religion, or gender. It rewards resourcefulness, initiative, hard work, perseverance, and dedication. Those succumbing to greed, addiction, laziness, or a "give-me" mentality are unlikely to thrive. They may revert to relying on the state or external support, hindering their ability to build a prosperous life through their own efforts.

Therefore, transitioning to market relations can create challenges for national identity development. The market offers a level playing field with equal opportunities for all, regardless of background. While those who effectively utilize these opportunities can achieve prosperity, those who don't must face the market's harsh realities. This, on the one hand, can lead to social stratification, and on the other hand, negatively impact national unity.

The negative impact of the market on national unity can be seen in the emergence of significant economic disparities among citizens. Even with the presence of initiative, resourcefulness, and determination across the population, these qualities may not be effectively used by everyone. This can lead to a division into two groups: entrepreneurs who are seen as driven and self-reliant, focused on their own well-being, and those who are perceived as lazy, greedy, and dependent.

These differences weaken national unity, which in turn can negatively affect the development of national identity. When material factors become dominant within a nation, individuals, regardless of their background, may prioritize their personal interests over the collective good. While these interests may sometimes align with national development, a focus solely on personal gain can slow the progress of national identity.

In the context of market economies, the appeal and unifying functions of national identity can diminish, potentially leading to the formation of sub-groups within the nation itself. This can create instability and chaos. The state has a crucial role to play in preventing such a situation.

If the state fails to implement measures to address these issues, the country may face significant challenges. However, it is important to acknowledge successful examples of navigating this transition. The five principles of transition to market relations developed in Uzbekistan, combined with strong social protection and a gradual approach, have demonstrably prevented the formation of sub-groups within the nation and the emergence of corruption. Notably, the implementation of these principles with a focus on national and spiritual revival has had a positive impact on the development of national identity and the successful implementation of reforms.

If, during the transition to market relations, only economic reforms were pursued while ignoring national and spiritual revival, this would certainly have a negative impact on the development of national identity. Ultimately, economic reforms might not have yielded the expected results. In the face of economic difficulties and declining living standards, prioritizing national and spiritual revival could have prevented major crises by channeling public energies towards a shared objective.

In the post-Soviet space, implementing national-spiritual revival became a central task in fostering national identity, aiming to address the thirst for cultural heritage. This process engaged everyone, regardless of their material circumstances, despite the challenges arising from market reforms.

However, today, material stratification within the nation due to market realities, as previously mentioned, poses a threat to the ongoing development of national identity. This is evident in the negative trends affecting our national spirituality. Many people prioritize material well-being over studying their heritage, customs, and traditions. The promotion of the Russian language and foreign spiritualities further complicates the picture.

For instance, some "entrepreneurs" adopt the selfish motto "I could give milk even if I was a goat," exemplifying the negative processes weakening national identity. It's unfair to solely blame the market, as mentioned earlier. A true mark of self-awareness and high spirituality lies in recognizing oneself as a representative of one's nation, with a sense of national pride, honor, and a commitment to its interests.

Material wealth should not lead to the individual psyche rejecting the concept of belonging to a nation. In the current transition phase, instead of blaming the market, the priority lies in nurturing within individuals a sense of loyalty and devotion to their people.

The fifth stage in national identity development coincides with the accelerating process of globalization. This stage presents a complex challenge: in the context of market forces, globalization can further hinder the development of national identity. It's crucial to remember that globalization can encompass different cultures and identities, not erase them. We must avoid being trapped in a narrative of inevitable cultural homogenization.

Globalization, a force reshaping economies and societies worldwide, presents a conundrum for nations seeking independent development. While it offers pathways to progress through technology and trade integration, it also poses risks to the very essence of national identity.

One key challenge lies in the asynchronous nature of these two developments. National identity, deeply rooted in history, culture, and shared values, evolves gradually. Conversely, globalization, fueled by rapid information and economic flows, unfolds at an accelerated pace. This disparity can leave developing nations feeling like they're constantly playing catch-up, struggling to preserve their unique character while embracing necessary advancements.

The economic dimension of this challenge is profound. Premature integration into the globalized market can expose developing nations to unfair competition, exacerbate existing inequalities, and leave communities feeling marginalized. This, in turn, breeds resentment and fuels internal divisions, making it even harder to foster a cohesive national identity.

Further compounding the issue is the cultural influence that often accompanies economic dependence. As developed nations become sources of technology, investment, and media, their values and practices can easily permeate societies undergoing rapid change. This can lead to a homogenization of cultures, diluting the unique traditions and customs that define a nation.

However, it's important to recognize that globalization is not a monolithic force. It presents both opportunities and risks, and navigating this complex landscape requires a nuanced approach. Here are some key strategies nations can adopt to mitigate the negative impacts and harness the positive aspects of globalization:

Selective engagement: Countries need to carefully evaluate the terms of globalization, prioritizing partnerships that foster sustainable development and cultural exchange while safeguarding national interests.

Investment in domestic capacity: Building a strong internal foundation is crucial. This includes prioritizing education, research, and infrastructure development to create a self-reliant economy and a skilled workforce.

Cultural promotion: Actively promoting and celebrating national heritage, including language, arts, and traditions, helps cultivate a sense of shared identity and belonging.

Critical media literacy: Equipping citizens with the ability to critically analyze information and cultural influences allows them to engage with the world while remaining rooted in their own values.

By adopting a proactive and strategic approach, nations can transform globalization from a threat to their identity into a force that empowers them to participate actively in the global community while preserving their unique essence. It's a delicate balancing act, but one that holds the potential for fostering inclusive and sustainable development for all.

Charting the Labyrinth: National Identity in the Face of Globalization's Tides

Globalization, a potent force shaping the world's political, economic, and cultural landscape, presents nations with a delicate balancing act. While unlocking access to advancements, knowledge, and opportunities, it also carries the potential to erode or homogenize the very essence of national identity. Understanding these vulnerabilities and devising effective strategies for protection is paramount for navigating this labyrinthine terrain.

Premature Integration: A Double-Edged Sword

Eager to catch up, developing nations might be tempted to rush into the globalized system before addressing internal disparities and societal concerns. This haste can backfire, exacerbating existing economic inequalities and social grievances. The influx of foreign goods, services, and ideologies, while offering economic benefits, can clash with cherished cultural values and traditions, creating alienation and undermining the unifying fabric of national identity. Imagine a nation rich in cultural heritage suddenly flooded with mass-produced goods and media narratives that resonate poorly with its traditional values. The resulting confusion and disconnect can breed discontent and threaten social cohesion.

Cultural Homogenization: The Erosion of Uniqueness

Another critical aspect is the inherent risk of cultural homogenization fostered by dependence on developed nations for technology and investment. While these imported elements can be catalysts for economic growth, they often come bundled with values and lifestyles that may not resonate with the recipient country's cultural norms. Over time, the pervasive influence of these external ideologies can erode the uniqueness that defines a nation, homogenizing its cultural landscape and diluting its distinctive identity. Think of a vibrant folk art tradition gradually fading away due to the popularity of homogenized global entertainment. This loss of cultural richness weakens the very foundation of national identity, leaving a sense of emptiness and disconnection.

The Time Lag and the Media's Amplification

Further complicating the equation is the time lag between developing nations catching up and developed nations continuing to advance. This creates a pressure cooker of sorts, where the rapid influx of external influences clashes with the internal process of forging a distinct national identity. The media, with its global reach and often Western-centric content, amplifies this pressure. Imagine a young generation bombarded with images and values that differ starkly from their cultural upbringing. This constant exposure can accelerate the erosion of traditional values and cultural practices, creating confusion and a sense of rootlessness.

A Nuanced Approach: Embracing Progress, Preserving Identity

However, safeguarding national identity does not necessitate rejecting globalization altogether. Instead, a nuanced approach is needed. Cultivating a strong sense of national identity must go hand-in-hand with embracing advancements that can empower economic and social progress. This requires striking a delicate balance between:

Promoting a deep understanding of national history, heritage, and cultural values through educational initiatives, cultural awareness programs, and community-driven activities. Imagine museums and schools actively engaging youth in exploring their cultural heritage, creating a sense of connection and pride.

Actively engaging with globalization on their own terms, selectively adopting technologies and investments that align with national development goals and cultural values. Think of a nation harnessing technology to modernize its agricultural sector while protecting its traditional farming practices and ensuring food security.

Nurturing a dynamic and inclusive national identity that acknowledges diversity within the population while fostering a sense of shared purpose and collective belonging. Imagine a nation celebrating its diverse ethnicities and regional cultures while uniting under a common vision for the future.

Inspiring Examples: Beacons of Hope

Several nations have successfully navigated these challenges, demonstrating that safeguarding national identity and embracing globalization are not mutually exclusive. South Korea, for example, embraced foreign technology and investment while fiercely protecting its cultural heritage through initiatives like promoting K-Pop and traditional arts globally. Thailand, while integrating into the global economy, emphasizes its unique Buddhist values and cultural traditions. These examples highlight the possibility of achieving economic progress while preserving the essence of national identity.

A Tapestry Woven Anew: Navigating the Crossroads of National Identity and Globalization

Globalization, a whirlwind of interconnectedness, sweeps across the world, reshaping landscapes and cultures with both exhilarating possibilities and daunting challenges. While it unlocks a treasure trove of scientific advancements, technological innovations, and investment opportunities, its relentless tide threatens to erode the very foundation of national identity, particularly for nations still charting their own course on the map of self-determination. Understanding these vulnerabilities and devising prudent strategies for cultural protection is paramount to traversing this complex terrain.

The Siren Song of Integration: A Premature Embrace

One of the key concerns lies in the seductive lure of unbridled integration into the globalized system. Eager to bridge the development gap, nations might be tempted to dive headfirst into the global marketplace before addressing internal economic disparities and social fissures. This hasty embrace can exacerbate existing problems, fueling public discontent and jeopardizing social stability. Moreover, the influx of foreign goods, services, and ideologies can clash with cherished cultural values and traditions, creating a sense of alienation and undermining the unifying fabric of national identity. Imagine a vibrant tapestry, woven with threads of shared history and customs, slowly unraveling under the relentless pressure of foreign influences.

Beyond Homogenization: Protecting the Wellspring of Culture

Another critical consideration is the potential homogenization of cultures due to an overreliance on developed nations for technology and investment. While these imported elements can be catalysts for economic growth, they often come bundled with values and lifestyles that may not resonate with the recipient country's cultural norms. Over time, the pervasive influence of these external ideologies can erode the uniqueness that defines a nation, homogenizing its cultural landscape and diluting its distinctive identity. Think of a vast meadow, once bursting with diverse wildflowers, slowly succumbing to the spread of a single, dominant species.

A Time Warp and the Media's Double-Edged Sword

Further complicating the equation is the "time warp" effect. Developing nations, striving to catch up, face a constant influx of external influences that clash with their internal process of forging a distinct national identity. The media, with its global reach and often Western-centric content, amplifies this pressure, potentially accelerating the erosion of traditional values and cultural practices. It's akin to a fast-forward button being pressed on cultural evolution, potentially bypassing crucial stages of organic development and leaving a nation feeling disoriented and adrift.

Beyond Dichotomy: Striking a Harmonious Balance

However, safeguarding national identity does not necessitate retreating into isolation or rejecting globalization altogether. Instead, a nuanced approach is needed. Cultivating a strong sense of national identity must go hand-in-hand with embracing advancements that can empower economic and social progress. This requires striking a delicate balance between:

Nurturing Roots and Reaching for the Sun: Nations must cultivate a deep understanding of their history, heritage, and cultural values. Educational initiatives that celebrate national narratives, cultural awareness programs that foster intergenerational transmission of traditions, and community-driven activities that revitalize customs and folklore are all vital tools. Imagine a nation's cultural identity as a majestic tree, drawing strength from its deep roots while reaching towards the sun with new growth.

Dancing with Globalization on Their Own Terms: Engaging with globalization selectively is key. Nations can adopt technologies and investments that align with national development goals and cultural values. They can also leverage global platforms to showcase their unique cultural offerings and engage in mutually beneficial cultural exchange. Think of it as a selective dance, choosing partners who respect and enrich your cultural identity, not seeking to dominate or overshadow it.

A Tapestry of Unity Woven from Diversity: Fostering a dynamic and inclusive national identity is crucial. This involves acknowledging and celebrating the diversity within the nation's population while fostering a sense of shared purpose and collective belonging. It's about creating a tapestry where individual threads retain their vibrant colors while weaving together to create a unified national image. Imagine a nation as a diverse orchestra, where each instrument contributes its unique melody to create a harmonious symphony, richer and more beautiful than any single voice alone.

A Future Woven with Hope: Continuity and Change Hand in Hand

By carefully navigating the complexities of globalization and nurturing a robust national identity, developing nations can harness the potential of both forces to forge a unique and prosperous future. The journey may be challenging, but the reward – a thriving nation with a strong sense of self, a vibrant cultural tapestry woven anew – is a beacon worth striving for. It's not about preserving a static monument to the past, but about embracing positive change while safeguarding the essence of what makes a nation unique. In this way, nations can chart a steady course, navigating the currents of globalization without losing sight of their own cultural North Star.

Imagine a nation as a voyager, embarking on a journey through the labyrinthine corridors of globalization. On one hand, the path beckons with dazzling lights, promising technological marvels, economic opportunities, and a vibrant exchange of ideas. On the other, it threatens to engulf the very essence of its identity, eroding cherished traditions and homogenizing its cultural landscape. This is the complex reality faced by developing nations, caught in the crosscurrents of globalization and the imperative to preserve their unique heritage.

The allure of globalization is undeniable. It offers a passport to progress, a chance to bridge development gaps and leapfrog technological advancements. However, this rapid integration can be a double-edged sword. Unbridled enthusiasm can lead to hasty adoption of foreign models, neglecting internal disparities and fueling social unrest. The influx of foreign goods and ideologies can clash with cherished values, creating a sense of alienation and undermining the unifying fabric of national identity. Imagine a bustling marketplace, where the familiar aroma of local spices is replaced by the sterile scent of mass-produced goods.

Furthermore, globalization often carries with it the subtle influence of dominant cultures. Overreliance on developed nations for technology and investment can lead to a subtle erosion of cultural uniqueness. Imported values and lifestyles, while potentially beneficial, can threaten to homogenize the cultural landscape, diluting the very essence of what makes a nation distinct. Think of a vibrant tapestry, its intricate threads gradually replaced by a monochromatic uniformity.

The challenge lies not in retreating from globalization altogether, but in navigating its complexities with a discerning eye. Cultivating a strong sense of national identity is not about erecting walls of isolation, but about fostering a deep understanding of one's history, heritage, and cultural values. This can be achieved through educational initiatives that celebrate national narratives, cultural awareness programs that bridge the generational gap, and community-driven activities that revitalize customs and folklore. Imagine a nation's identity as a majestic oak, drawing strength from its deep roots while reaching towards the sun with new growth.

Engagement with globalization must be strategic and selective. Nations can adopt technologies and investments that align with their development goals and cultural values. They can leverage global platforms to showcase their unique offerings and engage in mutually beneficial cultural exchanges. Think of it as a dance, choosing partners who respect and enrich your cultural identity, not seeking to replace it.

Finally, fostering a dynamic and inclusive national identity is crucial. This involves acknowledging and celebrating the diversity within the nation's population while fostering a sense of shared purpose and collective belonging. It's about creating a tapestry where individual threads retain their vibrant colors while weaving together a unified national image. Imagine a diverse orchestra, where each instrument contributes its unique melody to create a harmonious symphony.

By navigating the labyrinth with prudence and fostering a robust national identity, nations can harness the potential of both globalization and their own heritage. The journey may be challenging, but the reward – a thriving nation with a strong sense of self, a vibrant cultural tapestry woven anew – is a beacon worth striving for. It's not about preserving a static monument to the past, but about embracing positive change while safeguarding the essence of what makes a nation unique. In this way, nations can chart a steady course, navigating the currents of globalization without losing sight of their own cultural North Star.

Navigating the Rapids: Safeguarding National Identity in a Globalized World

The world dances to the rhythm of globalization, a relentless tide of interconnectedness that sweeps across borders, cultures, and economies. While its currents offer exciting opportunities for progress and exchange, they also pose a delicate challenge for developing nations, particularly those still forging their distinct identities. Like a small boat navigating a rapid, these nations must deftly navigate the powerful forces of globalization to avoid losing their cultural essence, yet harness its potential for growth.

The Erosion of Identity: A Looming Threat

One of the most significant dangers lies in the potential homogenization of cultures. As foreign goods, services, and ideologies flood in, they can subtly erode the unique tapestry of traditions, values, and beliefs that define a nation. Imagine a vibrant mosaic, its intricate tiles slowly replaced by bland uniformity. This loss of cultural distinctiveness can lead to a sense of alienation and disconnect, particularly among younger generations who may find their own heritage overshadowed by the allure of the "global."

The Time Lag and the Media's Double-Edged Sword

Further complicating the picture is the time lag between developing and developed nations. The rapid influx of external influences clashes with the internal process of forging a national identity, creating a pressure cooker environment. The media, with its global reach and often Western-centric content, amplifies this pressure, potentially accelerating the erosion of traditional values and cultural practices. It's akin to a fast-forward button being pressed on cultural evolution, potentially bypassing crucial stages of organic development.

Beyond Dichotomy: A Tapestry of Interconnected Threads

However, safeguarding national identity is not about retreating into isolation or rejecting globalization altogether. Instead, a nuanced approach is crucial. Nations must cultivate a strong sense of self while simultaneously embracing advancements that can empower economic and social progress. This requires striking a delicate balance between:

Nurturing the Roots: This involves fostering a deep understanding of national history, heritage, and cultural values. Educational initiatives that celebrate national narratives, cultural awareness programs that encourage intergenerational transmission of traditions, and community-driven activities that revitalize customs and folklore are all essential elements. Imagine a nation's cultural identity as a majestic tree, drawing strength from its deep roots while reaching towards the sun with new growth.

Engaging with the World on Their Terms: Nations can actively participate in globalization by selectively adopting technologies and investments that align with their national development goals and cultural values. They can leverage global platforms to showcase their unique cultural offerings and engage in mutually beneficial cultural exchange. Think of it as a selective dance, choosing partners who respect and enrich your cultural identity.

Weaving a Diverse Tapestry: Building a dynamic and inclusive national identity is key. This involves acknowledging and celebrating the diversity within the nation's population while fostering a sense of shared purpose and collective belonging. It's about creating a tapestry where individual threads retain their vibrant colors while weaving together a unified national image. Imagine a nation as a diverse orchestra, where each instrument contributes its unique melody to create a harmonious symphony.

Embracing Both Continuity and Change: A Tapestry Woven Anew

By carefully navigating the complexities of globalization and nurturing a robust national identity, developing nations can harness the potential of both forces to forge a unique and prosperous future. The journey may be challenging, but the reward – a thriving nation with a strong sense of self, a vibrant cultural tapestry woven anew – is a beacon worth striving for. It's not about preserving a static monument to the past, but about embracing positive change while safeguarding the essence of what makes a nation unique. In this way, nations can chart a steady course, navigating the currents of globalization without losing sight of their own cultural North Star.

4.3. FACTORS MAKING THE PROVISION OF NATIONAL AND SPIRITUAL SECURITY A NATIONAL IDEA

As we saw in the previous parts of our book, globalization is rapidly developing as a product of an objective stage in human and societal development. However, it appears unstoppable. We have cited numerous theoretical and empirical materials exploring potential crises arising from its impact on national spiritualities, the complex processes within national consciousnesses and identities, and its connections to modern civilization, with both positive and negative consequences.

Based on this information, we conclude that while restricting globalization itself is impossible, it carries the potential to link developing and less developed countries to highly developed ones first economically and intellectually, eventually leading to complete dependence. Simultaneously, claims have been made (by American scientist and statesman Patrick Buchanan) that Western natural population growth is declining, leading to future destruction by migrants. Further, opinions suggest that such fears are growing[1][lxxix].

So today, on the one hand, under the influence of globalization, titular nations embarking on the path of development and residing in less developed countries are experiencing internal processes within their national spirituality. On the other hand, this creates a situation where a new form of the Cold War threatens. This Cold War, similar to the one fought under the previous regimes of capitalism and socialism, could erupt between highly developed and now developing countries. Unless humanity takes steps to prevent it, new catastrophes may arise. Collaboration and balancing the interests of both parties are essential to avert this outcome.

However, the effectiveness of rapidly advancing globalization in achieving this balance remains questionable. Developed countries seem to see themselves as the primary beneficiaries in this process due to the unequal distribution of interests. Leveraging their economic, scientific, technical, and technological advantages, they can easily influence less developed nations embarking on the path of development. This influence extends beyond economy, science, engineering, and technology, rapidly gaining traction in the minds and hearts of people in developing and underdeveloped countries, affecting their attitudes towards spirituality, lifestyle, morality, and human values in general. As a result, these nations risk losing their distinct national and spiritual identities.

In such conditions, a natural question arises: If the sharp decline in the population in highly developed countries is mainly due to the titular nations, how can the "mass spirituality" they form today lead to the collapse of the spirituality of less developed nations in the future?

The answer to this question is as follows:

First, in developed countries today, state policy often requires migrants to master the language, values, customs, and traditions of the titular nations (as mentioned above). This may produce some results to a certain extent. Since migrants' primary motivation for coming to these countries is material gain, economic factors can offer some opportunity to sway their minds and hearts. Even if they live in these countries for many years, however, there's no guarantee they will retain their national identity.

Second, titular nations in developing and least developed countries may be unaware of the internal and external decline of their national spirituality. Economic problems in the current transition period may lead them to focus on solving daily economic and social problems, with a risk of becoming indifferent to this process. They may become accustomed to living under the influence of their more prosperous neighbors.

More precisely, titular nations in these countries may be actively striving to ensure that the "mass spirituality" they form is present in the minds and hearts of all people on the planet, both today and in the future. If we approach this issue in this way, we will always see that "in the minds of the nation's representatives, the ancestral heritage of their nation, national identity transmitted from generation to generation through heredity and parental genes, is preserved in any human condition, so the nation does not die."

Does this contradict the concept that "maybe it will improve"? Of course not! As noted above, the two sides—those who can somehow win in the current process between maintaining the dominance of titular nations in developed countries and losing time for titular nations in less developed countries—are a priority for the future. The main struggle is not to waste time, but to use it effectively. Along with economic and other factors, the level of self-preservation in the national mentality plays a leading role.

True, this process also has a "peak" (endpoint). But no one can predict how many generations it will take to form. Humanity needs to return to the same "top" and start all over again, returning to its national lands in the development of human consciousness and self-consciousness, which today is losing its "image" and identity. This is because a person is unique, a representative of a nation, and an heir to their ancestors. However, there is a dangerous aspect to this that has not yet reached its "peak" level.

The contradiction between the growing aspirations of the peoples of developing and less developed countries to preserve their language, customs, traditions, and values may ultimately lead to the complete destruction of today's civilization. If this happens, no one can guarantee that neither side will miss out on today's high levels of development and opportunities that it has achieved in a sustainable manner.

Today, we are witnessing such negative processes. A prime example of this is the emergence of calls for self-defense on both sides. If we take into account the fact that today, under various pretexts, the most developed countries are the only force interfering in the internal affairs of states, making it a practice to demonstrate their strength, such approaches have become a tradition. For titular nations, protecting their identity in less developed countries will become a major challenge.

Today, the intellectual potential of mankind has developed to an unprecedented level and reached the level of understanding everything. In such circumstances, there is a growing need to extend human life to take advantage of the opportunity to prevent the civilization it has achieved from collapsing, balancing the confrontation between the parties not by force, but by mutual benefit and education in self-defense. Of course, this is high politics in international relations. The focus of this policy on serving universal development remains an urgent task.

Today, it is possible to prevent the massive development of the use of force. This is a universal idea: to preserve the identity of both sides, to protect national spirituality from the negative consequences of globalization. While the threat may not seem significant for people living in developed countries, in practice, the impoverishment of national spirituality in them has reached a "peak" level. This is reflected in their search for protection from the processes of spiritual impoverishment. However, the spirit of domination prevails on the path to the formation of their "mass spirituality" and its spread across the globe.

The most surprising thing is that they also realize this nascent "mass spirituality" is formed due to the impoverishment of their national spirituality, and their progressive intellectuals are promoting the idea of preserving national spirituality from this. Unfortunately, these ideas have not yet reached the level of the national idea that has been forming in these countries for many years, and the prevalence of the tendency towards dominance in the national consciousness does not allow for this. So, it is true that today "mass spirituality" is being formed, and nations following the path of development are destroying national spirituality from within and without. In such conditions, the preservation of our national spirituality and ensuring its security remain key tasks in our national development.

There are opportunities. The challenge is to understand the current difficult situation and to use these opportunities effectively. Therefore, the main factors that make our national and spiritual security a national idea are:

1. The impact of today's globalisation on our national spirituality, the development of the national intelligentsia above the level of speed;

2. The continuation of our national and spiritual revival, the in-depth study of our spiritual and material heritage that has not yet reached our people, its transmission to our people and, on this basis, the improvement of our national spirituality in accordance with contemporary developments. 3;

3. To make the national heritage an integral part of the consciousness and world view of modern youth, and to prevent feelings of alienation from national spirituality from arising in their minds, enriching their consciousness at the expense of national and universal values;

4. To achieve the state status of our national language within the limits established by the current legislation;

5. Strengthening the activity of the intelligentsia in protecting the national spirituality from the negative consequences of globalisation, achieving freedom from the feelings of "passive" observation and indifference in their psyche;

6. Development of rural cultural and spiritual life at the peak of globalisation, enriching the minds of the rural population with universal human ideas, acquaintance with the causes of continuing tragedies and strengthening the focus on maintaining conservative relations in the development of national spirituality;

7. Consistent improvement of the idea of national development, effective use of propaganda means in the consciousness and practice of the people of our country, increasing the activity of the media and the Internet and other means available in the country to protect our national spirituality from external negative influences;

8. Establishment of the rule of law and consistent development of democratic values.

Of course, the practical application of each of the above tasks involves several main areas. If their meaning and possibilities are not revealed, they will remain at the level of dry conversations. So let's try to comment on them:

The first factor is the development of our national intelligentsia, which exceeds the speed of the impact of today's globalisation on our national spirituality. What role can an intellectual play in protecting national spirituality from the negative consequences of globalisation?

First of all, it should be noted that a national intellectual is an elite with a high intellect that has grown and matured within a nation and has developed the ability to quickly understand the positive and negative processes taking place in national development. Before considering the role and significance of the national intellectual in protecting national spirituality and the nation as a whole from the negative consequences of globalisation, let us first focus on the meaning and content of the term "intellectual".

In scientific literature and various dictionaries, there are different opinions on the concepts of "intellectual", "intellectual property" and "intelligence". They are interpreted in different ways. In particular, in "Philosophy: an encyclopaedic dictionary", "Intellect (lat. Intellectus - intellect, perception, understanding) in the broadest sense: human activity based on full knowledge of the nature of what is happening and manifested by it; in the narrowest sense: it refers to a person's ability to think.

According to the National Encyclopaedia of Uzbekistan, "Intellect (lat. Intellegence - to be educated) is a social class of intellectuals who occupy a certain place in the social system and are mainly engaged in intellectual work"[2]. "Intellect (lat. Intellectus - to know, understand, comprehend) is the mental abilities of a person: the ability to accurately reflect and change life, the environment in consciousness, the ability to think, read, learn. to know the world and social experience; the ability to solve various problems, to make decisions, to act rationally, to foresee events[3]. The Explanatory Dictionary of Spirituality defines the basic concepts as "intelligence" (Latin inlectus - intelligence, perception, mind) - in the broad sense: human activity based on full knowledge of the nature of events and manifested through them; in the narrow sense: the ability of human thinking, reasoning... "[4], if we state that "intelligence (Latin Intellegence - to be educated) is a social class of the intelligentsia that occupies a certain place in the social system and is primarily engaged in mental labour activity[5], in the recently published "Encyclopedic Dictionary of Philosophy", intellect (Latin: Intellectus - to know, to understand, to perceive) is a person's mental ability; the ability to accurately reflect and change life and the environment in consciousness, thinking, reading and learning, understanding the world and accepting social experience; solving various problems, making decisions, acting rationally, the ability to foresee events, perception, memory, thinking, speech, and so on. are part of the intellect"[6][lxxx].

In addition to the above, other dictionaries define the concept of "intelligence" differently. In particular, the "Concise Political Dictionary" (revised and revised second edition), published by Russian scientists and translated into Uzbek, defines the concept of "intelligence", and not the concept of "intelligence", as follows: from the intelligentsia - consciousness, intelligence) - social stratum of people engaged in intellectual, mainly complex[7], creative work. Similar views are expressed in other dictionaries. There is even an opinion that the concept of "intelligence" in Russian is an alternative to the Uzbek words "wise" and "clever"[8].

If you look closely at the above, you will find different translations of the word "intellect" from the Latin word "Intellectus" in Uzbek. In particular, in one dictionary it is called "knowledge, understanding, perception", in another - "reason, understanding, intellect", B. Isakov called it "an alternative to the Uzbek words" wise "," smart ". So to this day there are different relations. Of course, they are different. Because in dictionaries and literature each author expresses a relationship according to which aspect he or she prioritises.

In our opinion, in order to understand the essence of the concept of "intelligence", it is necessary to pay attention to at least two aspects: firstly, to whom and to what it is applied, and secondly, it is a simple mind, perception, intelligence. It is knowledge, understanding, perception or human thinking, not the ability to think.

Because if we look at it in the same way, it is no different from the general potential that all human beings have. Moreover, all of the above will be available to one degree or another. In this sense, "intelligence" can be seen not as a simple "indicator", but as a highly developed concept that is an indicator of the ability to influence something. Its lexical meaning in dictionaries and other literature also changed when it was translated into Latin. This makes it somewhat difficult to understand its meaning. Thus, in our opinion, intelligence is a combination of highly developed scientific, technical, technological intelligence capable of strongly influencing the known mind, "thinking", "knowledge", the ability to understand the environment, events and phenomena, as well as changes in them. clear. On the basis of these indicators, it will be possible to recognise and understand different levels of intelligence.

Now, when applied to "nation", it is understood in the context of its intellect, its ability to show what it is capable of, its unique ability to create material and spiritual wealth, its spirituality, thinking, mental and physical abilities. There are some differences between the terms "intelligence" and "intellectual potential". "Intellect" is the specific national potential of the "nation", which distinguishes it from others by these existing "complex" indicators, the national intellectual potential not only distinguishes a nation from others, but also its achievements in science, technology, universal with them. y you can understand the contribution to development, an indicator of strength, power and available opportunities in protecting itself from external negative influences.

More precisely, the difference between national "intelligence" and "intellectual potential" in this definition is that the former refers to the mentality of the nation, the existing indicators of intelligence, knowledge and thinking and their development, the influence on general development, protection from external harmful influences. Obviously, even in real development, a nation, with the intelligence, knowledge and thinking it possesses, can influence general development and protect itself from external harmful influences. At the same time, it can rise to the level of a nation with its own intellectual potential only if it develops it on the level of general development, raises it to the level of material power and strengthens its "I".

The presence of such potential today will be of great practical importance for the future of any nation. Turning now to the role of national intellectual potential in protecting the nation and national spirituality from its negative consequences in the context of globalisation, we would like to emphasise that even if globalisation itself is a new stage in human development, this does not mean its status as a material being. This is only manifested in the fact that the achievements of science and technology in the field of science, technology and modern mass communication with the intellect, knowledge and talent of mankind are approaching the unity of the globe as a material force. So, when we think about the impact of globalisation here, it can be emphasised once again that it is based on intellectual potential.

Why, then, can the national intellectual potential be one of the important factors in ensuring the nation and its national and spiritual security?

The reasons are as follows: First, as mentioned above, the national intellectual is the leading elite that has grown up from within the country in the creation and application of new scientific discoveries that have led to his high intelligence, knowledge, talents and national development; second, unlike other strata of the nation, the national intellectual quickly recognises the "pain points" of the nation, feels them in his mind and heart, and takes the initiative in strengthening national unity in overcoming them; Thirdly, it plays a leading role in the formation of the national idea, implements it in the minds and hearts of the representatives of the nation, in their minds and hearts, in such values as nationalism, patriotism, national pride, pride, responsibility for the future of the nation, inter-ethnic harmony and versatility; Fourthly, because of its potential, it anticipates to some extent the negative processes taking place in national spirituality and helps to inform the representatives of the nation about the possible consequences. Considering these aspects, the national intellectual is an integral part of the national spirituality and an important factor in protecting it from external negative influences.

Today, the tasks of a national intellectual to protect national spirituality from the negative consequences of globalisation are expanding more than ever. In our opinion, they are reflected in the following:

a) First of all, to develop school education on the level of today's globalisation, to strengthen its activities. Today, young people who graduate from any school should be actively involved in the acquisition of modern knowledge, awareness of the achievements of science, technology, people with a high level of intellectual potential;

b) Today's intellectuals must realise that the school is the centre of enlightenment, which first of all forms the main force of the nation's future, and then take an active part in its implementation in the minds of all people in society. Despite the fact that in our country a lot of attention is paid to school education, a lot of money is spent on its development and strengthening of its material base, there is a growing need for a gradual increase in the level of knowledge of students in accordance with modern requirements. If school education is not consistently improved according to today's requirements, it will be difficult to achieve the expected results in both secondary and tertiary education. This is because a student who graduates from a school with a shallow education can enter higher education institutions and, no matter how hard he tries, become a "higher" educated person with a shallow education. This is confirmed by our long experience. To solve the same problem, intellectuals must take the lead in the nationwide task of raising school education to a higher level;

It is not only their financial interests that are at stake, therefore it will be of practical importance to fully realise that loyalty to the future of the nation is a responsibility. It is necessary to make it clear in the minds and hearts of the collective of schools where the national intelligentsia is trained that the most urgent task is to increase the responsibility of teachers in raising the prestige of schools with the state language (Uzbek). It is no secret that today many parents in our country feel a sense of insecurity and send their children to schools and classes where the language of instruction is Uzbek. Although they are more expensive (i.e. the cost of language learning), it is not news that they try to send their children to schools and classes that teach in English and Russian, depending on their ability. Incidentally, it should be noted that the more foreign languages our people know, the more opportunities they have to go out into the world and bring success to our country. However, this should not be done at the expense of reducing the prestige of the mother tongue. The first is the decline of our mother tongue, as in the former Soviet Union, the rise of Russian and the danger that Uzbek will be reduced to the level of an "auxiliary" language used in everyday life, not in science. On the other hand, the fact that the national language is not taught at an adequate level in schools leads to a decline in its prestige among young people, which in turn leads to a weakening of the national spirit and an impoverishment of national spirituality;

d) The consistent improvement of the national intellectual potential should be a constant emphasis not only in the cities, but also in the heads of regions, districts and villages. Taking into account the attention paid by the leadership of our country to increasing the intellectual potential of young people, comprehensive support for talented young people should be provided, including material support for gifted children at school, as well as assistance in continuing their studies at leading foreign universities. "The level of a nationwide challenge for local leaders, farmers, entrepreneurs and other community organisations. It is necessary for all representatives of the nation to realise that its implementation today will bring practical results tomorrow.

Today, if the state does everything possible to support talented young people, such as the state prize named after Zulfiya. Zulfiya, presidential scholarships, various grants and sending them to study abroad, then good deeds for the development of the national intelligentsia will be carried out at the level of their villages and towns. and we cannot buy technological advances from abroad, we will rise to the level of overseas sales.

The formation and development of the national intelligentsia should become the sacred dream and practice not only of the state but also of every representative of the nation. If we do not realise today that raising our national intellectual potential to the highest level is the basis of our national development, we must teach our people, especially our youth, that tomorrow we will become intellectually dependent on others and will not be able to participate in globalisation on an equal footing. If we do not do this, we may not be able to reach the level we dream of tomorrow. Therefore, it is necessary to ensure the leadership of our national intelligentsia in the relevant fields.

Japan, which suffered the greatest loss of national intellectual potential during the Second World War, and Germany, whose housing industry was completely destroyed during the war, are now among the developed countries with a population of about 1.5 billion people in 20 years. the need for China, India and other countries with a population of more than one billion people to sell their intellectual potential in the world market, make a worthy contribution to world development and form a sense of national identity in our youth. Because time is changing so fast that people do not have time to realise its speed, to understand the essence of this process, to preserve their identity in it, which in turn leads to a high development of the national intellectual potential. Today we feel that its role in preserving the nation in the process of globalisation is growing day by day.

The swift advancement of globalization highlights the pressing issue of national intellectual participation. This involves recognizing the necessity to compete with developed countries in order to capture the global market by utilizing our intellectual potential. However, this awareness appears to be lagging behind the rapidly evolving processes. However, an important factor in the future of our nation is the ability to utilise the achievements of others and sell more of our own.

Today, the experience of countries around the world confirms that the primary driver of the globalization process is not the wealth of underground resources, but the highly developed intellectual potential of a country. Countries with a high intellectual potential, strength, intelligence, talent, knowledge, determination, and willpower will be able to develop new resources to ensure the growth of their nation and attract development for their people. The day of resources may come to an end, but these countries will continue to thrive. In this regard, developing national intellectual potential is crucial in protecting the nation and its spirituality from the negative consequences of globalization. This will enable equal participation with developed countries. On May 20, 2011, First President Islam Karimov issued a decree titled 'On measures to strengthen the material and technical base of higher educational institutions and radically improve the quality of training highly qualified specialists'. The decree outlines the tasks facing higher educational institutions in the development of higher education. Its implementation will enable the development of the intellectual potential of our country to meet modern requirements.

The second crucial aspect of ensuring national and spiritual security is maintaining the ongoing national and spiritual revival that has taken place since gaining independence and continues to progress today. Much work has been done in this regard, and there is a wealth of literature available on the subject. Even foreign politicians and visitors to our country acknowledge the achievements made in this area. Our accomplishments are our own and cannot be taken away. However, if we do not limit ourselves and strive to understand tasks and problems while seeking solutions, the value of our achievements may decrease over time.

Our main task today is to

develop translations of scientific and educational manuscripts in Uzbek, which have been passed down from our ancestors, in order to continue the preservation of material monuments.

To enhance the promotion of our heritage, particularly among our people, and also at the international level. This will serve as a foundation for creating excellent scientific, artistic, and literary works that will positively contribute to the enrichment of the national spirit.

C) We rely on technology in our daily lives, including in the construction of housing and modernizing our customs, traditions, and values. It serves as the primary source for the formation of national spirituality in the 21st century.

Currently, work is being carried out in all of the aforementioned areas. However, the restoration and promotion of our heritage among the population is dependent on our national 'image' and psyche. Globalization can help prevent the erosion of our national spirituality. Until now, we have not been able to create works of art that celebrate our national and spiritual heritage, including its glory, originality, and beauty, which are no less significant than the heritage of other nations. Our heritage is universal and charming, as recognized by people worldwide. Although our material and spiritual heritage is as rich as that of any other nation in its positive influence on the glorification of man, spiritual maturity, perfection, universality, and nationality, there is a lack of works of art dedicated to presenting it at the level of our people. We are interested in historical films from Japan, China, and Turkey, not to deny their necessity, but to enrich our national spirit with our own heritage. Today, there is a desire and need to appreciate high-quality works of art that glorify our heritage and provide spiritual nourishment. However, the level of satisfaction does not meet the demand due to various objective and subjective reasons. It is often claimed that there is insufficient funding to create works of art based on the heritage of our ancestors. In market conditions, obtaining money is difficult as it is not freely given and the state requires accountability for any funds provided. It is important to consider this objective situation, as well as the financial responsibilities of a large family. However, when it comes to safeguarding a nation's future, including its national spirituality, security, and opportunities, every citizen must draw upon the legacy of our ancestors. This legacy is the lifeblood of our spirituality and enables us to rise to the challenge of contributing to the spiritual nourishment of our people. It is important to maintain objectivity and avoid subjective evaluations, while ensuring clear and concise language with a logical flow of information. Additionally, the use of precise subject-specific vocabulary is encouraged to convey meaning accurately.

However, those who propagate 'mass spirituality' and implant it in the minds of people worldwide are now earning and squandering money. It is important to note that most of these funds are not allocated from the state treasury but come from those who know how to earn. On the one hand, they win competitions in the field of national spirituality, and on the other hand, they receive significant benefits. Using their experience can also be effective in protecting our national spirituality from the violence of 'mass spirituality' and ensuring its sustainable security.

Today, we have another opportunity to create works of art that can withstand the negative effects of globalization, based on our national and spiritual heritage. The financing problem could be solved if the Oliy Majlis improves the regulatory documents that provide loans to individuals and legal entities from banks in our country, with certain benefits for their creation, as well as strengthens control over their implementation. Today, banks provide loans to entrepreneurs, farmers, and those employed in production. As a result, the country's economy is developing, and the well-being of our people is improving. This practice can also be applied to create scientific works of art. Repaying a loan can be challenging at first. However, creating works that can compete with foreign art will meet the growing needs of our people. Both parties will benefit.

Educating writers, artists, playwrights, scientists, and professionals to take bank loans without fear and use them to create art is also important. It is possible that the created works may fail to meet people's expectations or may not be effectively promoted, leading to bankruptcy. Therefore, there is a concern in this regard. However, enriching our national spirituality through the heritage of our ancestors is crucial for ensuring our national and spiritual security. In this sense, one should not hesitate to make use of such opportunities.

When we believe that our national and spiritual revival is rooted in the heritage of our ancestors, it is important to note that there is another issue at hand. This issue stems from the indifference of both the public and experts in the field towards contemporary works of art and literature. The principle of 'I don't touch you, you don't touch me' has become a prevalent practice in literature and art. This has led to the popularization of market-based, low-quality works. Unfortunately, objective evaluation and constructive criticism are not common practices. As noted by the literary critic Shukhrat Rizo, many individuals, including politicians, economists, officials, and artists, are afraid of criticism. The reasons for this fear are unclear. If the criticism is accurate, it reveals the essence of a person or event. It exposes intentions, motives, interests, hypocrisy, sincerity, and capabilities. Although it may be frightening and uncomfortable, it is necessary for growth and improvement.

There would be many topical speeches under the headlines of criticism, such as 'two opinions on the work', 'open letter', 'attitude', and 'debate'. Even now, there is a need for a benevolent approach that speaks boldly in analysis, convinces the creator, improves their writing, and satisfies their next job. Impartial and honest criticism is essential. It is a challenge for development to prevent the production of works that lack talent, sincerity, and are created solely for commercial purposes, whether they are presented on screen or stage[10]. This requires proper public scrutiny.

This approach is not only applicable to literature and art but also to defended dissertations and published monographs. It highlights the growing need for the continuation of national and spiritual revival. We are discussing not only works of art and art but also the entirety of the heritage left to us by our ancestors in the fields of science and education. The spirituality of a nation is multifaceted, and it is practically important to protect it from external negative influences for the harmonious development of science, literature, art, philosophy, and the dedication of the nation's representatives.

When considering the need to preserve our ancestors' heritage, it is important to emphasise the significance of reviving traditional folk culture. This culture is created by the people themselves and holds an invaluable place in our value system. It is a treasure that gives strength and inspiration to the mind and psyche. According to Professor U. Karabaev, traditional folk culture was developed to meet the historical and spiritual needs of ethnic groups through their intellectual and creative activities. Karabaev's statement highlights the importance of traditional folk culture in our lives. This heritage is passed down from generation to generation, polished and improved over the centuries, and plays a crucial role in the spiritual development of people. It has a moral healing effect on our society and helps to stabilize humanity[11]

During the years of independence, our country has made significant progress in restoring traditional folk culture. Specifically, the revival of Navruz and the participation of young people in folk dances, sayings, and costumes from each region inherited from our ancestors have had a positive impact on developing love for our land and interest in its development. If popularity is increased, the ability to protect this national spirituality from external threats will expand, ensuring its security.

It is important to note that the national and spiritual revival of the Uzbek people is an ongoing process with a solid foundation, rich heritage, and a worthy place in world civilization. In this regard, the following views of First President Islam Karimov are worth citing. The assertion that our people are 'strong and energetic' is not without merit. The assertion that our people are 'strong and energetic' is not without merit. The assertion that our people are 'strong and energetic' is not without merit. It is my belief that the Uzbek people possess great strength and energy^{12} [lxxxii]. The discovery of this wealth and its use for the national and spiritual enrichment of our people, as well as meeting the growing needs of the rapidly changing modern world, remains a priority in our national and spiritual revival.

The second factor related to the security of our national spirituality is making our national and spiritual heritage an integral part of the consciousness and worldview of our youth. We present this task as an independent direction for two reasons. Firstly, the majority of our country's population are young people who require special attention in this area. Secondly, modern youth have varying attitudes towards national and spiritual revival, as well as the assimilation of their ancestors' heritage. Additionally, some youth imitate 'mass spirituality', which is becoming increasingly 'modern'. As children of the nation, they are aware of the importance of assimilating their land and ancestral heritage. It is crucial to avoid subjective evaluations and biased language, and to maintain a clear and logical structure with causal connections between statements. The language should be formal, value-neutral, and free from grammatical errors, spelling mistakes, and punctuation errors. Additionally, precise subject-specific vocabulary should be used when necessary. The content of the improved text must be as close as possible to the source text, and no new aspects should be added. They possess knowledge of science, technology, and modern communication, which drive globalization. However, many are influenced by 'mass spirituality,' making it challenging for them to preserve their national identity. Our national and spiritual revival is not keeping up with the rapidly changing needs of our youth. Rather than criticising them for enjoying the 'mass spirituality' that is formed on the spiritual and moral soil of foreign countries, or for their unwillingness to defend themselves to some extent, we need to offer an alternative 'product'. Otherwise, do we have the right to accuse some young people of being indifferent to spirituality and national values, as well as imitating foreigners? It is important to ask a fair question.

In October and November 2010, a sociological survey[13] was conducted by myself and my student Elbek Khalikov at the Department of Fundamentals of Philosophy and Spirituality of the Tashkent Chemical-Technological Institute, where I work. The results showed that 62% of residents, 60% of students, and 46% of employees were able to answer the survey questions, while 24% of residents, 29% of students, and 34% of employees responded with 'don't know'. Among the respondents, 14% of those in the district, 11% of students, and 19% of workers were unsure (see Figure 1).

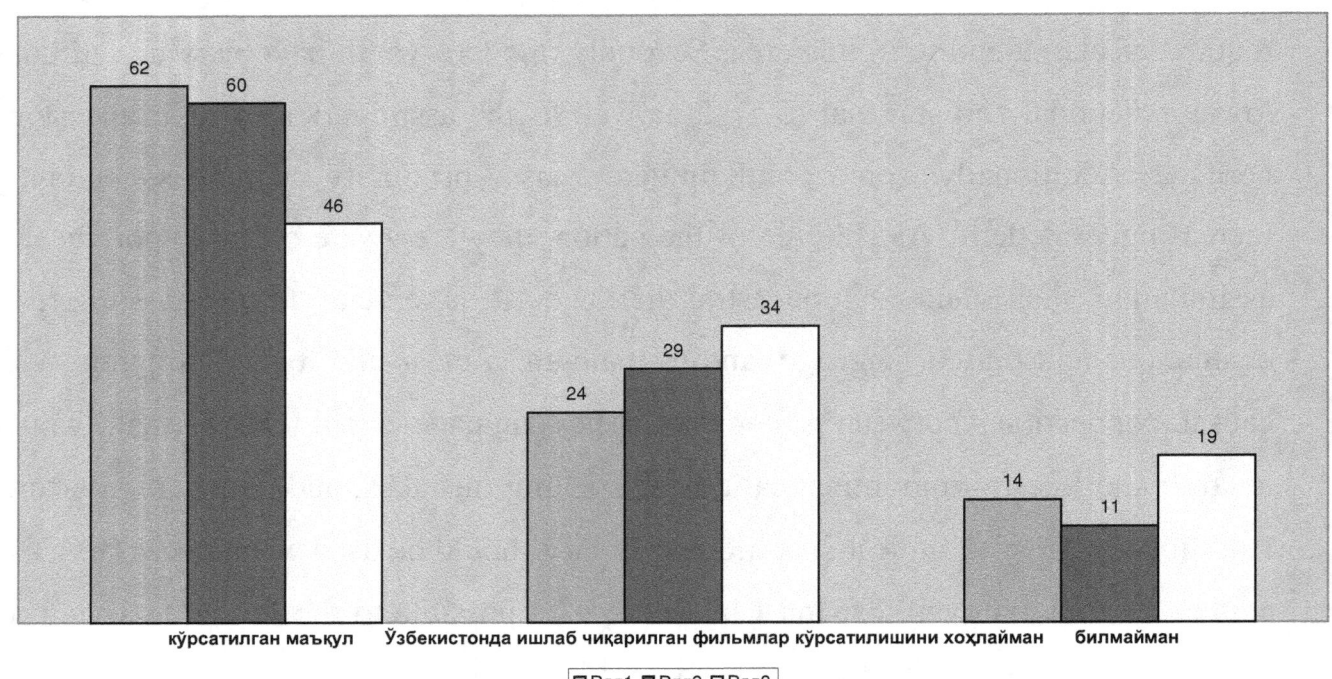

1-диаграмма. Ўзбекистон телевидениесида чет эл кинофильмлари кўрсатилишига муносабатингиз:

Foreign films in Uzbek language, although dubbed and broadcasted in Uzbekistan, maintain their original content and ideological message. Therefore, they can be considered as part of foreign television programs.

According to a survey, 56% of respondents expressed interest in watching foreign films on Uzbek television, while 44% preferred Uzbek films. This indicates a stable demand for foreign films in Uzbekistan. The reasons for this include:

The population of Uzbekistan is connected with the natural interests of the peoples of foreign countries in life, lifestyle and art. This connection is not necessarily related to activities carried out in Uzbekistan or ignored.

Given the significant impact of cinematography on the development of human consciousness and society, the comprehensive development of Uzbekistan's national cinema during the years of independence, and the creation of necessary material and spiritual conditions, new films are being produced that cover various topics related to history and contemporary life. For instance, the film 'Alpomish' has been produced, and 'The Last Days' has been reworked. It is pleasing to note that Uzbek films have received awards at prestigious film festivals. However, it must be objectively stated that a modern hero who can profoundly influence the education of young people has not yet been portrayed. Most of the films being produced depict the current reality, but fail to deeply explore its acute problems and remain distant from people's lives[14]

lxxxiii

Secondly, viewers seek exemplary and inspiring characters that contribute to the development of the market economy and democratic processes. If they cannot find such characters in national works, they turn to foreign works. For instance, a public opinion poll titled 'What programs would you like Uzbek television to broadcast?' revealed this trend. When surveyed, the majority of students indicated that they would watch a Korean television series called 'I Want to See Kim Nara', which tells the story of a girl who overcomes various challenges. This series was previously broadcast on Uzbek television.

Additionally, the Uzbek film industry currently fails to meet the demands of its audience in terms of both quantity and quality. It was heartening to see a full audience in attendance, not just during the premiere. In 2003, around 5-6 thousand viewers attended the Navoi Cinema Palace in Tashkent daily to watch the 'best film', but by 2010, this number had dropped to 700-800. Currently, 90% of films produced promote spiritual poverty, while only 10% strive for maturity. However, spiritually poor films can distract the audience. The film's audience was truly disappointed, which is a great tragedy[15][lxxxiv].

Generating interest in Russian cinema and theatre is crucial for safeguarding our spirituality against negative external influences. Television and film professionals have already produced films featuring characters that can deeply resonate with viewers, providing them with a profound understanding of life's meaning and noble ideals, while also serving as an inspiration for overcoming life's challenges. Therefore, there is no time to waste. According to the First President of Uzbekistan, Islam Karimov, introducing theoretical ideas about spirituality into public consciousness requires constant effort and thoughtful organization within the system. Without this, it is unlikely that we will achieve our goals or reach the hearts of the people. That is why today we have access to a wide range of media, including education, the press, television, the internet, theatre, cinema, literature, music, painting and sculpture. It is important to strengthen our efforts to meet the spiritual needs of people and keep up with the demands of the times[16][lxxxv].

The President assigns tasks to education personnel, the media, and those involved in educational work to address the issue of decreasing national spirituality among both the youth and older generations. The following example from journalist Bakhtiyor Khaidarov's life illustrates this trend. In recent years, several Korean drama series such as Summer Scent, Autumn Hair, Jewel of the Palace, Ruler of the Sea, The Last Queen, Jumong, and Song of the Prince have gained popularity. These dramas have increased our interest in the history of the Korean people and their unique spirituality. However, we have also experienced some strange events, as the saying goes: 'All good things come to an end.' The market for merchandise featuring Jumong heroes, such as T-shirts and baseball caps, as well as toy guns, is gaining momentum. On the street, there are boys named 'Jumong' holding a 'sword' and 'bow'. Additionally, I overheard a woman in the market recently calling someone 'So Seona!', which is a nickname for a compatriot from Korea. However, I am Uzbek and not So Seona. The woman's tone conveyed a sense of pride in the nickname.

In the past, Indian films influenced the names that were popular among our girls, such as Samira, Sunel, Ramesh, Radha, Indira, and Rita. It is possible that in the future, we may see an increase in Uzbek-Korean names. It is worth noting that the name mentioned in the example, Jaloliddin Manguberdi, is not relevant to the topic at hand, but rather a character from the show Jumong that the boy is imitating. It is evident that the individual in question has not viewed any cartoons depicting their heroism and bravery. While this may be understandable, it is not excusable. What about adults? A recent acquaintance of mine stated, 'My friend was awarded the Order of Igamberdi by the government.' Initially, I was unsure of what he meant. However, I later discovered that he was referring to his friend who had received the Manguberdi Order. Is it appropriate to laugh when an adult confuses Manguberdi with Igamberdi? Isn't it peculiar that a girl named Gulnisa is consistently referred to as 'Gulya', and Maksud as 'Max' in an attempt to appear modern?

While it is admirable to aspire to the accomplishments of others in various fields, it is important to avoid mere imitation and preserve one's cultural identity[17,lxxxvi].

The journalist's example is not an exaggeration. Unfortunately, negative situations like that can happen to anyone. Firstly, media outlets prioritize profits over critical analysis, resulting in the production of marketable content rather than informative journalism. The reasons for this are twofold. Secondly, they fail to learn from their mistakes and continue to prioritize sales over quality reporting. Unfortunately, many of these products are produced and marketed at the expense of the state. Additionally, the creation of new television programs that appeal to young people should not only meet demand but also promote national spirituality. It is important to avoid the negative impact of globalization on our cultural heritage. Thirdly, it is difficult to accept products that are deeply rooted in the former Soviet Union's consciousness and mentality, such as in art, artistic creativity, and media, excluding television, cinema, theater, and other areas. It is slow to get rid of inherited attitudes that conflict with our progress, such as imitation and faith, and to see them as the ultimate reality, albeit in a negative context. Efforts to achieve material well-being and prosperity are accelerating, but spiritual development lags behind.

To ensure that our national and spiritual heritage becomes an integral part of the worldview of young people, it is necessary to elevate literature, art, and media to a new level. Concerns about the necessity of relying on our national lands, particularly in the creation of works of art, may be dismissed as mere slogans or attempts to demonstrate nationalism. However, the empirical evidence presented above suggests otherwise.

If we do not prevent these processes of disintegration today, or at least maintain the current situation, it will be too late tomorrow. The main task is to enrich the minds and worldviews of our youth, not at the expense of the 'mass spirituality' that has formed in rapidly developing countries, but at the expense of our national and spiritual heritage, created by the heart and life experience of our ancestors. Realising this is a challenging task. It is not merely a matter of making a superficial change or promoting false slogans or materialistic desires. Rather, it involves developing internal potential, consciousness, and worldview while preserving our national identity and heritage. A careful approach is necessary to protect individuals from the negative effects of globalization. The expression of national spirit in works of art can help replace the 'mass spirituality' from abroad and satisfy the growing thirst of young people.

At the same time, it is important to note that there is a challenge in raising awareness among young people about works of art and culture that express the national spirit. The promotion of national and spiritual heritage, as well as works of art, is not keeping up with current demand. It is widely acknowledged that few young people choose to visit bookstores or museums to learn about the heritage, history, and sacrifices of our ancestors and people for our independence. It is worth noting that museums and theaters today have been directed by the country's leadership to educate young people, particularly schoolchildren, lyceums, colleges, and university students, in the spirit of patriotism, nationalism, and humanity. This is achieved by enriching their consciousness and worldview with our national and spiritual heritage. Additionally, one day a month has been declared as a day of spiritual enlightenment, where public transport is provided to other places. It can be concluded that this event is proving to be fruitful. This is a common trend among most young people. The desire for a national identity is being instilled in the consciousness and worldview of our youth. However, some of them are being educated through television, the internet, and other technical means. Additionally, in recent years, there has been an increase in the number of young people in the education system who are 'enriching' their spirituality with the help of these tools. The internet provides access to a vast amount of information, but it does not provide the same spiritual strength to the human heart and psyche as works of art, theatre, or cinema.

It is important to acknowledge that modern technology, such as television and the internet, can have the effect of dehumanising individuals. Television, the internet, and other technological advancements have been known to hinder the critical thinking abilities of young people. It is important to cultivate a culture of appreciation for literature, art, and other forms of creative expression from an early age. This will not only strengthen their connection to their national and spiritual heritage but also provide them with the necessary spiritual nourishment. To achieve this, it is necessary to elevate the effectiveness of current propaganda means and factors in our country to meet modern standards.

It is important to note that teaching Philosophy in higher education can enhance critical thinking and broaden students' perspectives on historical events and ideas. However, there is a need to update the curriculum to keep up with current trends and developments. Given that there are only two hours of lectures on the natural science views of Central Asian thinkers, or 16 hours of lectures on this topic in general, it is important to consider how our highly educated cadres can form philosophical thinking that is methodologically important for their fields and have sufficient knowledge of their scientific views. This issue should be discussed in detail with the relevant ministries and departments. Whether we like it or not, we cannot ignore this issue if we want to prevent the minds and hearts of our youth from being influenced by the ideas and ideologies of others. As the First President stated, maintaining the inviolability of a state's borders requires military power and armed forces, which are as essential as water and air. The protection of the spiritual integrity of our people, particularly the younger generation, is a matter of great concern. It is important to consider what we should rely on for this purpose[18][lxxxvii].

Thus, in addition to our work and achievements during the years of independence, aimed at integrating our national and spiritual heritage into the minds and worldviews of young people, we must also acknowledge that in today's rapidly changing and globalized world, 'mass spirituality' is a significant factor... Our national and spiritual heritage is rich and imbued with a sense of humanity. By making it an integral part of the minds and worldview of our youth, we can ensure our national and spiritual security and participate on an equal footing in globalization.

To ensure the security of our national spirituality in the context of globalization, compliance with our language at the level established by law must be achieved.

This year marks the 25th anniversary of the recognition of Uzbek as the state language. It is enshrined in the Constitution of the Republic of Uzbekistan as a crucial symbol of state sovereignty. Article 4 of the Constitution states that 'The state language of the Republic of Uzbekistan is Uzbek. The Republic of Uzbekistan respects the languages, customs, and traditions of all nations and peoples living on its territory and creates conditions for their development[19][lxxxviii]. Since gaining independence, significant efforts have been made to uphold this right as enshrined in our Basic Law. In the past, Russian lost its prestige, resulting in job applications being written in Russian and both large and small meetings being held in the language. This was the case even in fields such as natural, technical, technological, medical, and fundamental sciences. Additionally, yesterday's study of Russian in the countryside is a testament to its widespread use. Furthermore, social and humanitarian sciences were taught in Russian to freshmen in higher educational institutions. It was unfortunate that individuals who were not proficient in the Russian language, regardless of their job performance, were deemed 'illiterate' and faced discrimination. Dissertations in fields such as technical, technological, natural, medical, fundamental, and socio-economic sciences were written and defended in Russian, even if they were in the Uzbek language. It is worth noting that the use of the term 'Russian' in this context has led to certain thoughts, events, and processes. During the Soviet era, the Uzbek language was not used for scientific or everyday purposes. The materials of the congress, plenum, and other materials of the CPSU were promoted, as it was the 'core and driving force' of society in the former Soviet Union. Additionally, a single day of political preparation was announced once a month to inform the public about its daily activities. In April 1982, professors and teachers from the socio-political and economic sciences faculties of the Tashkent Polytechnic Institute named after Abu Rayhon Beruni, where I work as a professor, gathered at the party bureau of the faculty according to the list of students. In April 1982, professors and teachers from the socio-political and economic sciences faculties of the Tashkent Polytechnic Institute named after Abu Rayhon Beruni, where I work as a professor, gathered at the party bureau of the faculty according to the list of students. In April 1982, professors and teachers from the socio-political and economic sciences faculties of the Tashkent Polytechnic Institute named after Abu Rayhon Beruni, where I work as a professor, gathered at the party bureau of the faculty according to the list of students. We were ordered by the institute party committee to gather in the hall. The next day, we all arrived at the appointed place at the appointed time. We were divided into groups and assigned to various cities and large enterprises in the region. Our associate professor, who worked in our department (may they rest in peace), was sent to a chemical plant in Chirchik. Upon arrival, he began delivering a lecture in Uzbek. However, the deputy head of the company interrupted him and demanded that he switch to Russian. The following day, Academician Karim Sodikovich Akhmedov and a teacher were summoned to the regional committee by the Secretary for Ideology, the Secretary of the Party Bureau, and the Secretary of the Party Committee of the institute. The following day, Academician Karim Sodikovich Akhmedov and a teacher were summoned to the regional committee by the Secretary for Ideology, the Secretary of the Party Bureau, and the Secretary of the Party Committee of the institute. The following day, Academician Karim Sodikovich Akhmedov and a teacher were summoned to the regional committee by the Secretary for Ideology, the Secretary of the Party Bureau, and the Secretary of the Party Committee of the institute. They were instructed to expel him from the institute. The party committee of the institute gathered us to inform us about the recent events. The faculty announced their resignation to the secretary of the party bureau. Our teacher, an Uzbek lecturer who teaches in his native language and resides in Uzbekistan, faced similar experiences. There are numerous comparable examples.

There are numerous examples of the language's revival and development, which are a testament to our achievements. Today, when discussing the restoration of our language, it is important to acknowledge the elimination of violence and the opportunity to communicate in our own language throughout the country. However, it is crucial to consider whether its current development is sufficient to withstand the impact of globalization and prevent the erosion of our national identity. Answering this question is challenging. Currently, the use of the state language in everyday communication, including individual ministries, departments, enterprises, and public organizations, as well as in advertising and announcements, does not comply with the norms established by the law on the state language. Most of these organizations communicate with each other in Russian, rather than the state language, and receive responses in Russian. Unfortunately, many organisations are now writing information about employees in Russian and Uzbek. Advertising in Tashkent is mainly shown in Russian and other foreign languages, with only occasional use of Uzbek. Until recently, when boarding the Tashkent metro, passengers could imagine themselves in a Russian city, as all advertisements and announcements were in Russian. However, this is no longer the case.

At present, there is a growing trend to incorporate foreign words into the Uzbek language. For instance, while the term 'renovation' was once commonly used, it has now been replaced by 'Euromoyka'. Similarly, hotels that were once known as 'Druzhba' are now referred to as 'Dedeman', 'Versailles', 'Grand Mir', and so on.

One issue is the lack of qualified personnel to teach in Russian in rural schools. Additionally, many textbooks and manuals used in higher education, particularly in technical universities, are only available in Russian. This limits students to relying solely on their teachers' lectures. There is also no requirement for the translation of additional literature from Russian or other foreign languages into Uzbek. This could hinder the growth of our future employees into mature professionals. According to some of our scientists, certain scientific achievements published in English cannot be accurately expressed in any other language. For instance, Professor Sh. Egamberdiev, who holds a Doctorate in Physical and Mathematical Sciences, has made this claim: Currently, 96% of scientific and technical literature is written in English. Therefore, knowledge of English is essential for conducting scientific research in the field of natural sciences. It is important to remember this fact. Learning English is a more cost-effective and useful option than compiling an Uzbek dictionary of molecular biology, genetic engineering, nanotechnology, astrophysics, and other modern sciences. Moreover, given the current pace of development of modern science, we understand that ongoing discoveries, definitions of new technologies cannot be clearly expressed in any language other than English (word of the author - S.O.)"[20] [lxxxix]. The importance of learning English, as expressed by the teacher, is commendable. It is widely acknowledged that knowledge of multiple languages expands one's worldview and enriches one's spirit. Therefore, if the youth of our country become fluent in Russian, English, Chinese, Japanese, and other foreign languages, their intellectual potential will undoubtedly grow in line with the rapidly changing world. Today, young people are increasingly learning 3-4 languages, which is a positive development. However, it is important to remember that this should not come at the expense of our native language, Uzbek. While it is important to study foreign languages, we should not sacrifice our own language.

In terms of scientific research, it is important to note that during the 9th-12th centuries in Central Asia, renowned thinkers made significant discoveries in Arabic and Persian. These discoveries ultimately contributed to the Western Renaissance. However, it is worth noting that Western scholars did not replace their own language with Arabic and Persian, but rather translated the discoveries into their own languages. By studying the language used in countries where great scientific discoveries have been made, not only was their language preserved, but it also compelled people around the world to study it. This shows that studying and translating the language used in these countries can lead to global advancements in science, technology, and other fields. This process benefits us in two ways: 1) science advances and 2) our language becomes richer. It is important for scientists and intellectuals to care about this task. The task of developing our language was set by the first President of Uzbekistan, Islam Karimov, who stated that it is our responsibility to preserve, enrich, and enhance the prestige of our native language as heirs of the priceless wealth passed on from our ancestors. The Uzbek language should be expanded for use in important areas such as fundamental sciences, modern communication and information technologies, the banking and financial system, and the publication of etymological and comparative dictionaries. It is necessary to develop the required terms, phrases, concepts, and categories. This will serve the noble goals of understanding national identity and feelings of homeland. It is important to avoid subjective evaluations and use clear, objective, and value-neutral language. The language should be formal, avoiding contractions, colloquial words, informal expressions, and unnecessary jargon. The text should be grammatically correct and free from spelling and punctuation errors. The content of the improved text must be as close as possible to the source text, and the addition of further aspects must be avoided at all costs[21 xc].

Unfortunately, not all of our compatriots demonstrate sufficient activity in fulfilling this task. Examples of this have been provided above. In the early years of our independence, there has been a slight decline in the revival of our language. During the post-Soviet era, our language, customs, traditions, and values were violated. A lot of work was done to restore them in the first years of independence. The question of who is to blame for the decline arises. The answer lies with Uzbek intellectuals and their contributions to science, technology, and other fields. These discoveries should serve the development of all mankind and be translated into other languages. It is important for our national and spiritual security that Uzbek is learned in the same way as other languages.

If we do not ensure the safety of our national identity by following the state language law objectively, our efforts in other areas will not yield the expected results. It appears that the amendment of the 'State Language' law is currently being considered. Specifically: To improve control over the implementation of the law, the following measures are proposed: a) strengthening control mechanisms; b) introducing significant fines for violating language requirements in correspondence between advertising, ministries, departments, enterprises, and public organizations; and c) imposing personal responsibility on the first head of a city, district, region, ministries, departments, enterprises, and public organizations for monitoring compliance with the state language as prescribed by law. D) To increase the activity of our entire intelligentsia in assisting people of other nationalities and ethnicities living in our country to learn the official language, as well as to improve the quality of translations of scientific, technological, and other achievements from foreign languages into the official language. It is crucial to have impeccable knowledge of foreign languages without neglecting the promotion of our native language, not only in our country but also worldwide. This way, we can effectively utilize its capabilities to safeguard our national identity.

Another factor in ensuring our national and spiritual security is the development of rural cultural and spiritual life in accordance with the requirements of the growing level of globalization. This includes:

(a) Familiarizing the rural population with the changes taking place in the world, especially the process of globalization, the factors and means that affect the erosion of our national spirituality.

(b) Instilling in them the idea of market relations, particularly that they are not limited to full state assistance or social protection. Hard work, creativity, and dedication of each person are key to prosperity.

(c) Preserving existing relationships in consciousness that perpetuate the national language, mentality, customs, traditions, and values, while enriching and improving them with universal values.

(d) Accelerated development of rural infrastructure.

Of course, it cannot be said that the rural population today is unaware of the processes of globalization taking place in the world. They, like the townspeople, are forced to live under strong information pressure. They also have access to modern telecommunications, computers, the internet, mobile phones, and can be aware of even the smallest changes taking place in the most remote parts of the world.

However, the awareness of the negative impact of these tools on the erosion of our national spirituality lags behind the level of need for it today. The main reason for this is the imitation forming in their minds, an "example" of the process of assimilating "mass spirituality" in cities.

Today, pursuing a policy of simply bringing the village closer to the city, as in the former Soviet times, is not a viable solution. Back then, the goal of "bringing the village closer to the city" was achieved only through the development of rural infrastructure. This approach turned the population not into active creators, but into obedient workers loyal to ideology, with their mentality limited to a one-sided view of cotton as he only source of development.

Instead, we need to focus on empowering the rural population by fostering their cultural and spiritual identity, while preparing them to engage with the globalized world effectively.

It is true that the reforms carried out in our countryside since independence eliminated this practice, but remnants of such views still linger in the minds of the rural population raised in the Soviet era. It can be difficult for them to grasp that they need a wider range of activities to thrive. In particular, the process of harmonizing farming with entrepreneurship is developing slowly. The population lacks initiative and the courage to effectively use the opportunities created by the state, given the current level of demand and the prevailing mindset of expecting financial assistance.

Ultimately, these factors all contribute to the lagging of market relations in the minds of the population behind the demands of today's globalization processes and the slow pace of infrastructure changes.

What does this have to do with ensuring the security of our national spirituality? The connection is profound. All of the above are issues related to improving the well-being of the rural population. If we can overcome these negative shortcomings, it will lead to an increase in their well-being, confidence in their future, and the spiritual strength of their nation and people. It will also foster a sense of national identity. In this sense, improving the well-being of the rural population and developing a modern production structure are leading factors in ensuring our national and spiritual security.

With the advent of infrastructure in rural areas, the consciousness of the population will grow, and the desire for creativity and self-sufficiency will increase.

Now let's consider the need to preserve a conservative attitude towards the national language, customs, traditions, and values in the mentality of the rural population, while also enriching it with universal values. It is well-known that Uzbekistan is an agrarian country, with two-thirds of our population living in rural areas. While this poses certain challenges, it also presents a positive aspect: the rural population's inherent attentiveness to changes in their mentality contributes to the preservation of national and spiritual foundations. This factor of conservatism played a positive role in safeguarding national spiritual and moral values even under Soviet rule.

Today, when we analyze the factors of the relative stability of our national language, customs, traditions, and values during the Soviet era, it becomes clear that the conservative spirit in the mentality of the rural population had a positive impact. In the mentality of the urban population, the spirit of conservatism about change is not as strong as that of the rural population. Since they do not live in a territorially fragmented state, they live in an organized state, they live under relatively large information pressure, and in a spiritual state they are also prone to new emerging innovations. Their data exchange will be faster. All this will, to some extent, play a role in the penetration of external influences on the national spirituality of the urban population. Of course, this does not mean that they are the main culprits in the collapse of national spirituality, but rather that there is a growing need to change their mentality towards national spiritual security. We want to promote the idea of strengthening the conservative spirit of preserving national spirituality in the rural mentality and adapting it to modern changes. There is a growing need for the active participation of the state, public organizations, persons responsible for the development of spirituality, scientists, literary and artistic figures, in short, all intellectuals in the harmonious organization of these two processes. In particular, we are witnessing the popularization of traditional folk culture, songs, games, costumes, and dresses, which are unique and have no analogues in our country. The selfless people of our country are working hard to prepare and hand them over to our people. We will be able to prevent threats to our national spirituality in the process of globalization by revealing and popularizing what has not happened and inspiring it to our people, especially our youth. Because it is in this heritage that the spirit of the ancestors, the light of the soul, traditions, experience, and philosophy of life are reflected. That is why they do not lose their nationality, their value increases over time, and they remain an important source of education for each new generation. New carefree games, cut off from the folk heritage of the new era – non-artificial "news" will go away, they will remain only in the history of that period. But folk games created and revived by people themselves, based on the heritage of their ancestors, other works of art, will not die but remain immortal and universal. In preserving the same heritage, the leading factor may be the convergence of the mentality of the rural population with the urban one. In this sense, the development of spirituality and enlightenment in rural areas at the level of globalization, raising them to the level of central cities, will be of practical importance for national and spiritual security.

Another factor in ensuring national and spiritual security is the increased activity of the national intelligentsia. The intelligentsia is an integral part of the country's intellectual potential. However, it's important to distinguish between two different concepts: intellectuals and the intelligentsia.

Intellectuals are individuals with high intelligence and expertise in specific fields, such as scientists, artists, designers, technologists, modern farmers, and entrepreneurs. They contribute to society through their discoveries, innovations, and creations, enriching the intellectual life of the nation.

The intelligentsia, on the other hand, is a broader group that includes not only intellectuals but also teachers, educators, engineers, doctors, and technicians. They play a crucial role in disseminating knowledge and translating intellectual potential into reality for the benefit of society, particularly young people.

Both intellectuals and the intelligentsia are essential for a harmonious society.

Given this distinction, let's explore the role of intellectuals in protecting national spirituality from negative influences in the globalized world.

The Uzbek people have a rich history of producing talented intellectuals who have significantly shaped the nation's identity and aspirations. They played a key role in the struggle for independence and continue to contribute to the country's development and the education of younger generations in the spirit of patriotism and national identity.

The role of the intelligentsia is indeed enormous. As Professor N. Kamilov aptly stated, "Reason shines brightly like the sun." This highlights the crucial role intellectuals and the intelligentsia play in guiding society towards progress and safeguarding its cultural and spiritual heritage. A nation with a strong and dedicated intelligentsia is better equipped to navigate the challenges of globalization and protect its unique identity[22][xci].

Today, we have an intelligentsia making a great contribution to the development of the country, drawing on the heritage of our ancestors and the achievements of modern science. While many of them earn less than an "entrepreneur" who buys and sells goods from one market to another, we are grateful that we have intellectuals who are happy to contribute to reforms, strengthen our confidence in the future of our nation, and make knowledge acquisition practically important in sustainable development.

Despite living modest lives, some intellectuals have a strong sense of belonging to the fate of the nation and country. They are highly respected among our people and, like true intellectuals, spread enlightenment among our youth. It would be unfair not to admit this.

Among them are teachers who taught the alphabet to young people at school, teachers who teach students in lyceums, colleges, and universities, scientists and educators who inspire them with the spirit of patriotism, nationalism, and humanity, and writers, poets, and artists who strive to bring joy to our people through their work. These are important pillars of our country, selfless individuals who shape its intellectual potential. It is impossible to imagine a country and a nation without them. This is a fact that does not require proof.

Therefore, over the years of independent development, our country has paid great attention to intellectuals, creating all the necessary conditions for them to thrive and meet the demands of the modern world. We can say with confidence that a new generation of intellectuals is being formed today.

However, this does not mean that our entire intelligentsia is actively involved in the life of our society, that all the problems of forming a new intelligentsia have been resolved, or that the potential of the intelligentsia is being fully utilized. In this regard, a number of tasks still need to be solved. These are:

a) Broad involvement of the intelligentsia in raising the level of education and upbringing to the modern level. This applies not only to school teachers (this goes without saying), but also to the involvement of the entire intelligentsia in this process. Raising school education to a new level should become a national task. This includes academics, journalists, poets, writers, artists, and others who can boldly raise school issues and leverage their contributions to inspire students to learn science.

b) Eliminating delays in the formation of the political consciousness and culture of the population, especially young people. We must acknowledge that today, part of the intelligentsia is preoccupied with everyday life and the processes taking place in society. Additionally, our national spirituality is affected by "mass spirituality."

c) Recognizing that the development of our national language and spirituality is one of the main tasks of the intelligentsia in their preservation and transmission to the next generation, it is advisable to avoid neglecting their mentality. In this respect, if we compare their activities today with those in the early years of our independence, we can see that their involvement has decreased over the years. It is unfortunate that some intellectuals believe that "our language has been assigned the status of a state language, and now it will develop independently." In fact, if a law is not widely applied, it may remain on paper, especially if the intelligentsia does not actively participate in its implementation.

Today, the popularity of our language lags behind the level of demand in communication, science, technology, and other areas due to the indifference of the intelligentsia. Generally, if national spirituality is impoverished, "enriched" by external influences, then this is due to the helplessness and irresponsibility of the national intelligentsia.

Only if the intelligentsia becomes the leading force in ensuring the security of national spirituality, if it is intellectually strong and selfless on the path of national development, will it be possible to participate on an equal footing with highly developed countries in today's rapidly developing globalization and to protect national spirituality from its negative consequences. It will be easy for an intellectually crippled and impoverished nation to fall into the trap of globalization and "assimilate" with other nations. In this sense, in the modern, rapidly changing world of globalization, the national intelligentsia is becoming an important factor in ensuring national and spiritual security.

One important factor in ensuring national and spiritual security is the advancement of the concept of national development, its integration into the consciousness of our nation's people, particularly the youth, and the responsible use of appropriate communication tools.

Turning national and spiritual security into a national idea means protecting it from the growing threats to the national and spiritual in the process of globalization. The idea of national development, which includes the effective use of equal opportunities with developed countries, is called to become an integral part of it.

The idea of national development is intertwined with national and spiritual security. Because if the nation's goals and objectives are clear and implemented effectively, and if it can use available opportunities effectively, the nation will develop and be able to ensure its national security. In this sense, ensuring national and spiritual security is reflected in a specific idea, and this idea, in turn, becomes a material force only when certain factors are combined.

National and spiritual security cannot be ensured by force or violence. Here, we are talking about materiality not for the human body, but for its consciousness, worldview, and values, that is, about an "abstract" factor that has not become material. If this "abstraction" materializes, it will be easier to take possession of a person with their whole being and integrate them into the desired "melody". When we view a person as the "creator" of a nation, the main factor that makes the nation dependent on them remains the key factor in shaping consciousness, worldview, and heart. Therefore, in ensuring national and spiritual security, the priority remains to protect the consciousness, worldview, and heart of the nation from harmful ideas.

The idea of national development, combining ensuring national and spiritual security, is not only a theory but also an integral strategy for protecting national spirituality from the negative consequences of globalization. It combines a clear unity of ideas and practices. Its characteristic feature is that it embodies clear mechanisms for achieving the main goal. If these mechanisms work, efficiency can be achieved. However, the problem is that they are being used beyond the power of globalization to change the world. Using them at this level is not easy; it is very difficult. This is because the diversity of material interests and lifestyles within the nation, especially the growing need for material needs in a market economy, to some extent has a negative impact on national and spiritual security. Therefore, to ensure national and spiritual security, empty words, slogans, and platitudes like "this must be done" or "national unity is necessary" will not work. It will be of practical importance to convey to the minds of our people, especially our youth, the essence of the threat globalization poses to our national spirituality. We must make it our national idea that if we do not unite and protect it today, the next generation will never forgive us. Its transformation into a national idea means that all members of the nation, regardless of financial status, gender, profession, occupation, place of residence, and age, should actively defend our national spirituality to the best of their ability.

Of course, ensuring national and spiritual security does not require separation from other nations or indifference to their spirituality, customs, traditions, and values. Instead, their active participation in this process is expected. After all, globalization has a negative impact not only on the Uzbeks but also on the spirituality of other nations and peoples living in our country. Therefore, the active participation of all our citizens in transforming national and spiritual security into a national idea and practice will surely be successful. Understanding the identity of any nation and protecting it from various harmful influences are integral parts of universal human values.

Another factor in ensuring national and spiritual security is achieving the rule of law and consistently developing democratic values in our country. Their significance lies in the fact that where the rule of law prevails, there is equality for all, regardless of nationality, language, customs, traditions, and values. This creates conditions that are very important for societal development. In a country where laws are enforced, peace and stability reign, interethnic harmony and interreligious tolerance flourish, and all problems that arise are solved through cooperation and dialogue among the population.

Awareness of everyone's responsibility for their actions is also associated with the importance of the law. In a country where the rule of law prevails, citizens are aware of the potential influence of preconceived ideas and violent ideologies from abroad. This awareness unites the entire population into a single, strong force against such threats. This, in turn, strengthens national unity and ensures national and spiritual security. Conversely, where laws are not prioritized, national and spiritual disintegration occurs. When laws are violated, instability arises, leading to new threats to national identity and cultural values.

The development of democratic values is also an important factor in ensuring national and spiritual security. Their place and role:

a) Where democratic values develop, the activity of the masses in governing the state increases, and their political consciousness and culture grow. This, in turn, has a positive effect on the development of society and the state.

b) As democratic values develop, existing problems in the life of society will naturally arise, and their solutions can be found through the interaction of the population.

c) The development of democratic values itself is a high indicator of national and spiritual development, leading to an increased sense of self-awareness among the representatives of the nation. Conversely, the development of each nation's self-awareness helps to ensure its unity in protecting its national spirituality from external threats.

d) The development of democratic values also holds practical importance for the formation of a public spirit in understanding any problem in the context of globalization. This plays a role in ensuring national and spiritual security by bringing issues to light instead of allowing them to fester in secrecy, facilitating public participation in finding solutions.

Thus, in the context of globalization, ensuring national and spiritual security has become an urgent task. Today, the effective use of the above factors remains of practical importance. After all, it is becoming increasingly clear that humanity cannot save itself without ensuring national and spiritual security.

CONCLUSION

From the analysis of the relationship between globalization and national and spiritual security on a number of theoretical and empirical materials, it becomes clear that any concept does not arise spontaneously, but rather as a reflection of various societal problems and the need to solve them. "National and spiritual security" is not a random concept, but rather the need to protect national spirituality from the impact of various threats that undermine it, caused by the process of globalization today.

Today, analysis of the escalation of globalization shows that under its influence, the achievements of science, technology, and technology are rapidly gaining popularity, serving the development of countries and the peoples living in them. However, while exploiting these same gains creates inequality, globalization is emerging as a driving force. It does not only allow highly developed countries, as well as the nations and peoples living in them, to develop even faster, but it also hinders the nations and peoples entering the path of development, and those living in them, from approaching them. This is because today, achievements in the field of science, technology, and modern communications are primarily made in highly developed countries with great intellectual and material power.

In developing countries, there is a risk that these capabilities will not be sufficient in today's fast-paced world and that they will become more dependent on others due to the growing trend to buy finished products rather than create their own. Given the impossibility of curbing globalization, the nation has a growing need to activate itself in the preservation of national spirituality through the search for and effective use of factors that impede this process.

The results of our research show that if a nation does not realize its limitations in achieving complete self-sufficiency and relies solely on the achievements of others, it will inevitably become dependent on those "others." This is because other countries' achievements never reach developing nations in their pure form; they come bundled with the spirituality, way of life, morality, and psyche of the originating culture. These developed nations not only promote their achievements but also their underlying values. This natural penetration into the lives of developing nations can lead to a weakening of their own unique spirituality, essentially an "enrichment" at the expense of their own hidden cultural identity. Thus, the trend towards a weakening of national spirituality is a growing concern.

Analysis of these processes reveals that, similar to other events and processes, there is a potential culmination point for the "enrichment" of the national spirituality of developing countries at the expense of the spirituality of highly developed nations. This can occur in two scenarios:

a) If developing nations and peoples on the path of progress develop an awareness of external threats to their own spirituality and a sense of self-awareness.

b) If a developing nation experiences a "thirst for its own land" after becoming "saturated" with the spirituality of others and finding it insufficient to fulfill its own spiritual needs.

However, this process is not easy; it is complex and can lead to significant contradictions and conflicts. Firstly, it takes a relatively long time, and this duration further complicates the process. Ultimately, its success depends on the nation's capabilities, its commitment to the cause, and its potential to effectively utilize its resources.

Another difficult problem in this process is that highly developed countries do not allocate funds for the development and popularization of "mass spirituality" formed by each other, taking into account the needs of nations and peoples embarking on the path of development in the context of globalization. This, of course, significantly complicates the growing hunger of peoples on the path to development. Consequently, developing countries need to prioritize allocating funds for the preservation of national spirituality, in accordance with their level of economic development and its transmission to future generations.

Throughout our research, we have encountered another complex problem. This issue is also rooted in the material stratification that occurs in modern society, where market relations are formed in our country. As everyone knows, the market has its own unique characteristics. Those who are resourceful, enterprising, and able to adapt to these characteristics can effectively utilize methods of earning money, leading to wealth. Conversely, those who cannot adapt struggle to acquire the resources necessary for daily life, often finding themselves trapped in a difficult situation. This disparity has a negative impact on national unity, weakening its overall cohesion. On the other hand, the conservative attitude of the less affluent segment of the population towards national spirituality serves as a means of survival. More specifically, some wealthy members of the nation, unknowingly, compete with each other through violence, potentially setting a dangerous precedent. The increasing popularity of such actions poses a significant threat, as these affluent individuals, unwittingly, become catalysts for the disintegration of our national spirit. This situation reflects the proverb, "Where is the cure for my trouble?" Indeed, preventing the internal erosion of national spirituality is arguably more challenging than mitigating the consequences of external influences. Therefore, a growing need exists for collaborative efforts between the intelligentsia, intellectuals, and public organizations of our country to prevent such a detrimental development.

An analysis of the possibilities of national and spiritual security in the context of globalization indicates opportunities for the development of national intellectual potential at the peak of globalization, the continuation of the national-spiritual revival, and the transformation of the national-spiritual heritage into an integral part. We can ensure our national and spiritual security by achieving the state status of our language at the level established by law and integrating a number of other factors into the daily lives of our compatriots. The main thing is that they, whoever they are, actively participate in the development of these factors and realize that ensuring their national and spiritual security is a National Idea. If every representative of our nation forms this idea in their consciousness and worldview, we will be able to protect our national spirituality from the threats of globalization, take a worthy place in world civilization on par with developed countries. We will be able to take an active part in preserving the civilization that humanity has reached.

BIBLIOGRAPHY
INTRODUCTION

[1] Karimov I.A. High spirituality is an invincible force. - Tashkent: "Manaviyat", 2008. - B. 12.

[2] Karimov I.A. Let the ideology of our society serve to make people a people, a nation a nation. - Tashkent: Uzbekistan, 1998 .- B. 4.

[3] Uzbekistan and Central Asia. - Center for Political Studies. Information and analytical bulletin. IX-2007. - S. 42-45.

[4] This source. - B. 42-45.

[5] This source. - B. 42.

[6] This source. - B. 44.

[7] This source. - B. 45.

[8] Globalistics: an international interdisciplinary encyclopedic dictionary. - Moscow-St. Petersburg-New York, 2006 .- p. 163.

[9] Holbekov M. Globalization in literature. // Tafakkur, 2006. №4. - b. 20-23.

[10] This source.

[11] Kodirov A. Traditional society and the strategy of its modernization. - Tashkent: TDYUI, 2006 .- p. 90.

[12] Ochildiev A. Globalization and ideological processes. - Tashkent: Muharrir, 2009 .- p. 64.

[13] Umarov B. Contradictions of Globalization: Economic, Social and Spiritual Aspects. - Tashkent: Manaviyat, 2006 .- p. 7.

[14] Saidov U. Globalization and intercultural communication. - Tashkent: Academy, 2008. - p. 7-8.

[15] Philosophy: Encyclopedic Dictionary (Compiled and Editor-in-Chief K. Nazarov). - Tashkent: Sharq, 2004 .- p. 169.

[16] Philosophy: A Brief Glossary. - Tashkent: Sharq, 2004 .- p. 162.

[17] Philosophy: Encyclopedic Dictionary (Compiled and Editor-in-Chief K. Nazarov). - Tashkent: Sharq, 2004 .- p. 167-168.

[18] See Uzbekistan and Central Asia. - Center for Political Studies. Information and analytical bulletin. IX-2007. - S. 44.

[19] Globalistics international international encyclopedic dictionary. Moscow - St. Petersburg - New York, 2006 .- B. 163.

1.2. DIALECTICS OF GLOBALIZATION AND CIVILIZATION

[1] Independence: Explanatory popular science dictionary. Edited by A. Jalolov and K. Khonazarov. - Tashkent: Sharq, 1998 .- B. 236.

[2] Philosophy: A Brief Glossary. Managing editor: Doctor of Philosophy A. Jalolov. - Tashkent: Sharq, 2004 .- B. 347.

[3] Philosophy: Encyclopedic Dictionary (Compiled and Editor-in-Chief K. Nazarov). - Tashkent: Sharq, 2004 .- B. 446.

[4] National Encyclopedia of Uzbekistan. Volume 9 - Tashkent: State Scientific Publishing House "National Encyclopedia of Uzbekistan", 2005. - B. 548.

[5] Fundamentals of Philosophy. - Tashkent: Uzbekistan, 2005 .- B. 348.

[6] Western philosophy (Compiled and editor-in-chief K. Nazarov). - Tashkent: Sharq, 2004 .- B. 225-226.

[7] See "Philosophy" (textbook). Edited by E.Yu. Yusupov. - Tashkent: Sharq, 1999 .- B. 208, 212-213.

[8] See Sulaimonova F. East and West. - Tashkent: Uzbekistan, 1997.

[9] Tulenov Y. Philosophy of values. - Tashkent: Uzbekistan, 1998 .- B. 85-108.

[10] Leningrad University Bulletin. 1974, no. 11. Issue 2. - P. 59.

[11] Kuznetsov B.G. Understanding by science of the problem of its impact on civilization. - V book.: Mechanics and civilization of the XVII-XIX centuries. – Moskva, 1979.

[12] See Sociology and the Present. Vol. 1. – Moskva, 1977 .- S. 375-376.

[13] Davidovich V.E. Culture and social progress. - Philosophical Sciences, 1978. №3. - S. 6.

[14] Egorov A. Aesthetic problems. - Moskva, 1974 .- p. 255.

[15] See Conrad N.I. West and East. - Moskva, 1972 .- p. 453, 476.

[16] Ochilova N.R. The influence of modern civilization on the spiritual image of a person: dissertation author's abstract for the degree of candidate of philosophical sciences. - Tashkent, 2010 .- B. 11.

[17] Spengler O. Zakat of Europe. / Per. with him. and try it on. I.I.Maksankova. - Moskva, Thought, 1998. - 606 p.

[18] See Uzbekistan and Central Asia. - Center for Political Studies. Information and analytical bulletin. IX-2007. - S. 44.

1.3. GLOBALIZATION, CIVILIZATION AND NATION

[1] Sadulla Otamuratov, Sarvar Otamuratov. Spiritual recovery in Uzbekistan. - Tashkent: Yangi asr avlodi, 2003; Otamuratov S. Philosophy of National Development (Political and Philosophical Aspects). - Tashkent: Academy, 2005; Otamuratov S. Globalization and the Nation (Political and Philosophical Analysis). - Tashkent: Yangi asr avlodi, 2008.

[2] Karimov I.A. Uzbekistan on the threshold of the XXI century: threats to security, conditions of stability and guarantees of development. - Tashkent: Uzbekistan, 1997 .- B. 69.

[3] Khudoyberganov A. Political globalization: the foundations of formation and features of manifestation. // Society and management. 2009, no. 4. - B. 37.

[4] Otamuratov S. Globalization and the Nation (Political and Philosophical Analysis). - Tashkent: Yangi asr avlodi, 2008 .- B. 43.

[5] See O. Toshboev. The threat of "mass culture". // Tafakkur. 2008, no.1. - B. 16-21; Erkaev A. Globalization: Information Crisis and Mass Culture. // Tafakkur. 2008, no. 4. - B. 10-17; Odilkhonova Sh. What is "popular culture"? // Tafakkur. 2010, no. 2. - B. 85-86; Shukhrat Rizo. If benevolence is the main criterion ... // Tafakkur. 2010, no. 3. - B. 4-15; Saidov U. Globalization and intercultural communication. - Tashkent: Academy, 2008. - B. 48-57., Samarov R. Information and psychological security // Journal of Protection +, 2009, No. 09 (59). - B. 14-15.

[6] See Saidov U. Crowd culture. // Tafakkur. 2008, no.2. - B. 4-9; Najmiddin Komil. Compassionate love saves the world. // Tafakkur. 2008, no. 3. - B. 10-17; Shukhrat Rizo. If benevolence is the main criterion ... // Tafakkur. 2010, no. 3. - B. 4-15.

[7] See Kukarkin A.V. Bourgeois society and culture. Under total. ed. A.N. Yakovleva. - Moskva: Politizdat, 1970. - B. 371-379; Mass literature and the crisis of bourgeois culture in the West (State collection). – Moskva: Science, 1974; Pigrov G. Cultural aggression. - Moskva, 1986; Smolskaya E.P. "Popular culture": entertainment or politics? – Moskva: Thought, 1986. and others.

[8] Patrick DJ. Buchanan. Death of the West. Translated from English by A. Sergeev. - Moskva, 2005.

[9] Huntington S. Cradle of Civilization? "Clash of Civilizations?" 1993 year

[10] See Arguments and Facts. 2011, no. 6. - S. 2.

[11] See Arguments and Facts. 2011, no. 4. - S. 2.

[12] See Arguments and Facts. 2011, no.8. - S. 8.

[13] See Source. - B. 8.

2.2. Spirituality of the nation

[1] Karimov I. A. High spirituality is an invincible force. - T.: "Ma'naviyat", 2008. - B. 11.

[2] See: Guseinov A.A. Great pluralists. - M.: 1995. - B. 36.

[3] Karimov I. A. Without historical memory there is no future. - T.: Sharq, 1998. - B. 10.

[4] Karimov I. A. High spirituality is an invincible force. - T.: "Manaviyat", 2008. - B. 4.

[5] Karimov I. A. Without historical memory there is no future. - T.: Sharq, 1998. - B. 24.

[6] Karimov I. A. Without historical memory there is no future. - T.: Sharq, 1998. - B. 21.

[7] Karimov I. A. High spirituality is an invincible force. - T.: "Manaviyat", 2008. - B. 25-26.

[8] Karimov I. A. High spirituality is an invincible force. - T.: "Manaviyat", 2008. - B. 19.

[9] Jalolov A.M. Responsibility for independence. - T.: Uzbekistan, 1996. - B. 249.

[10] Kasimov B. National awakening: courage, enlightenment, sacrifice. - T.: Ma'naviyat, 2002. - B. 260.

[11] Kasimov B. National awakening: courage, enlightenment, sacrifice. - T.: Ma'naviyat, 2002. - B. 259-260.

[12] Scenes of reality. 96 classical philosophers. Fates, proverbs, aphorisms. Compiled and translated by Said Joraeva. - T.: Generation of the new century, 2002. - B. 57.

[13] Karimov I. A. Without historical memory there is no future. - T.: Sharq, 1998. - B. 21.

[14] Sadulla Otamuratov, Sarvar Otamuratov. Spiritual revival in Uzbekistan. - T.: Generation of the new century, 2003. - B. 186-187.

[15] See: T. Makhmudov. About "Avesta". - T.: Sharq, 2000. - B. 5.

[16] Yusupov E.Yu. Spiritual foundations of human development. - T.: University, 1998. - B. 38.

[17] Jabbarov I. Uzbeks (traditional economy, lifestyle and ethnoculture). Second edition, corrected and expanded. - T.: Sharq, 2008. - B. 8.

2.3. The concept of national-spiritual security and the reasons for its occurrence.

[1] National Encyclopedia of Uzbekistan. Volume 9. - T.: State scientific publishing house "National Encyclopedia of Uzbekistan", 2005. - P. 355.

[2] Philosophy: encyclopedic dictionary (Compiled and executive editor K. Nazarov). - T.: Sharq, 2004. - P. 251.

[3] The idea of national independence: basic concepts, principles and terms (a brief annotated practical dictionary). - T.: Generation of the new century, 2002. - P. 87-88.

[4] Kuznetsov V.N. Sociology of security. – M.: Book and business, 2003. – P. 82.

[5] Mitrokhin V.I. Conceptual foundations of Russia's national security strategy. // Socio-political magazine. – M., 1995. No. 6. – P. 23.

[6] System analysis and safety modeling. Textbook (N.A. Severev, V.K. Dednov). – M.: Higher School, 2006. – P. 27.

[7] Yanovsky R. Social dynamics of global change: sociology of a chance for Russia for a decent and safe life for its people. – M.: Book and business, 2001. – P. 63.

[8] Kravchenko A.I. Sociology and political science. – M.: Publishing house. Center "Academy", 2000. – P. 273.

[9] Science and security of Russia: historical, scientific, methodological, historical and technical aspects. – M.: Nauka, 2000. – P. 157.

[10] Skvortsov A.S., Kruglov D.A. Trends in changes in the content of military threats to the military security of the Russian Federation in the medium term / Military security of the Russian Federation in the 21st century. Collection of scientific articles. Under the general editorship of A.V. Kvashnin. – M.: General Staff of the RF Armed Forces, 2004. // http://www.mvlast.ru/geopolitics/russia_war_security.doc

[11] Voloshko V.S. Military policy: problems of ensuring the military security of the Russian Federation / Military security of the Russian Federation in the 21st century. Collection of scientific articles. Under the general editorship of A.V. Kvashnin. – M.: General Staff of the RF Armed Forces, 2004. // http://www.mvlast.ru/geopolitics/russia_war_security.doc

[12] This source.

[13] Samarov R.S. Methodological foundations of security. - T.: Academy, 2010. - P. 14.

[14] Esaev F.M. ŸProblems of improving military-political activity in the national security system of Uzbekistan: abstract of a dissertation for the degree of candidate of political sciences. - T., 2011.

[15] Ishmukhamedov A.E. Economic security (textbook). - T.: TDIU, 2004. - P. 18.

[16] Abulkasimov Kh.P. Economic security. - T.: Academy, 2006. - P. 6.

[17] Samarov R. Methodological foundations of security. – Tashkent: Academy, 2010. – P. 74.

[18] Karimov I.A. The ideology of national independence is the people's faith in a great future. - T.: Uzbekistan, 2000. - B. 6-7.

[19] Karimov I. A. High spirituality is an invincible force. - T.: "Manaviyat", 2008. - P. 12.

PART THREE. THREATS TO NATIONAL SPIRITUALITY UNDER GLOBALIZATION

3.1. Basics of threats to national spirituality

[1] See: History of political and legal doctrines. Ancient world. – M.: Nauka, 1985. – B. 237.

[2] Confucius. Sayings / Confucius; [transl. from ancient China; comp., translation, comment. I.I. Semenenko]. – M.: Eksmo, 2009. – P. 57.

[3] Plato. Laws (translation from Russian by Urfon Otahon). - T.: Yangi asr avlodi, 2002. – P. 122.

[4] This source. – pp. 95-96.

[5] Scenes of reality. 96 classical philosophers. Fates, proverbs, aphorisms. Compiled and translated by Said Joraeva. - T.: Yangi asr avlodi, 2002. – P. 98.

[6] Bobojonov H., Satlikov A. "Avesta" is an invaluable cultural heritage. - Khiva, Khorezm Mamun Academy, 2000. - P. 25.

[7] See: Boboev H., Hasanov S. "Avesta" is a reflection of our spirituality. - T.: Adolat, 2001. - P. 12.

[8] Boboev H., Hasanov S. "Avesta" is a reflection of our spirituality. - T.: Adolat, 2001. - P. 34.

[9] National Encyclopedia of Uzbekistan. Volume 12. - T.: 2006. - P. 114.

[10] Jabbarov I. Treasure of ancient culture and spirituality. - T.: Uzbekistan, 1999. - P. 115.

[11] Boronov K. Deep roots of spirituality and enlightenment of our people. - T.: Nauka, 2003. - P. 28.

[12] Jabbarov I. Treasure of ancient culture and spirituality. - T.: Uzbekistan, 1999. - P. 130.

[13] This source.

[14] See Farabi Abu Nasr. City of virtuous people. – T.: Publishing house "People's Heritage" named after. A. Kadyri, 1993. – P. 86.

[15] This source. – P.186.

[16] Zhabborov I. Antik madaniyat va manaviyat hazinasi. – T.: Ozbekiston, 1999. – P. 150; 155.

[17] Shihobiddin Muhammad an-Nasawiy. Sulton Jaloliddin Manguberdi hayoti tafsiloti. (K.Matekubov tarzhimasi). – T.: Ozbekiston-Yozuvchi, 1999. – 432 pages

[18] See: Jabbarov I. Treasure of ancient culture and spirituality. - T.: Uzbekistan, 1999. - P. 151. Information about the Arab historian Ibn al-Assir: Shihabiddin Muhammad an-Nasawi. Details

of the life of Sultan Jalaluddin Manguberdi. (translation by K. Matekubov). - T.: Uzbekistan-Yozuvchi, 1999. - P. 22.

[19] Nizamuddin Shami. Zafarnoma. - T.: Uzbekistan, 1996. - B. 370.

[20] Code of Timur. - T.: Publishing house named after Gafur Gulam, 1991. - P. 37.

[21] See: Mominov I.M. The place and role of Amir Temur in the history of Central Asia (according to written sources) Second edition. - T.: Nauka, 1993. - P. 23.

[22] See: Otamuratov S., Khusanov S., Ramatov J. Fundamentals of spirituality (textbook). – T.: Publishing house "People's Heritage" named after. A. Kadyri, 2002. – P. 119-128.

[23] Karimov I. A. High spirituality is an invincible force. - T.: "Manaviyat", 2008. - . 45.

[24] See: Excerpts: Majidi Hasani. Invasion into Turkestan. - T.: Nur, 1992. - P. 39.

[25] See: This source. - pp. 37-46.

[26] See: This source. - P. 37.

[27] See: This source. - P. 38.

[28] See: This source. - P. 15.

[29] See: Kasimov B. National awakening: courage, enlightenment, sacrifice. - T.: Ma'naviyat, 2002. - p. 233, 235.

[30] See: Kasimov B. National awakening: courage, enlightenment, sacrifice. - T.: Ma'naviyat, 2002. - P. 233, 235.

[31] Alimova D.A., Golovanov A.A. Uzbekistan during the period of the authoritarian Soviet system: the consequences of political and ideological oppression (1917-1990). - T.: Uzbekistan, 2000. - P. 10.

[32] This source. - P. 25.

[33] This source. - P. 27.

[34] This source. - P. 57.

[35] Kasimov B. National awakening: courage, enlightenment, sacrifice. - T.: Ma'naviyat, 2002. - B.S.

[36] This source. - P. 30-31.

[37] Karimov I. A. High spirituality is an invincible force. - T.: "Manaviyat", 2008. - P. 12.

3.2. External threats affecting national spirituality

[1] Karimov I.A. Uzbekistan on the threshold of the 21st century: security threats, conditions of stability and guarantees of development. - T.: Uzbekistan, 1997. - B. 4.

[2] Pakhrutdinov Sh. Threat is a destructive force. - T.: Academy, 2001. - B. 11.

³ This source. - B. 138.

⁴ Spirituality: Key Concepts and Glossary. – T.: Publishing house named after Gafur Gulam, 2009. – B. 546-547.

⁵ Karimov I. A. High spirituality is an invincible force. - T.: "Manaviyat", 2008. - B. 110-127.

⁶ Karimov I. A. High spirituality is an invincible force. - T.: "Manaviyat", 2008. - B. 11.

⁷ Otamuratov S. Globalization and nation (political and philosophical analysis). - T.: Generation of the New Century, 2008. - B. 45.

⁸ Saidov U. Globalization and intercultural communication. - T.: Academy, 2008. - B. 35.

⁹ The people's word. April 16, 2009

3.3. Internal threats against national spirituality and the process of their implementation

¹ Karimov I.A. High spirituality is an invincible force. - T.: "Manaviyat", 2008. - P. 120.

² Karimov I.A. High spirituality is an invincible force. - T.: "Manaviyat", 2008. - P. 143.

³ Shukhrat Reza. The path to the heart. // Thinking. 2009, No. 2. - P. 25-26.

⁴ Kadyrov R. Human trafficking is a global problem. // People's word. October 17, 2008

⁵ Boliev A. The trap of lust. // People's word. February 18, 2009

⁶ This source.

⁷ Kadyrov R. Human trafficking is a global problem. // People's word. October 17, 2008

⁸ National Encyclopedia of Uzbekistan. Volume 6. - T.: State scientific publishing house "National Encyclopedia of Uzbekistan", 2003. - P. 26.

⁹ Report of the Religious Committee of the Cabinet of Ministers on Freedom of Conscience and Freedom of Religion, International Religious Freedom. 09/19/2008. http://www.diyonat website

¹⁰ Asadullaev M. About the harm of the life ego or noise to human health. // People's word. August 8, 2008

¹¹ This source.

¹² Botaev F. Indifference? Or Indifference? Or national impostor?... // People's Word. May 28, 2011

¹³ This source.

¹⁴ More about this: Otamuratov S. Philosophy of national development (political and philosophical aspects). - T.: Academy, 2005. - P. 36-37.

4.2. Features of awareness of national identity in the context of globalization

[1] See: Atamuratov S. National identity and international education. – T.: Uzbekistan, 1991; Spiritual revival in Uzbekistan. - T.: Yangi asr avlodi, 2003 (together with Sarvar Otamuratov); Philosophy of national development (political and philosophical aspects). - T.: Academy, 2005; Globalization and nation (political and philosophical analysis). - T.: Generation of the new century, 2008. etc.

[2] Kasimov B. National awakening: courage, enlightenment, sacrifice. - T.: Ma'naviyat, 2002. - P. 4.

[3] Kholmatov G.M. The role of political views of the Jadids of the Fergana Valley in the formation of ideas of national independence (political and philosophical analysis): Abstract of a dissertation for the degree of candidate of political sciences. - T., 2011.

[4] See: Otamuratov S. Globalization and nation (political and philosophical analysis). - T.: Yangi asr avlodi, 2008. - P. 117.

4.3. Factors of national ideas ensuring national and spiritual security

[1] See: Buchanan P. The Death of the West. How dying populations and immigrant invasions threaten our country and civilization (book abstract). Published on the website 01/01/2007. http://www.perspektivy.info/oykumena/europe/smert_zapada.htm; Huntington S. Clash of civilizations in the transformation of the world order (new post-industrial wave in the West). – M., 1999.

[2] Philosophy: encyclopedic dictionary (compiled and executive editor K. Nazarov). - T.: Shark, 2004. - P. 168.

[3] National Encyclopedia of Uzbekistan. Volume 4. - T.: 2002. - P. 179.

[4] Spirituality: Key Concepts and Glossary. – T.: Publishing house named after Gafur Gulam, 2009. – P. 213.

[5] That source. – P. 214.

[6] Philosophy: encyclopedic dictionary. - T., 2010. - B. 139.

[7] Brief political dictionary. Completed and revised second edition. - T.: Uzbekistan, 1983. - P. 132.

[8] Isakov B. Intellectual responsibility. - T.: Manaviyat, 2008. - P. 7.

[9] Resolution of the President of the Republic of Uzbekistan "On measures to strengthen the material and technical base of higher educational institutions and radically improve the quality of training of highly qualified specialists." // People's word. May 21, 2011

[10] Shukhrat Reza. If kindness is the main criterion... // Thought. 2010, No. 3. - B. 4-15; Saidov U. Globalization and intercultural communication. - T.: Academy, 2008. - P. 48-57.

[11] Karaboev U. Cultural problems. - T.: National Encyclopedia of Uzbekistan, 2009. - P. 40.

[12] Karimov I.A. Without historical memory there is no future. - T.: Shark, 1998.

[13] See: The survey was conducted in September-November 2010 as part of a thesis prepared by department researcher E. Kholikov on the topic "The negative impact of foreign television programs on the information security of Uzbekistan and the problems of eliminating it."

[14] Karimov I.A. High spirituality is an invincible force. - T.: "Spirituality", 2008. - P. 146.

[15] The theaters are roaring. Where are you, audience? // Newspaper "Dunyo". 2010, 22 (435) – no. - P. 4.

[16] Karimov I.A. High spirituality is an invincible force. - T.: "Spirituality", 2008. - P. 129.

[17] Khaidarov B. Imitation – virtue or vice? // Mushtum (Uzbek magazine of humor and humor). 2009, No. 6. - P. 6.

[18] Karimov I.A. High spirituality is an inexhaustible power. - T.: "Spirituality", 2008. - P. 115.

[19] Constitution of the Republic of Uzbekistan. - T.: Uzbekistan, 2008. - P. 4.

[20] Thinking. 2011, No. 1. - P. 13.

[21] Karimov I.A. High spirituality is an inexhaustible power. - T.: "Spirituality", 2008. - P. 87.

[22] Najmiddin Kamil. Love saves the world. // Thinking. 2008, No. 3. - P. 16.

CONTENT

INTRODUCTION 4

PART ONE. THEORETICAL AND METHODOLOGICAL FOUNDATIONS OF THE GLOBALIZATION PROCESS 8

    1.1. The revolutionary essence of "globalization" 9

    1.2. Dialectics of globalization and civilization 29

    1.3. Globalization, Civilization and Nation 53

PART TWO. INTERCONNECTION OF GLOBALIZATION AND NATIONAL SPIRITUAL SECURITY 78

    2.1. The nation of man and the nature of its manifestation in the context of globalization 79

    2.2. The spirituality of the nation 96

    2.3. The concept of national and spiritual security and its causes 122

PART THREE. THREATS TO THE NATIONAL SPIRITUAL IN THE CONTEXT OF GLOBALIZATION 147

    3.1. Fundamentals of Threats to National Spirituality 147

    3.2. External threats affecting national spirituality 176

    3.3. Internal threats to national spirituality and the process of their implementation 197

PART FOUR. FACTORS OF ENSURING NATIONAL AND SPIRITUAL SECURITY 219

    4.1. Development of national identity in the process of globalization trends 219

    4.2. In the context of globalization of national identity functions ... 249

    4.3. Factors making the provision of national and spiritual security a national idea 275

    Conclusion 313

    Bibliography 316

www.ingramcontent.com/pod-product-compliance
Lightning Source LLC
LaVergne TN
LVHW081333080526
838199LV00086B/3798